THE MIDDLE AGES IN THE HIGHLANDS

THE MIDDLE AGES IN THE HIGHLANDS

ISBN 0 9502612 1 1

Published by
The Inverness Field Club 1981

Printed by
John G Eccles Printers Ltd, Inverness

Contents

Introduction

Over many years the Inverness Field Club has been fortunate in the distinguished and erudite persons who have addressed it. The frequent references in scholarly writings to the Transactions of the Society show clearly the value placed upon such lectures by students of Highland history, archaeology and field studies.

However, the annual programmes of talks and excursions are somewhat random, without planned sequence, and in recent years the Club has supplemented these with occasional periods of extended study of a body of related subject matter, followed by publication of the lectures given. In 1970 came "The Dark Ages in the Highlands", now sadly out of print, in 1977 "The Moray Firth Area Geological Studies", still in regular demand, and now there is the present volume "The Middle Ages in the Highlands".

The preceding study week drew enrolments from all over Scotland, from England and even from overseas. That this was so was largely due to the calibre of the speakers, all of whom are acknowledged authorities in their various specialities. The Field Club is greatly indebted to these guest speakers with whose kind permission the series of papers is now published. They are also grateful to the local firms who recognised the worth of the enterprise by giving their financial support. The reading public cannot fail to give similar recognition.

ALAN B. LAWSON
President, Inverness Field Club.

Acknowledgements

The Editor here has the pleasant duty to thank all those who have been involved in the production of this small book, particularly Professor Geoffrey Barrow, who was Chairman of the Week of Lectures and Excursions in July, 1980.

First come thanks to the writers of the papers, who came to give their lectures to an international audience at Eden Court, Inverness. Their names will be found in the Table of Contents, but thanks are also due to Edward Meldrum, a Past-President of the Field Club, who has drawn the sketches that will be found scattered through the pages.

The Week of Lectures was made possible by the generous support of the following: Bingham Hughes and MacPherson, Estate Agents; The Caledonian Hotel; Esso Petroleum; Fraser and McColl, Ironmongers; The Inverness Courier; Leisuropa Ltd., Sports Specialists; Leslie, Coiffeur de Dames; Macrae and Dick, Motor Engineers; Marks and Spencer; Savo Electronics; Shell U.K.

This publication has been helped by a grant towards the printing of the Architectural Paper from The Civil Service Department. It has also been helped by the Highlands and Islands Development Board.

Mr William Jolly, who was our first President, said in 1875, "Many good men are deterred from joining . . . by the idea that great erudition, much scientific knowledge and elaborate papers are asked for and necessary to constitute efficient membership. Our objects, as a local association, are much less ambitious and much more human and sensible. We are all learners." I am sure that Mr Jolly would agree that the "great erudition, much scientific knowledge and elaborate papers" that are collected here are also both "human and sensible."

LORAINE MACLEAN OF DOCHGARROCH, Editor.

Tradition does not mean that the living are dead; it means that the dead are alive.

HAROLD MACMILLAN, December 1958.

EXCURSIONS

L. MACLEAN OF DOCHGARROCH

There were three Excursions during the Week, all aimed at enlarging the background of the lectures.

The first Excursion took place on Monday afternoon, when a bus-load and a number of cars met at the then new car park above Urquhart Castle (531286), the largest mediaeval stone castle in the Inverness District. Mr John Dunbar, who had given his paper on Architecture in the Middle Ages in the morning, was the expert in charge and he explained the development of Urquhart Castle from a prehistoric dun to its prime, represented now by the ruins of the 13th century enclosure walls and the shell of the great Towerhouse, rebuilt by the Grants of Grant after 1509, and partially reconstructed in 1627. Now an Ancient Monument, the castle has been ruinous since it was blown up after the 1689 Jacobite Rising, but its popularity is such that in the summer of 1978, over 76,000 people visited it.

On Tuesday evening another bus-load set out from Eden Court to visit several mediaeval castle locations to the east of Inverness. Mr Edward Meldrum, a Past President of the Field Club, was in charge. The first pause was at Cawdor, where it was pointed out that there had been two castles on different sites. The earliest timbered earthwork castle has vanished, although its remains were visible in the 18th century, but the later towerhouse castle is now open to the public (847498). The first stop was at Rait Castle (894524). This involved a walk and some surprise at the way that vegetation, much of it prickly, had shot up since quite a number of members had visited it individually earlier in the year.

Although Rait does not stand very high, this ruined stone manor hall of the early 14th century has a splendid view of the Moray Firth and of the threatening storms coming south from the Sutherland Hills. The return, fortunately down hill, to the bus was much speeded by the sight of the dark grey clouds and most people congratulated the bus driver, who had backed his huge bus a considerable distance from the road up a very taxing course to the farm.

The next stop was at Auldearn Castle Hill, the N.T.S. site (917556). By then the promised rain had arrived, but this did not deter the party, and the driver, from walking the short distance to where the dovecot stands inside the earthwork ramparts of the 12th century mote hill castle. Once again the commanding position of the fortified site was clear, with fine views all round, even if only intermittently seen through the rain. King William the Lion (1165–1214) occupied the timber castle at Auldearn, or 'Ulerin' in some records, during his expeditions to subdue the North; he is recorded as having signed royal charters here.

The return route was through Nairn to Ardersier, missing the magnificent, but 18th century, Fort George, to a stop below its early mediaeval predecessor, the motte known as Cromal Mount (782555). "Can you see the pole on the skyline? Well, it is just to the right of that, but there is not much left of it."

The rain had lessened, but the clouds had darkened the evening and the bus paused where both Castle Stuart (741498), the third of the Mackintosh castles of Petty, and the earthwork motte, the site of the first castle of the De Moravias, just west of Petty Church (739498) could be seen and spoken about. Then a speedy return to Inverness ended a damp, but enjoyable evening.

The full day Excursion was to the north and east of Inverness. The first stop was a Beauly Priory (528467), where the Reverend Donald Maclean of Dochgarroch, a Field Club Member, described the lay-out and history of the ruined building. Others joined in, pointing out various details that had caught their eyes. From there the bus and several attendant cars went on to Fortrose where, with the help of an enormous mediaeval key, the party packed itself into the 'Undercroft' of the once great cathedral church of the diocese of Ross (729567). Here the speaker was Miss Noel Wilby who, as the author of an, alas, then unobtainable little book on Fortrose, was eminently suitable to be our mentor. Very little remains of the cathedral, thanks to the depredations of O. Cromwell and others, but the magnificent ruins of the south aisle still remain and gave shelter during a sudden heavy storm.

The procession crossed the Cromarty Firth by the new bridge and arrived at the church of Logie Easter, by no means a mediaeval building, but it has a splendid car park for lunch, and the church was opened for us by the Reverend A.G. MacAlpine, who lives at the old Manse and who showed us the, surely mediaeval, Drowning Pool (779756) in his garden. Mr MacAlpine joined the party and the next stop was Fearn Abbey (837773), considered by some to have been the place where the Book of Kells was actually written. The surviving part of the Abbey is now the parish church. Here the minister, the Reverend Mr Macfarlane, met the party. He had arranged all sorts of visual aids, and made sure that everything was explained at length.

The final stopping place was Tain Collegiate Church (781824) where Mr MacAlpine, looking at the assembled learned people, said that this was a foretaste of Judgement Day, and then proceeded to give a fascinating account of this "Valhalla of the North", calling on his audience to support, or disagree with, his opinions.

This made a very lively end to the various places seen, and several visitors said that their ideas of what there was to see in "The Highlands" had been much enlarged — there was much more to the region than just the West Coast.

Rood Tower and South Aisle
Fortrose Cathedral ★79

THE SOURCES FOR THE HISTORY OF THE HIGHLANDS IN THE MIDDLE AGES

G.W.S. BARROW

The first source for medieval highland history — as distinct from more or less secondary authorities — which I ever encountered was, I think, the *Geographical Collections* of Walter MacFarlane of MacFarlane, completed in 1749.[1] It was not a direct encounter for I did not become acquainted with the Scottish History Society's edition till many years later. I learned of MacFarlane because at an early stage in my life I was an avid reader of the works of Seton Gordon. Seton Gordon took careful advice on Gaelic place-names from the great William Watson, some time Rector of Inverness Royal Academy (one of the six schools of which I can claim to be a former pupil) and later Professor of Celtic at the University of Edinburgh. Whether Seton Gordon got to know about Macfarlane's collections through William Watson or referred to them simply because they are the chief example of a sadly small class of topographical, geographical and historical works written about Scotland in the pre-tourist era, he certainly made effective use of picturesque extracts from MacFarlane in his 'Highways and Byways' books.[2] Since it may not be obvious in what way statistical and geographical information gathered parish by parish in the seventeenth and early decades of the eighteenth century can constitute a source for medieval history, let me give you three instances, two particular and one general, of how MacFarlane's — or Sir Robert Sibbald's — parish informants may throw light on periods much earlier than their own or at least give us important clues which might be followed by present and future archaeologists. An account of Durness written in 1726 refers to a 'mannour house' of Lord Reay called Balnacille. 'This mannour having been church lands of old, there was to be seen, (till this last year that it was thrown down for building a new house) the ruines of an old wall about eight or nine foot thick and in some places thirty foot high, without any window thereon, it seemd to extend on the one side one hundred foot long, and in breadth fourty foot; there is no tradition by whom it was built, or for what purpose; it seems to have been some old monastery'.[3] Again, it is (as far as I know) only a brief note in MacFarlane's collection which makes tantalizing mention of the road built between Blair Atholl and Ruthven in Badenoch by 'David Cuming Earle of Athoill' — presumably either John Comyn who built the first castle at Blair in 1269 or one of the earls of Atholl named David, i.e. Hastings or Strathbogie, a road called *rathad an fhiona* ('wine road'), 'layd with calsay in sundrie parts'.[4].

Finally, one of the most valuable features of MacFarlane's collections is the listing of fairs and markets. If the burghs of medieval Scotland are plotted upon a map, or a series of maps — as is done in the MacNeill-Nicholson *Historical Atlas* — the all-too-familiar dichotomy of a well-endowed lowland region and a virtually empty highland region appears in one of its starkest manifestations. But if we plotted the regular markets and fairs of Scotland whose existence by, or before, the sixteenth century is certain or may be reasonably inferred, the picture would be markedly different. The editors of MacFarlane for the Scottish History Society list seventeen fairs and markets in the Highland region (including within that region upland

Aberdeenshire and Banff).[5] Most of these not only bore the names of saints and must consequently antedate the Reformation, but also more particularly bore the names of Celtic and other native saints, which indicates an origin far back in the medieval or even 'dark age' centuries.

Geography and topography form the essential groundwork of any systematic approach to Highland history. Behind the pioneering labours of Timothy Pont, Robert and James Gordon, Robert Sibbald and others as we find it gathered together by MacFarlane, there are even earlier topographical essays such as Archdeacon Monro's *Description of the Western Isles* (1549), edited with an admirably simple yet informative apparatus by the good dean's fellow-clansman R.W. Munro[6] and the geographical notes prefaced to Fordun's *Scotichronicon* (c.1370).[7] To an extent which we cannot yet fully grasp these pieces of geographical lore anent the Highlands may derive from treatises now lost. E.g., Bower tells us that in Loch Awe is the isle of Inishail wherein is the parish kirk but, quite separately, he lists 'Loch Awe 24 miles long where are three castles'.[8] Now John MacDougall of Lorn writing to Edward II in 1308 or 1309 told the English king that he had 'three castles in his keeping and a loch 24 miles long' — surely both have been referring to the same geography textbook or at least common stock of well-remembered lore. Similarly, Monro's list of the isles begins in the extreme south with Man, continues with Ailsa, Arran, Bute and the Cumbraes, moves across by way of the Mull of Kintyre to Rathlin before proceeding steadily northward up the west side of Kintyre and Lorn, and eventually, only when Kerrera has been dealt with, embarks on a lengthy description of Islay. The *Scotichronicon* list likewise begins with Man and the islands of the Firth of Clyde, whence it moves, like Monro's list, by way of Rathlin and Gigha. Here, however, the order differs from Monro, for Islay and Colonsay are taken before Jura, while Mull and its satellites are dealt with before we are told of Kerrera 'where King Alexander II died'. Moreover, the *Scotichronicon* list is appreciably weaker on the northern Hebrides than Monro, listing only ten islands north of Coll and Tiree as against thirty-five to the south, whereas Monro enumerates 125 in each sector.

The *Scotichronicon* list has recently been discussed in much detail by Mr Basil Megaw and Mr William Scott.[10] Their discussion has made only a passing reference to Donald Monro's list and has been concerned chiefly to establish whether or not there is any relationship between Fordun's text and the list of islands in a forged papal bull purporting to have been issued by Pope Gregory IX in 1231 but more likely to have been fabricated at the end of the fourteenth century, or even later.[11] Mr Scott has usefully reminded us of the report by Robert de Torigni, abbot of Le Mont Saint Michel, that in 1166 the kingdom and bishopric of the Isles was thought to contain 32 islands.[12] If we exclude from Fordun's forty-five the islands not in Sodor diocese, e.g. the Cumbraes, Rathlin and Lismore, we have a total of 31.[13] This seems to me too close to Robert de Torigni's total to be coincidental.

Messrs Megaw and Scott do not bring into their discussion the much shorter list of western isles given in Reginald of Durham's book of the miracles of Saint Cuthbert, composed in the late twelfth century[14] This begins in the north with Uist and Lewis and ends with Islay, Iona and Mull, misplacing Bute which is the only Clyde island listed by Reginald. During the twelfth and thirteenth centuries the Hebrides fell into two clearly differentiated sectors, north and south, the one based on Lewis or Skye, the other on Man.[15] Although I would agree with Mr Scott[16] that Fordun's list of islands — a comparatively elaborate essay in topography — cannot be derived from, or even very closely related to, the forged papal bull, and although I would further agree that information has probably been fed into Fordun's account from some Scottish royal or governmental source, I would nevertheless be inclined to agree with

Mr Megaw that Fordun's list and that of the forged bull may both go back to a single source of information about the islands originating in the kingdom of Man and the Isles.[17] In that sense I would agree that the way of looking at the islands represented by the *Scotichronicon* and Archdeacon Monro derives ultimately from a Manx viewpoint, and (especially in view of the precision of Torigni's total of 32 in 1166) possibly from a Manx list.

Reginald of Durham's list, by contrast, might be thought to derive from the *milieu* either of the family of Somerled of Argyll (whose son Dugald visited Durham in 1175)[18] or of the family of Reginald, eldest son of Guthred king of Man, who held some position of power in the northern Hebrides before his father's death in 1187.[19]

In addition to these lists there is another much briefer one contained in Pope Innocent III's solemn privilege of 1203 for the abbey of Iona,[20] newly and controversially re-founded as a house for Benedictine monks.[21] Unlike the Manx bull allegedly of Gregory IX this bull of Pope Innocent is undoubtedly genuine, although the original is lost and the text survives only in the Register. Beside certain individual churches and lands the privilege lists the Outer Isles ('Insegal'), Mull, Iona itself, Colonsay, Oronsay, Canna and the little Calve Island in the Sound of Mull. This grouping differs from both the Fordun-Monro list and Reginald of Durham's list and may be said to be 'Iona-orientated'. It surely derives from written documents, doubtless charters given to the abbey by Reginald (Raonall) son of Somerled which like the original bull have long been lost.

If we add up all the information regarding the Highlands and western isles contained in these lists, whatever their exact provenance may have been, and compare it with the paucity, vagueness and unreliability of the Highland information to be found on the mid-thirteenth-century map of Matthew Paris and the mid-fourteenth-century map among the Gough MSS in the Bodleian Library[22], we are bound to be impressed by the contrast between the fairly high quality of topographical and geographical knowledge apparently available in Scotland between the thirteenth and sixteenth centuries and the extremely inadequate level of such knowledge available in the south of England. We need hardly be surprised by the unwillingness of a North Riding of Yorkshire jury in 1251 to admit to any certainty regarding the death of Walter Bisset: 'they know not the day of his death, nor can they know it. For he died far away, in Scotland, in a certain island called Arran. Some say he died the Tuesday *before* Michaelmas; others that he died the Tuesday *after*, at Vespers; the truth is not yet known'.[23]

We may use these geographical excursions to illustrate an important contrast between the early and late middle ages as far as the sources of Highland history are concerned. Just as most of the early written geography of Scotland seems to be highland and island geography, so in the period between the coming of Christianity and c.1100 most of the historical source material we have — admittedly not abundant — seems to be remarkably biased towards the Highlands, or at least towards the west. This is strikingly seen in the fact that the most informative corpus of annals we possess for events in Scotland before the ninth century is what Dr John Bannerman has called the 'Iona Chronicle',[24] what Dr Marjorie Anderson has called the 'Iona Annals'.[25] Whether or not we accept the belief that a proportion of the material in these annals is derived from annalistic entries actually written in the land of the Picts — and then copied at Iona, copied again at Bangor in a supposed 'Ulster Chronicle', and eventually incorporated into the surviving annals of Ulster, of Tigernach and of Clonmacnoise — whether or not we are disposed to see any Pictish provenance for the information about Scotland contained in these Irish collections, we must be struck by the high proportion of items dealing with places and/or persons in what are now the Highlands and Islands. For example, among the fortresses mentioned (as Dr Bannerman has pointed out)[26] with special prominence, Etin (Edinburgh) and Dundaff near Stirling are clearly Lowland places, while Dunottar may be regarded as borderline. But Dunadd, Dundurn, Dunollie and Dunaverty are all Highland localities, and I should also be prepared to argue a Highland location for *Castellum Credi*, the scene of a 'pitiful battle' between two Pictish armies in A.D. 728, when Angus son of Fergus (Onuist son of Urguist) was the victor and an obscure Alpin the vanquished.[27] *Castellum Credi* has often been identified with Scone[28] on no stronger grounds than the phonological resemblance between *Credi* and *Credulitatis*, in the light of the name *Mons Credulitatis* 'hill of credulity', sarcastically given to Scone by the writer of the so-called *Chronicle of the Kings of Scotland* at A.D. 906.[29] I think it is not so much the credulity of the Picts as our own which is strained by this identification. The plain fact is that we have a place-name Cretyn, Credyn, Crethy, well-attested from 1207,[30] and exceptionally familiar in our own times as Crathie in Braemar. Crathie is only a mile or two from Kindrochit (now Braemar) whose church of St Andrew was said to have belonged to St Andrews cathedral foundation in the twelfth century as a result of an alleged gift of Kindrochit by Angus son of Fergus King of the Picts.[31]

The Highland and Hebridean bias of annalistic sources for the period before A.D. 800 continues to be reflected in the wholly Irish annals for the tenth and eleventh centuries, allowing for the fact that Scandinavian incursions had the effect of cutting off not only the Northern Isles but also and increasingly the Western Isles and even the West Highland seaboard from contact with Irish church centres, where annals or chronicles were of course written. And it is not only in annalistic writings that we can see this bias. It characterizes a number of the early lives and legends of the Saints, for although we possess biographies, e.g. for Cuthbert and Kentigern, which are set in what are now the southern Lowlands of Scotland, we are notably lacking in saints' lives which have for their background the eastern Lowlands north of Forth.[32] For the Highlands on the other hand we have lives of the saints of Iona, — most notably, of course, Adamnan's Life of Columba — as well as a good many lives of Irish and other saints not specially (or not at all) connected with Iona but associated as far as their missionary labours were concerned with northern or western Scotland. Incidentally my reference to Adamnan's *Columba* prompts me to ask how often we have heard the confident assertion that the Loch Ness Monster is mentioned in this late seventh-century biography? The story has become such an immovable part of tourist lore that it is perhaps pointless to quote (in translation) what Adamnan actually wrote.[33]

'At another time, when the blessed man was for a number of days in the province of the Picts, he had to cross the River Ness. When he reached its bank, he saw a poor fellow being buried by other inhabitants; and the buriers said that, while swimming not long before, he had been seized and most savagely bitten by a water beast (*aquatilis bestia* or *belua*)'. When Columba tempted it with the bait of a tasty young monk, Lugne MacMin, who had been commanded to swim across the river, 'it suddenly swam up to the surface, and with gaping mouth and with great roaring rushed towards the man swimming in the middle of the stream'. In other words we have no 'Loch Ness Monster' but a river beast, an *each uisge* perhaps, of a type familiar in Gaelic folk-lore. There is a contrast between this fierce river-dwelling carnivore and the shy, elusive vegetarian creature of modern imagining, keeping itself strictly to the loch and only on rare occasions surfacing from the stygian depths, which must be inescapable to anyone save a hardened fabricator of tourist publicity.

Even Bede, in his *Historia Ecclesiastica* (not, of course, in his *Life of Saint*

Cuthbert), has almost as much to say of Highland localities and personalities as he has of Lowland in the admittedly short and rare passages which touch on any part of what is now Scotland. Yet we must be grateful for his mention of Bridius son of Meilochon 'a very powerful king' (*rex potentissimus*),[34] for his remarkably precise mensuration of Iona as consisting of '5 hides by English measurement'[35] (5 hides, as the common Wessex place-name Fifehead reminds us, was a normal village settlement among the Anglo-Saxons), for his careful statement anent the division of the Pictish nation into those who dwell beyond (i.e. to the north of) and 'within' (i.e. to the south of) the steep and rugged mountain ranges,[36] and for his account of how Nechtan son of Derile, King of the Picts, having received from Abbot Ceolfrith of Jarrow the lengthy letter of instruction as to the best method of calculating the date of Easter, 'without delay put his words into effect by royal authority. For at once the 19-year Easter cycles were dispatched throughout all the provinces of the Picts by public decree, to be transcribed, learned and observed, the erroneous 84-year cycles having been totally discarded'.[37] This last passage shows us quite unequivocally what it could mean to be a very powerful Pictish king and how inapplicable to the Highlands in the early eighth century would be any of the weary generalizations we so often hear of the late medieval Scottish realm, namely that the King's writ did not run effectively north of the Highland line.

Thanks to the careful work of Dr Bannerman we are now able to appreciate that by far the earliest description of the civil administration of any part of North Britain is that contained in the *Senchus Fer nAlban*, dating ultimately from the mid-seventh century.[38] The description deals with Scottish Dalriada, the south-west area of the Highlands which became the sheriffdoms of Argyll and Tarbert, eventually simply of Argyll. The significance of this tract for our knowledge of the almost wholly undocumented social and political structure of the Pictish kingdom has not yet been worked out, but it hardly seems rash to guess that further study of the *Senchus* in conjunction with place-name and other evidence for Scotland generally, especially for Galloway and the country north of Forth and Clyde, will throw a good deal of light on an area of early Scottish history which is still very obscure. To mention one small point by way of illustration, Dr Bannerman has drawn attention to the basic importance in the Dalriadic system of the unit of five houses or households, which in turn constituted a quarter of a davoch or ounceland (*tir unga*).[39] This poses the question of whether some of the place-names embodying Gaelic *cóig*, 'five', usually interpreted as referring to *fifths*, may not originally have referred to *fives*, i.e. 'five house units'. Among these names are Pitcog in the Carse of Gowrie, Pitcox near Dunbar in East Lothian and Pentecox (formerly Pet(h)cox) between Edinburgh and Dalkeith, all Pictish hybrids perhaps indicating five-household settlements.[40]

* * * * * *

As we move from the Dark Ages and early Middle Ages into the central medieval period from the late eleventh to the early fourteenth century, we are aware of a dramatic shift in the balance between Highland and Lowland source material. Anyone who has read the Bannatyne Club's gallant but alas! never completed essay in local history, the *Origines Parochiales Scotiae*, and compared the articles on Lanarkshire and Border parishes with those for Argyll or maritime Inverness-shire will appreciate the contrast. 'The church of Kilmorich [at the head of Loch Fyne]' (I quote at random) 'of which we have no early record . . . In 1511 Sir John Finlosoun was vicar'; of Kilviceuen in the Ross of Mull, 'there seems to be no mention of this parish before the year 1561'; of Canna, 'the paroche kirk of Kannay is mentioned by Archdeacon Monro in 1549'; of Duirinish in Skye, 'In 1501 Kilmory in Watternes

[Vaternish] was one of the vicarages of the parsonage of Snizort';[41] and so on and so on. There seem to me to be two areas in which modern scholarship has very materially redressed the imbalance which used to prevail and make our history of Scotland from the death of Malcolm Canmore to the reign of Robert I overwhelmingly a history of Lowland Scotland. The first area concerns the Scandinavian element. The last fifty or sixty years have witnessed a steady advance in the study of Norse saga and genealogical source-material and in the evaluation of Scandinavian terminology and structure in the formation of place-names. As far as Scotland is concerned, this really began with Alan Orr Anderson's remarkable collection and analysis of the *Early Sources of Scottish History*, without whose guidance most of us would surely have left all but the most popular and translated sagas or saga-type sources severely alone. Much more recently we have had Professor Nicolaisen's masterly survey of the chronology of Norse settlement in northern and western Scotland as evidenced in place-names,[42] and Dr Megaw's important re-assessment of 'Norseman and native in the kingdom of the Isles'.[43] Moreover, the relationship between the west highlands and isles generally and the medieval kingdom of Scotland, the *regnum Scottorum*, has been illuminated by the studies of Professors A.A.M. Duncan and A.L. Brown from the Scottish, and of Professor Arne Johnsen from the Norwegian, point of view.[44] Thanks to the work of these and other scholars we are beginning to have a much clearer understanding of the fascinating amalgam of Gael and Norseman which provides the historical background to the late medieval Lordship of the Isles, the beginnings of the so-called 'Highland Problem' in Scottish and British history, and burgeoning of clans and the 'clan system' which for so many — unfortunately, in my view — constitutes the be-all and end-all of Highland history.

The second area of advance in documentary studies has been the remarkable opening up of the Roman treasure-chest, the Vatican Archives, which has been largely the product of a post-Second World War generation of scholars all of whom, however, would gladly acknowledge the inspiration and pioneering labours of the late Annie Isabella Cameron or Dunlop. There is no single respect in which the *Origines Parochiales* of a century ago would have been more amply supplemented (in the documentary as distinct from the archaeological sphere) than by the mass of information, much of it wholly new, dealing with the ecclesiastical — and to a considerable extent with the secular political — history of the Highlands and Islands in the later middle ages. Much of this information is available only on microfilm in the University of Glasgow, but some important contributions have already been made in published editions of sources, and even of the unpublished material a great deal has already been incorporated into definitive reference works such as Professor Donald Watt's *Fasti*[45] of the medieval church and Dr Ian Cowan's *Parishes of Medieval Scotland*[46] and his revised edition of the late Dr Easson's work on Scottish monastic and other religious houses.

A fairly rapid glance through the volume of *Scottish Supplications* for 1428-32,[47] for example, shows entries for the Highland parishes of Abriachan, Abernethy, Abertarff, Ardclach, Balquhidder, Boharm, Contin, Croy, Dingwall, Glassary, Inverallan, Kilarrow, Kilmallie, Kingussie, Kirkmichael, Luss, Mortlach, Moy, Petty, Strath or Kilchrist in Strathswordale (Skye), Torosay, Uig, and for the Valliscaulian priory of Beauly. An even more casual dip into the pages of the SHS edition of Pope Clement VII's letters to Scotland[48] yields the information that in 1392 Euphemia countess of Ross petitioned for separation from her husband Alexander Stewart earl of Buchan (the 'Wolf of Badenoch') on the grounds of his persistent adultery with a woman of Ross diocese named Mariette Nighean Eachainn, by whom he had had children[49] — this evidently Gaelic-speaking lady was surely the mother of

Alexander earl of Mar, who won, or at least did not lose, the battle of Harlaw in 1411. In the decree of the bishops of Moray and Ross of 1389 printed in the *Registrum Moraviense*, she appears merely as Mariota filia Athyn (*rectius*, Achyn).[50] Here the new evidence from the papal archives nicely confirms the surmise made as long ago as 1911 by the late Dr William Mackay of Inverness that the name of the Wolf of Badenoch's mistress was Mairead daughter of Eachan and that she must be seen as a Gaelic-speaking highland woman; a surmise which for Dr Mackay formed part of the evidence which led him to believe that the battle of the Red Harlaw was in no way a conflict between Gael and Sasunach.[51]

Again, in 1393, Pope Clement gave a dispensation to Hector Maclean, bachelor, and Mary (Mor), spinster, daughter of Colin Campbell, of the dioceses respectively of the Isles and Argyll, to marry within the prohibited degrees 'in order to establish peace and harmony among their families and friends, whereas until now there have only been wars, dissensions, murders and other grave scandals'.[52] A similar dip into the *Letters of Pope Benedict XIII* shows that in 1403 a dispensation was given to Lachlan Maclean (of Duart) to marry Anna daughter of William Macleod, even though Anna had been previously betrothed to Rory Macleod and then to Neil Maclean — both kinsmen of Lachlan — 'in order to prevent dissension and unrest in the lands of the noble man Donald lord of the Isles whose subjects they are'.[53] On their marriage the parties must subscribe to the building fund of Iona Abbey which has collapsed. In both these volumes, more particularly among Benedict XIII's letters, there is mention of a high proportion of Highland parishes. I have counted references to some 36 different Highland parish churches in a period of 25 years. Moreover, these papal records are an invaluable repertory of Highland personal names, from which we can not only derive much biographical information but also learn more about the method of forming personal names, including women's names, in the Scottish Gaedhealtachd.

In singling out for special mention the areas of Scandinavian linguistic and political study and of exploitation, much of it for the first time, of the immensely rich resources of the Vatican, I have not been unmindful of two other disciplines through which our understanding of the medieval Highlands has been and is being enlarged. The first is that of genealogy. The centrality of kinship and descent in Celtic society has resulted in the compilation and preservation of a great quantity of genealogies or pedigrees, mostly in Ireland and Wales, but also in Scotland and in any case often dealing with Scottish Highland families, wherever the information happens to have been collected. Far more of Archdeacon Monro's sixteenth-century compilation is taken up with genealogies of the clans than with the geographical treatise on the western isles, already discussed.

Some of the earliest serious work on Highland genealogy was carried out by Walter MacFarlane, with whose geographical collections this talk began. Unfortunately MacFarlane, though serious, was not critical of his sources but, jackdaw-like, gathered in a good deal of rubbish.[54] The first large-scale critical study was undertaken by W.F. Skene, who grasped the crucial importance of Irish and Welsh MSS for this purpose. Skene printed many Highland genealogies for the first time in an appendix to his greatest work *Celtic Scotland*, first published in 1876.[55] Of Skene it has been justly said that 'All those who condemn him use his books',[56] and also that his work 'underestimates the complexity of the evidence'.[57] Certainly without Skene not only the historiography of the Highlands but also our whole way of looking at the history of Scotland would have been poorer.

In recent years notable advances in Highland and especially Scoto-Irish genealogical study have been made by David Sellar, often building upon Skene's theories but able to use a much wider range of scholarly expertise including access to facsimiles and accurately edited texts of some of the key MSS.[58] Here, perhaps, I need only make special mention of Mr Sellar's seminal work on the origins of the Campbells and the interesting families — some well-known, some obscure, and some extinct — who occupied Cowal and Knapdale in the twelfth, thirteenth and fourteenth centuries. Mr Sellar's investigations have had as one of their purposes an attempt to test the traditional genealogies, presumably preserved by hereditary shennachies or other members of the learned order in Celtic society, against different and independent historical evidence, poetry, chronicles, charters etc. On the whole the genealogies seem to stand up to the test remarkably well, but that does not mean that we should take anything handed down by bards or shennachies at its face value — far from it.

A good idea of the complexity of the evidence and of the need for critical control of the wilder flights of fancy still alas! to be found in modern literature can be gained by studying the work of Jean Dunlop and R.W. Munro — better known to us all as Mr and Mrs Munro or simply as Jean and Billy — which has been mounting up steadily over the years until it has now reached the proportions of a *magnum opus*.[59] Much of this, of course, is post-medieval in the strict sense, but nearly all the clans as we know them today have their origins in the medieval period and a few, such as the MacDonalds, Campbells and MacDougalls can trace their beginnings from the thirteenth century with in some cases a proven ancestry back into the twelfth century or even earlier. One refreshing feature of this modern work (as it seems to me) is that it is informed by a sense of how the history of the Highlands and their clans has been part of the history of Scotland as a whole. This awareness of the essential unity of Highland and Lowland history also characterizes Sir Ian Moncreiffe's book on *The Highland Clans* (1967)[60] which, besides, is full of curious lore of every kind, some at least having a direct relevance for the Highlands in medieval times.

The names of Jean and Billy Munro allow me to move easily from the discipline of genealogy to that of charter scholarship, for they are now splendidly far advanced with their edition of the written acts of the Lords of the Isles, putting to shame the slothful editors of the *Regesta Regum Scottorum*. Not for the first time the Lords of the Isles will have stolen a march on their natural liege lords the Kings of Scots.

Charters are one obvious way of demonstrating the Highland-Lowland unity already mentioned, for with the exception of the famous Gaelic land-grant of Donald lord of the Isles (1408)[61] all the Highland charters known to us conform to the diplomatic pattern laid down in the twelfth century. As holder of the Sir William Fraser Chair I ought, if only out of piety, to make special mention of Fraser's editing of Highland charters. In the course of his life-time's task of producing elaborately documented histories of the ancient landed families of Scotland, Fraser succeeded in including a substantial amount of Highland material — we need only think of his volumes on the chiefs of Grant, the Colquhouns of Luss, the early earls of Lennox and Menteith, the Sutherland family and the earls of Cromartie; and in addition to these collections we must bear in mind his searches on behalf of the Historical Manuscripts Commission. But even though Fraser towers above other Scots charter scholars of the second half of the nineteenth century his work must not be allowed to obscure the extensive and solid editorial labours of Cosmo Innes and others associated with the Bannatyne, Spalding and other clubs. Thanks to these learned and able antiquaries of the last century the Highlands have, on the whole, not been ill served in the matter of making texts of surviving charters available.

Several smaller but not unimportant collections of private charters have been published either individually or through learned societies, e.g. in Charles Fraser-

Mackintosh's *Invernessiana* (1875), in the *Highland Papers* series of the Scottish History Society edited by Sheriff MacPhail, notably including the Glassary Writs preserved by the Scrymgeour family, constables of Dundee,[62] and the Lamont muniments calendared for the Scottish Record Society.[63] One thirteenth-century document edited by MacPhail for the Scottish History Society is the oldest example I know of a wadset. It deals with the estate of Coille Bhrochain, 'the wood of the porridge', beside the Pass of Killiecrankie, neatly disposing of the legend that the wood got its name from the hasty breakfast that Robert the Bruce took there after the rout of Methven, for the name 'Kelbrochachyn' was clearly long-established before 1282.[64] In another stray document of the early fourteenth century dealing with Kinrara and with Dalnavert by the confluence of Feshie and Spey we have a grant to Malmoran of Glencharny including as the 'capital messuage' the site of the residence of Scayth son of Ferchard (Shaw MacFarquhar or Farquharson).[65] This supposed ancestor of the Shaws of Rothiemurchus was surely descended from Ferchar son of Seth (Farquhar MacShaw) who was steward of Badenoch under Walter Comyn in the 1230s.[66] Thirteenth-century 'stewards' of Badenoch and Lochaber are a most unusual and (as far as I am aware) unexplained phenomenon, and it is only charters which reveal their existence. Somewhere at Dalnavert there is still to be found the site of this official's *manerium* or manor house. A final example of what can be yielded by charter evidence concerns the Isle of Man but certainly has Highland implications. Mr Megaw, in the paper already referred to, was concerned to refute the extraordinary thesis recently put forward by Mrs Margaret Gelling, namely that the Gaelic tongue was driven out of Man entirely by the Norse settlement of the ninth century, and did not return until after 1266.[67] The ruling dynasty of Man retained the Norse personal names of their Viking ancestors, but, as Mr Megaw pointed out, they often had Gaelic nicknames and they were aided by Gaelic-named officers. The register of the little priory of St Bees on the Cumberland coast contains a mid-twelfth century charter of King Guthred of Man (d.1197) witnessed by his foster-brother Gillocrist,[68] surely further evidence that the *milieu* of the Manx kings at that time was as much Gaelic as Norwegian.

As far as royal charters and other acts are concerned there is what can only be described as a dramatic contrast between the period 1100-1306, when documents directly relating to the Highlands are noticeably few and far between, and that from 1306 onwards. The reigns of David II and the early Stewarts in particular were evidently marked by a close attention to Highland land ownership and land lordship. The most casual examination of the surviving lists of missing royal charters reveals a sudden outburst of grants to Highlanders or of Highland estates (or both), which to a student of twelfth and thirteenth-century Scotland is like a lifting of the curtain which in the earlier period has hidden so much from us. Although there are important regional peculiarities in some of these charters — e.g. naval service instead of knight's or archer's service — there is absolutely no suggestion that king, council or *capella regis* ('chancery') was conscious that grants and infeftments of landed estates in the Highlands or in the Isles differed in any fundamental respect from those made by the Crown elsewhere in the realm. This impression is confirmed by the treatment of the Highlands in the *Exchequer Rolls* and other records of central government.

Of course there are some notable gaps in the medieval charter coverage for the Highlands. Whereas much of the oldest archive of the cathedral church of the Holy Trinity of Elgin — the cathedral of the diocese of Moray — has been preserved and gives us priceless information about Badenoch, Strathspey and Strathdearn, the corresponding archives of Dunkeld, Ross and Caithness have been lost. Only a handful of charters survive for the abbey of Kinloss and the priories of Beauly and

Pluscarden, practically nothing for the houses of Urquhart, Ardchattan or Iona. Burghs in the Highland area — in any case very few in number in the medieval period — have not done any better than religious houses as far as the survival of their earliest muniments are concerned. Of the four charters which Inverness is known to have received from King William the Lion, the burgh long ago managed to lose three.[69] No early charters survive for Auldearn, Nairn, Tain or Tarbert, and only a handful for Elgin and Dingwall. The fate of the muniments of Cromarty is to say the least, obscure. Remarkably, Rosemarkie or Fortrose had a charter from Alexander II or III, now lost, whose gist is preserved in a confirmation of James II. The somewhat unhappy accident that at least one duke of Argyll has been an antiquarian scholar has actually resulted in the once sizeable — reportedly still sizeable — corpus of charters at Inveraray never being edited or published in full or in any adequate form. The fact that the muniments of several families preyed on or harassed by the Campbells have perished would matter less if the Campbells themselves had made it their business to lay before the public the documentary evidence which would have constituted the basic source material for much of the late medieval history of Argyll. Unfortunately, the Argyll family has tended to sit on its early muniments like the proverbial dog in the manger.

* * * * * *

In any survey of the sources of medieval Highland history, however compressed, some reference must be made to what may be regarded as in one sense a particularly solid and permanent document, namely the stone buildings and carved stone crosses and grave slabs, some of them inscribed, in which the Highland area is a good deal richer than is popularly believed. The pioneer work of recording and interpreting these monuments was carried out in the last (or very early in the present) century by John Stuart,[70] Joseph Anderson,[71] Romilly Allen,[72] MacGibbon and Ross[73] and others, and much of this work has stood the test of time remarkably well. But in more modern times we have the majestic panorama of description, measurement, analysis and documentation slowly and all too sumptuously unrolled by the Royal Commission on Ancient and Historical Monuments. The Commissioners have now carried out their hosting through Kintyre, Lorn, Mull and North Argyll.[74] The Stirlingshire volumes deal with some buildings of the Highland border. But at the present rate of progress few of us will be spared to see volumes for the remainder of the Highland region completed on the same generous scale. It is not the least mournful consequence of Scotland's always being last in the queue that major public projects of this kind, in which our country is invariably far behind England and Wales, fall victim with special force to blanket economies in state spending.

Any impatience we may feel over the measured tread of the Ancient Monuments Commissioners must to a great extent be disarmed by the promptness and yet at the same time the exemplary thoroughness of their volume on *Late Medieval Monumental Sculpture in the West Highlands* (1977).[75] Drs Kenneth Steer and John Bannerman have between them presented us with an edition — in the fullest and best sense of that word — of what must now be regarded as the most important single family of documents for the history of any Highland region in the later middle ages. It will be a good while before the contents of this truly sumptuous and most attractive volume are properly digested; no doubt we shall be hearing more about it in the course of our Conference. For the present, however, it is agreeable to conclude a review of the sources for the medieval history of the Highlands on such a high note. Messrs. Steer and Bannerman have ensured that the middle ages go out not with a whimper but a bang.

FOOTNOTES

1. *Geographical Collections relating to Scotland made by Walter MacFarlane*, ed. A. Mitchell and J.T. Clark (Scottish History Society, 3 vols., 1906-8).
2. See, e.g., S. Gordon, *Highways and Byways in the Central Highlands* (Macmillan, 1948).
3. MacFarlane, *Geog. Coll.*, i, 193.
4. Ibid., ii, 598: 'Rad na pheny' for *rathad an fhiona*, 'road of the wine'.
5. Ibid., i, pp. xviii-xix; iii, pp. xxii-xxiii. A work of about the same date which, like MacFarlane's collections, has information relevant for the medieval period, is Martin Martin's *A Description of the Western Islands of Scotland* (2nd edn, London, 1716), now available in a photographic facsimile (Edinburgh, 1970).
6. *Monro's Western Isles of Scotland and Genealogies of the Clans, 1549*, ed. R.W. Munro (Edinburgh, 1961).
7. Johannis de Fordun, *Chronica Gentis Scotorum*, ed. W.F. Skene (2 vols., Edinburgh, 1871-2), i, 43-4; *Joannis de Fordun Scotichronicon cum Supplementis et Continuatione Walteri Boweri*, ed. W. Goodall (2 vols, Edinburgh, 1759), i, 45-6.
8. *Chron. Bower*, i, 47 (Inishail), 46 (Lochawe).
9. [G.W.S.] Barrow, *Robert Bruce [and the Community of the Realm of Scotland]* (2nd edn, Edinburgh, 1976), 255.
10. B. Megaw, 'Norseman and native in the kingdom of the Isles', *Scottish Studies*, xx (1976), 1-44; W.W. Scott, 'John of Fordun's Description of the Western Isles', *Scottish Studies*, xxiii (1979), 1-13.
11. The text of the bull was printed by R.L. Poole in *SHR*, viii (1911), 259. It is surprising that its authenticity was not suspected by Dr Poole, the foremost English scholar of his day in matters concerning the medieval papal chancery. It may not be fanciful to read into the comments added to Poole's article by Dr J.M. Thomson, the Scottish record scholar, a degree of scepticism with regard to the document's genuineness. See Megaw, art. cit., 29-34; Scott, art. cit., 2-5.
12. Cf. Lawrie, *Annals*, 115.
13. Man, Arran, Holy Island (Lamlash), Bute, Pladda, Inchmarnock, Sanda, Gigha, Islay, Texa, Colonsay, Jura, Scarba, Lunga, Eileach an Naoimh, Garvellach (= Dun Chonnuill), Mull, Cairnburghmore, Iona, Inchkenneth, Coll, Tiree, Muck, Barra, Uist, Rum, 'Fuleay' (Canna?), 'Assek' (Eigg or Raasay?), Skye, Lewis and St Kilda, making thirty-one or thirty-two if 'Benwewyl' (Benbecula), located in Uist, is counted separately. The selection of islands is, of course, odd in some respects, especially in its apparent omission of either Eigg or Raasay, and its inclusion of some very small islands. The list in *Chron. Bower*, i, 45 adds the isle of 'Alissay' (Ailsa) between Arran and Holy Island, and 'Alesay' between Little Cumbrae and Pladda (a second reference to Ailsa?).
14. *Reginaldi monachi Dunelmensis libellus de admirandis beati Cuthberti virtutibus*, ed. J. Raine (Surtees Soc., 1835), 251.
15. Anderson, *Early Sources*, ii, 313-4, 456-60.
16. W.W. Scott, *Scottish Studies*, xxiii, 2-4.
17. B. Megaw, *Scottish Studies*, xx, 31 and xxiii, 13.
18. Lawrie, *Annals*, 204.
19. Anderson, *Early Sources*, ii, 313.
20. *Diplomatarium Norvegicum*, vii (1867), 4-5 (no. 4), Anagni, 9 December 1203 (also in *Life of Saint Columba written by Adamnan*, ed. W. Reeves, *Historians of Scotland*, vi (Edinburgh, 1874), 353-5.)
21. Anderson, *Early Sources*, ii, 363.
22. For these maps see i.a., [G.W.S.] Barrow, [*The*] *Kingdom* [*of the Scots* (1973)], 369-70; *The Early Maps of Scotland* (Royal Scottish Geographical Soc., 1973), 4-6.
23. *Yorkshire Inquisitions of the Reigns of Henry III and Edward I*, ed. W. Brown (Yorkshire Archaeological Soc., Record Series), i, (1892), 26-7.
24. [J.] Bannerman, *Studies* [*in the History of Dalriada* (1974)], 9.
25. [M.O.] Anderson, *Kings and Kingship* [*in early Scotland* (1973)], 12.
26. Bannerman, *Studies*, 15-16.
27. Ibid., 15; Anderson, *Early Sources*, i, 224.
28. Ibid., n.l.; Anderson, *Kings and Kingship*, 141.
29. Anderson, *Early Sources*, i, 445.
30. *Cambuskenneth Registrum*, no. 26 (p.47), May 1207, Crelyn for which read Cretyn. See also no. 67. For later thirteenth-century forms see *Miscellany of the Scottish History Society*, vi (1939), 41, Creghi, 66, Grethy (read Crethy); *St Andrews Liber*, 355, Crehy.
31. *Chron. Picts — Scots*, 183; W.F. Skene, *Celtic Scotland* (2nd edn., 1886), i, 297-8.
32. One notable exception is the Life of Saint Serf; *Chron. Picts — Scots*, 412-20.
33. *Adamnan's Life of Columba*, ed. with translation by A.O. Anderson and M.O. Anderson (1961), 387.
34. Bede, *H*[*istoria*] *E*[*cclesiastica Gentis Anglorum*, ed. C. Plummer], i, 133 (in the Loeb edition, i, 341).
35. Bede, *HE*, i, 133; Loeb edn, i, 341.
36. Bede, *HE*, i, 133; Loeb edn, i, 340-1.
37. Bede, *HE*, i, 346; Loeb edn, ii, 361 (which omits to translate *iussu publico*, 'by public decree').
38. Bannerman, *Studies*, 27-156.
39. Ibid., 135-6, 141.
40. On these names see [W.J.] Watson, [*History of the*] *C*[*eltic*] *P*[*lace-*] *n*[*ames of*] *S*[*cotland* (1926)], 407, 410. Conceivably these names contain the compound *cóic-thige*, 'five houses', cited by Bannerman, *Studies*, 135, n.8, from the *Críth Gablach*.
41. The passages quoted will be found in *OPS*, ii, pt. I, 82, 304, 339, 358.
42. W.F.H. Nicolaisen, 'Norse settlement in the Northern and Western Isles', *SHR* xlviii (1969), 6-17; idem, *Scottish Place-names: their study and significance* (1976), 84-120.
43. See n.10 above.
44. A.L. Brown and A.A.M.Duncan, 'Argyll and the Isles in the earlier middle ages', *PSAS*, xc, 192-220; A.O. Johnsen,

'The payments from the Hebrides and the Isle of Man to the crown of Norway, 1153-1263', *SHR*, xlviii (1969), 18-34. See also Barrow, *Kingdom*, 362-83.
45. D.E.R. Watt, *Fasti Ecclesiae Scoticanae Medii Ævi ad annum 1638*, Second Draft (1969).
46. I.B. Cowan, *The Parishes of Medieval Scotland* (SRS, 1967).
47. *Calendar of Scottish Supplications to Rome, 1428-32*, ed. A.I. Dunlop and I.B. Cowan (SHS, 1970), *passim* (references in index).
48. *Cal[endar of Papal Letters to Scotland of] Clement VII [of Avignon, 1378-94*, ed. C. Burns (SHS, 1976)].
49. Ibid., 181 (Mariette 'Nilzarre' or, better, 'Enyenachyn').
50. *Moray Registrum*, 353 (Mariota filia Athyn, better, Achyn).
51. W. Mackay, *The Battle of Harlaw: its true place in history* (Inverness, 1922), 19-20.
52. *Cal. Clement VII*, 188-9.
53. *Calendar of Papal Letters to Scotland of Benedict XIII of Avignon, 1394-1419*, ed. F. McGurk (SHS, 1976), 103.
54. *Genealogical Collections concerning families in Scotland, made by Walter MacFarlane, 1750-1*, ed. J.T. Clark (SHS, 2 vols., 1900. See particularly vol. i. 36-40, 54-407; ii, 301-331, 357-79, 484-512.)
55. In the second edn (1890), iii, 458-90 (Appendix VIII).
56. Anderson, *Early Sources*, i, p. lxxxviii.
57. F.M. Stenton, *Anglo-Saxon England* (2nd edn, 1947), 702.
58. W.D.H. Sellar, 'The origins and ancestry of Somerled', *SHR*, xlv (1966), 123-42; 'Family origins in Cowal and Knapdale', *Scottish Studies*, xv (1971), 21-37; 'The earliest Campbells — Norman, Briton or Gael?', ibid., xvii (1973), 109-125.
59. Among a number of publications which might be listed special mention should be made of the following: J. Dunlop, short histories of clans Chisholm, Mackenzie (both 1953), Gordon (1955) and Mackintosh (1960); and R.W. and J. Munro, *Tain through the centuries* (1966); R.W. Munro, *Monro's Western Isles* (1961), *Kinsmen and Clansmen* (1971) and *The Munro Tree, 1734* (privately printed, 1978).
60. I. Moncreiffe and D. Hicks, *The Highland Clans* (London, 1967).
61. Edited in A. MacDonald and A. MacDonald *The Clan Donald* (3 vols., Inverness, 1896-1904), i, 513-4 (facsimile facing p.1).
62. *Highland Papers*, ii, 114-226.
63. *Lamont Papers*, (SRS, 1914).
64. *Fraser Papers*, 217-9.
65. *Spalding Miscellany*, iv (1849), 125-6 (Scayth filius Ferchardi).
66. *Moray Registrum*, nos. 85 (Fercardus filius Seth), 86 (Fercardus senescallus de Badenach).
67. Megaw, *Scottish Studies*, xx, 5-6.
68. *The Register of the priory of St Bees*, ed. J. Wilson (Surtees Soc., 1915), no. 43.
69. The surviving original is edited in *RRS*, ii, no. 176, the texts of the remaining three ibid., nos. 213, 388, 475.
70. J. Stuart, *The Sculptured Stones of Scotland* (Spalding Club, 2 vols., 1856-7).
71. J. Anderson, *Scotland in early Christian times* (1881).
72. J.R. Allen and J. Anderson, *The Early Christian Monuments of Scotland* (1903).
73. David MacGibbon and Thomas Ross, *The Castellated and Domestic Architecture of Scotland* (5 vols., 1887-92; photographic facsimile edn, 1971); eidem, *The Ecclesiastical Architecture of Scotland* (3 vols., 1896-7).
74. *RCAHM, Argyll*: i, Kintyre (1971); ii, Lorn (1975); iii, Mull, Tiree, Coll and Northern Argyll (1980).
75. K.A. Steer and J.W.M. Bannerman, *Late Medieval Monumental Sculpture in the West Higlands* (RCAHM, 1977).

Tombstone (undated) at St. Oran's, Iona, of Angus, son of Sir Angus mac Donald of Islay.

THE LORDSHIP OF THE ISLES

JEAN MUNRO

The Lordship of the Isles held a prominent position in the history of the Highlands in the medieval period, both in the Hebrides and in much of the mainland. In working on the record of the MacDonalds as Earls of Ross as well as Lords of the Isles, it is hard to put together a straight narrative from the various sources available, and so I thought that the most useful thing that I could do would be to try to unravel the thread of events for you.

Dr John Bannerman has made a study of social conditions under the Lordship in the 15th century, which I would recommend to those who want to know more on that topic.[1] This is only one of the fields in which recent work has helped towards an understanding of the lordship and its origins.

In Gaelic tradition the title king or lord of the Isles goes back to Somerled who lived in the 12th century but David Sellar has shown that Godfrey, son of Fergus, who died about 853 is an authentic ancestor of Somerled.[2] At his death Godfrey was described as a lord or lord of the Hebrides.[3] But after his time Norse overlordship and settlement of the west fill the gap of some 300 years until the emergence of a separate Norse dynasty in Man and the Isles under Godfrey Crovan in c.1079. His predecessors had already been called in Gaelic *Ri Innse Gall*— King (or ruler) of the Hebrides. Somerled, who married the grand-daughter of Godfrey Crovan, was first recorded as ruler in Argyll but extended his power into the islands. This brought conflict with his brother-in-law solved by a territorial division which left Somerled in possession of the Islay and Mull groups but not of Man, Lewis or Skye. This division remained until the death of the last king of Man in 1265. Somerled's descendants formed three branches called after his son and grandsons — the clan Dougal later associated with Mull and Lorn, the clan Donald with Islay, Kintyre and Morvern and the clan Ruari with the Uists and Garmoran (Moidart, Arisaig, Morar and Knoydart). Dr Bannerman suggests that until the 14th century the family was led by representatives of one or other group in succession following the Irish pattern. At first they kept considerable independence both from Scotland and Norway, although they owed allegiance to the former for their mainland and the latter for their island territories. In 1266 Norway ceded the Hebrides to Scotland and the island rulers became much more directly involved in Scottish affairs — for example representatives of all three of the branches attended the council at Scone which recognised the Maid of Norway as heir to the throne in 1284.[4] The wars of independence soon emphasised this involvement and upset the balance between the three groups of Somerled's descendants. The clan Dougal backed Balliol and although their leaders later recovered a good deal of their land they never again dominated the scene. The clans Donald and Ruari backed Bruce, and the close association of Angus Og the leader of the clan Donald with Bruce gave that branch a pre-eminence which was enhanced by the fact that the male line of clan Ruari came to an end when Roderick was murdered at Elcho in 1346 and that the heiress, his sister Amie, was already married to Angus Og's son and heir John who thus inherited the Uists and Garmoran.[5]

It is with John, son of Angus Og, that I propose to begin a more detailed study, as this is the period on which our study of the charters of the Lords of the Isles for the Scottish History Society is being based, extending from about 1350 to 1493. This period includes four lords John, Donald his son, Alexander *his* son, and finally again a son, John.

John Macdonald of Islay succeeded Angus shortly after the death of King Robert Bruce in the family lands in Islay and also in Mull and other possessions granted to his father by Bruce. Unlike his father, John was not a dedicated Bruce man and indeed he is found attached to the English interest when Edward Balliol gave him a charter in 1335[6]. But after the defeat of Balliol and his supporters, David II pardoned John and his Macruari brother-in-law. To John, he gave the islands of Islay, Jura, Colonsay, Mull, Coll, Tiree and Lewis, and the mainland districts of Morvern, Lochaber, Duror and Glencoe.[7] On the mainland the Macdougalls had only the lands between Appin and the south boundary of Lorn. This charter and John's succession to Uist and Garmoran established what was to be the lordship of the Isles and very soon afterwards John himself uses the designation not just of John of Isla but also *Dominus insularum* or lord of the isles. One of the first recorded instances of this style occurs in an indenture or treaty with John Macdougall of Lorn dated in 1354.[8] This sorts out the rights of each party to island properties in Argyll — Macdougall accepting Macdonald's right to Mull, Tiree and part of Jura, while Macdonald apparently relinquished Coll and parts of Tiree.

In 1350 while King David was still a prisoner in England, John of the Isles married Margaret, daughter of the Steward of Scotland, later Robert II[9] — John's earlier marriage was put aside on some pretext but he kept the Macruari lands. The long argument over the payment of the King's ransom found John, as one of the leading magnates of Argyll, absenting himself from Parliament and allying himself with his father-in-law in opposition to the King's policy. David had a bargaining factor in an act of revocation passed in 1367[10] which would have borne heavily on John but which was not consistently put into effect. It was probably this that brought him to agree to a second reconciliation and at Inverness in 1369 John made 'the most complete and unqualified submission' offering his father-in-law as security and handing over as hostages his son Donald and a grandson called Angus. He also undertook to obey royal officials and to pay contributions.[11] This was of course made easier when King David died early in February 1371 and was succeeded by John's father-in-law Robert II.

John called 'good John of Isla' by a later cleric[12] appears to have been liberal in his support of the church, as his ancestors had been — the poet did them less than justice when he called them 'a race that made no war on the church.'[13] The MacVurichs say that John made donations to Iona, roofed over chapels on Eilean Finlaggan and two other islands and equipped them with 'all their appropriate instruments for order and mass and the service of God':[14] the Macdonald shennachie adds that 'he mortified much land to the church in his time' and mentions the parish church in Benbecula and 'the little oratory in Grimsay' as having been built at his expense.[15] There is good evidence that the 5 major religious foundations in the west and the isles were founded by descendants of Somerled and in the case of Saddell abbey[16] perhaps by Somerled himself or his son Reginald, who is also credited with the transformation of Iona into a Benedictine abbey[17] and with founding the Nunnery there whose first prioress was a daughter of Somerled.[18] Ardchattan priory was founded by Reginald's nephew Duncan son of Dougall about 1230[19], while Oronsay priory was founded or perhaps transferred to Augustinians by good John himself, before 1353.[20]

The diocese of Argyll was mostly mainland and came directly under the Pope from about 1250.[21] The church of the isles was officially part of the diocese of Trondheim from 1153 although a cathedral for the southern part of the diocese called Sodor was being built at Peel in the isle of Man from about 1230. But the patronage of the Scottish part of the see was transferred to Alexander III in 1266.[22] In 1349 the Pope was sending copies of a letter about the bishop-elect of Sodor not only to John Stewart of Bute and John Macdonald of Islay but also to the people of the city and diocese of Trondheim — however the letter said that the bishop-elect need not visit Trondheim personally.[23] During the lifetime of John Lord of the Isles the separation of the Isles even from Man was coming about. In about 1330 a group of canons and local clergy of Skye elected a bishop at Snizort but it was not until 50 years later (in 1387) that the great schism in the papacy, during which Scotland supported the opposite side from England and Man, brought about a complete separation; and from that date the diocese of the Isles was established with Snizort as its not very convenient cathedral.[24] The relations between the Church and the Lordship require further study, but the problems are obvious — language, remoteness and claims of general barbarity. In 1433 Angus bishop of the Isles, who was a son of Donald, lord of the Isles, was asking for Papal licence to move his cathedral from Skye to some 'honest place' within his diocese — nothing seems to have been done.[25] In 1462 Bishop Lauder of Argyll after a rough reception in Lismore told the Pope that 'on account of strife raging between temporal lords and other magnates of his diocese he was unable to reside safely and befittingly in Lismore and to exercise jurisdiction, and his subjects as well clerics as seculars cannot convene to him in one place within his diocese without danger of their lives'. He asked for permission to live in Glasgow or some other suitable place within two days journey of the bounds of his diocese.[26] But only ten years later Angus bishop of the Isles and natural son of the former bishop Angus was requesting that he could have a house on the mainland where he could maintain episcopal state when called away from the Isles and suggesting Kilberry in Knapdale as he already had a life canonry of the church there before he went to the Isles.[27]

We return to John lord of the Isles to record his death about 1386 — he was taken ill at Ardgour and 'while yet alive' carried to his castle of Ardtornish where he died three days later surrounded by monks and priests — he was buried, as his ancestors had been, at Iona.[28]

He was succeeded by Donald the eldest son, not by his first Macruari marriage by which he had three sons, but by his second marriage to Margaret Stewart by which he had another four sons. It is evident from events, and endorsed in the chronicles, that this arrangement was supported or at least not actively opposed by Donald's half brothers — the eldest was already dead leaving a son; the second, Godfrey at one time held Uist;[29] and the third Ranald had a charter including Moidart, Arisaig and Morar with Castle Tioram[30] which became the country of his descendants the Clanranald.

Some sources say that Donald was a minor at the time of his father's death but I find this hard to believe as he had apparently been a hostage for his father in 1369,[31] and in any case we know that his parents were married about 1350. Another story is that he was educated at Oxford — Balliol being the college usually mentioned. This arises from a safe conduct granted in 1378 to Donald described as 'clerico' son of 'Johannis de Insulis'.[32] This is certainly another Donald and almost certainly another John — de Insulis is the style used by other members of the lord's family but very seldom by the Lord of the Isles himself except occasionally by English and other foreigners.

There are two important items to consider during Donald's period of rule in the Isles. The first is the famous and unique Gaelic charter by which on 6 May 1408 he granted to Brian Vicar Mackay several parcels of land in Islay in recognition of his services to Donald and his father and in return for the gift of 'four cows fit for killing for my house every year.'[33] There are learned arguments over whether or not this charter has a feudal basis but two things certainly cause it to stand out — one is that it is *signed* by two people, Donald himself and Fergus Macbeth and that the names of three witnesses with their marks are spread below the text in a way more usual in later documents. It is not the literacy that is unusual but the shape and the layout of the charter. The other thing is that the grant is made 'for ever and ever' 'to the end of the world' which has no feudal parallel that I know — the more usual form being to mention a specific period or to remain silent on the duration. There are texts of quite ordinary Latin charters which Donald granted to Maclean of Duart (just as Gaelic a family as Mackay in Islay) in 1390 and 1409[34] and the confirmation charter he gave to the abbey of Inchaffray in 1410 has survived in the original.[35] So the Gaelic charter doesn't represent just a stage in the development of Donald's secretariat — and the question must be, if one why not more? As far as we know there is no similar example in Ireland either. One theory is that island charters, more likely to be in Gaelic, suffered more than their mainland counterparts and there are many references to charters being destroyed — Maclean of Coll rather grandly informed the authorities in 1528 '*registrum combustum est*' when he applied for a confirmation of a previous royal charter[36] — and certainly the lordship 'register' if there ever was one, has long since disappeared. Another theory is that a more traditional verbal type of grant was common. The formula, very likely in Gaelic, is said to have gone something like this 'I Macdonald, sitting upon Dundonald, Give you a right to your farm from this day till tomorrow and every day thereafter, So long as you have food for the great Macdonald of the Isles.'[37] In 1772 Professor John Walker wrote to Lady Kaimes 'I beg, Madam, you'll ask My Lord, if among the many Charters he has ransacked he ever found one of this tenor.' Well, among those that have been 'ransacked' on our behalf in the S.R.O. and elsewhere we have found nothing of the sort.

Donald's other claim to fame is, of course, the battle he fought at Harlaw near Inverurie in 1411. The origins of this are quite as controversial as the Gaelic charter. There are two extremes of interpretation of Donald's motives in undertaking this invasion of the east of Scotland — one is that he was aiming to take over the earldom of Ross and the other is that he was aiming to take over the crown of Scotland. Donald's claim to the earldom of Ross was in right of his wife Mary or Mariota Leslie. This was fairly straightforward, as in the normal way she was the successor to her niece Euphemia who was still very young — certainly under 13 — in 1411. The succession had already gone through the female line when Euphemia's grandmother succeeded *her* father in 1371/2.[38] On the death of Alexander Leslie Earl of Ross in 1402, Donald might have expected the official wardship of the infant heiress. But Alexander had married a Stewart and by 1405 Albany had taken over his grand-daughter and was calling himself 'Lord of the ward of Ross'.[39] The power of the Albanys was getting very strong in the Highlands. Recently Mar had been acquired by one of them in very dubious circumstances and Donald may well have had good reason to suspect that Ross would be similarly swallowed up. There may have been more than that, for after the mysterious death of David Duke of Rothesay in 1402 and the death of Robert III in 1406 at the time of the capture by England of his son James, the Regent Albany looked to be swallowing up not just Ross but all Scotland. Donald was probably one of the few magnates and certainly the only one in the Highlands capable of withstanding the Albanys. In 1407 his nephew Hector Maclean

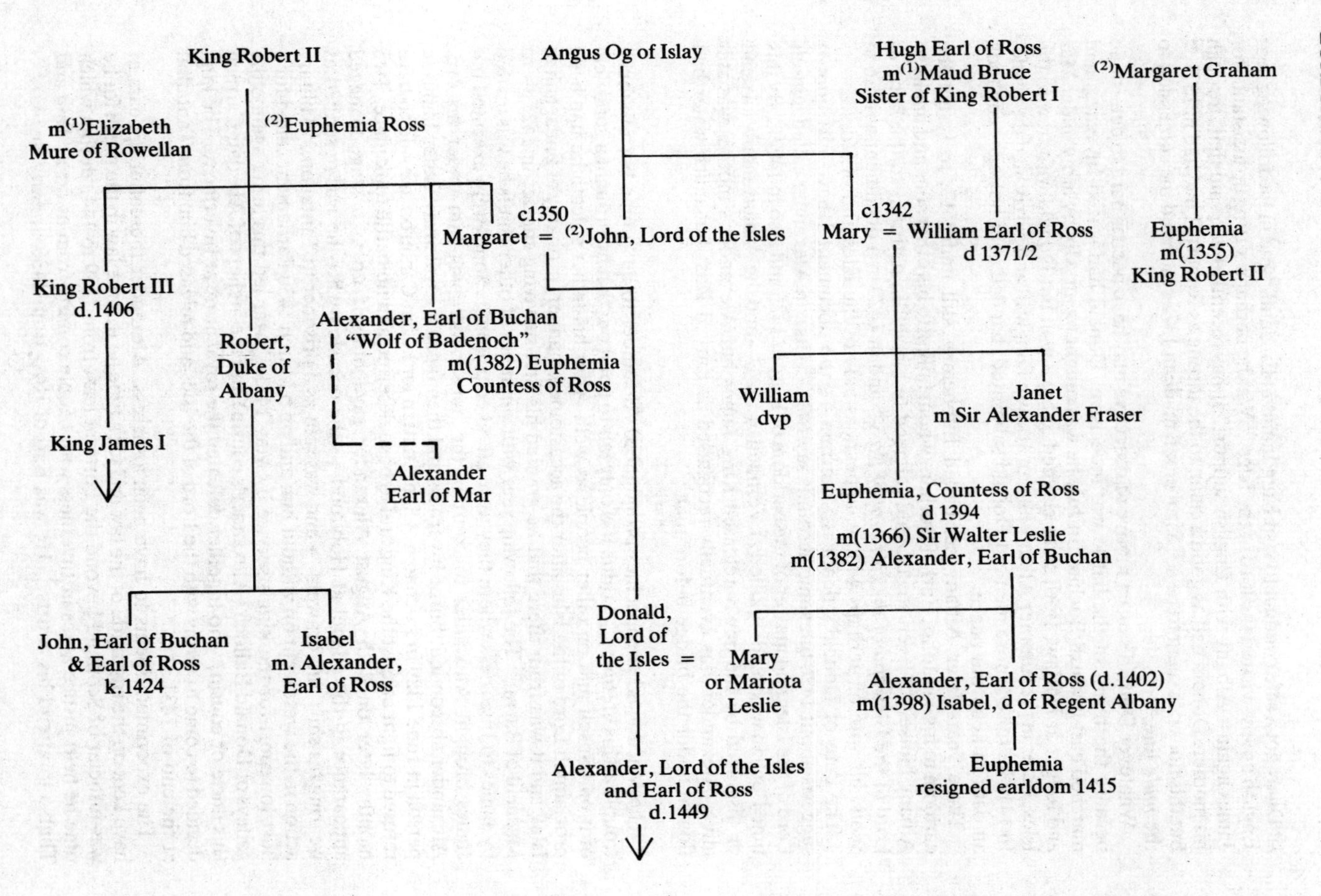
King Robert II
m(1)Elizabeth
Mure of Rowellan
(2)Euphemia Ross
Angus Og of Islay
Hugh Earl of Ross
m(1)Maud Bruce
Sister of King Robert I
(2)Margaret Graham
c1350
Margaret = (2)John, Lord of the Isles
c1342
Mary = William Earl of Ross
d 1371/2
Euphemia
m(1355)
King Robert II
King Robert III
d.1406
Robert,
Duke of
Albany
Alexander, Earl of Buchan
"Wolf of Badenoch"
m(1382) Euphemia
Countess of Ross
William
dvp
Janet
m Sir Alexander Fraser
King James I
Alexander
Earl of Mar
Euphemia, Countess of Ross
d 1394
m(1366) Sir Walter Leslie
m(1382) Alexander, Earl of Buchan
John, Earl of Buchan
& Earl of Ross
k.1424
Isabel
m. Alexander,
Earl of Ross
Donald,
Lord of
the Isles =
Mary
or Mariota
Leslie
Alexander, Earl of Ross (d.1402)
m(1398) Isabel, d of Regent Albany
Alexander, Lord of the Isles
and Earl of Ross
d.1449
Euphemia
resigned earldom 1415

of Duart got a safe conduct to visit King James in England[40] and in the following year English envoys visited the lord of the Isles.[41] Was he perhaps setting up assistance for James against Albany with English support? It has recently been said that, through his mother, Donald had as good a claim to the throne as Robert II had had in 1371,[42] but this does not seem to be so, as an entail made in 1372 restricted the succession to the *male* line.[43]

Whatever Donald's exact motive or objective may have been is hard to determine because the result of the battle was indecisive. Donald had seized Inverness and marched east towards Buchan. In July he was caught by an Albany army under Mar and fought at Harlaw. Both sides claimed to have won but Donald withdrew to the Isles. Later in the summer Albany had an army in Dingwall and garrisoned the castle. In 1412 he raised more men but Donald submitted, handed over hostages and took an oath to keep the peace.[44]

Three years later Albany persuaded Euphemia, still under 17, to resign the earldom to his son John, Earl of Buchan, whom failing to his other sons and finally to Albany himself.[45] Even so, Donald referred to himself in petitions to the Pope as Lord of the Isles *and of the earldom of Ross*[46] and in 1420 in a document written in Scots, his wife or perhaps widow, appears as lady of the Isles and of Ross.[47]

The date of Donald's death is uncertain — the document I have just quoted suggests about 1420 but some accounts say 1423.[48] His son Alexander called himself Lord of the Isles and master of the earldom of Ross in 1426 and also in 1427.[49] By this time Buchan was dead — killed at Verneuil in 1424 — and the Albany family all dead or disgraced by the newly released King James but Alexander's mother was still alive. Alexander was eventually recognised as Earl of Ross but much water had flowed under the bridge before that.

The Macdonald shennachies pronounced Alexander to be 'a man born to much trouble all his lifetime.'[50] I think it is only fair to point out that he brought a good deal of it on himself and on other people as well. After his father's death he had been proclaimed Lord of the Isles after the accustomed manner, probably at Finlaggan in Islay and it was from there that he granted his first surviving charter in 1427 — to Macneill of Barra.[51] The following year with a number of other chiefs he was invited by James to Inverness where they were all taken prisoner. Some were executed but James brought Alexander to court in the hope of keeping him under his eye. Alexander absconded, burnt Inverness and then faced a royal army under James in person in June 1429 in Lochaber. Clan Chattan and Clan Cameron are said to have refused to fight against the King and to have deserted and no battle took place. Two months later on 27th August Alexander gave himself up at a stage-managed appearance in the chapel at Holyrood — the occasion when he was described as wearing his shirt and drawers — and was sent as a prisoner to Tantallon.[52] Military action in the west went on without him and on 6 March 1430 Parliament called for a host to report for the king's service by May 1431.[53] Mar led this army against the galleys of Donald Balloch (Alexander's cousin) and the archers of Alasdair Carrach (his uncle or cousin) who together defeated the royal army at Inverlochy. The king decided to come to terms with the Lord of the Isles and released him from Tantallon at the end of 1431.[54]

The experiment seems to have been a success. Alexander thereafter appears to have kept on the right side of the law and for a time he *was* the law in the north for he was justiciar of Scotland beyond the Forth at least from 1439 to 1443 during which time he held justice ayres in Inverness with people coming from as far as Tain and Thurso to attend his courts.[55] He was Earl of Ross from 1436 or early in 1437.[56]

Perhaps this is the place to consider the implications of Alexander's mainland commitments and see what effect they had on his position as Lord of the Isles. Apart from one charter now lost but mentioned in some detail in the 17th century by the first Earl of Cromartie as having been dated at Finlaggan on 7 January 1432/3 and granted to Macleod of Lewis,[57] his charters are dated in Inverness and Dingwall or around and are concerned with the earldom and Lochaber. It should be pointed out that the Leslies had never had a presence in Ross, so that there was probably a good deal to sort out since the last earl of Ross had died in 1372, and indeed Alexander was probably not in total control of his earldom for some time — he would therefore be anxious to bring in the local families of Urquhart, Innes, Rose, Calder and Mackintosh to whom he was granting charters. But there is still plenty of unrecorded time and no reason to imagine that he abandoned his hold on the lordship.

There are some problems concerning Alexander's marriage or marriages and some non-marriages also. In the Vatican papers there is an indult dated 1433 addressed to Alexander and his wife apparently called Jacobella.[58] But in 1445/6 his wife Elizabeth procured a Papal mandate to admonish him and his concubine. Elizabeth is thought to have been a Seton, but it seems possible that she was a Haliburton.[59] He had two illegitimate sons Celestine and Hugh whom we shall meet again — the former was almost certainly older than his one legitimate son John who seems to have been born about 1434. In 1445 three other sons Hugh, Alexander and Donald were legitimised but nothing further is heard of them.[60] Alexander had some advantage in church matters as his brother Angus was bishop of the Isles from 1426 at least until 1438 and probably until 1441.[61]

In view of his own conduct Alexander seems to have taken rather an unfairly high line when he protested to the Pope against the scandalous behaviour of a monk of Iona who is described in January 1443/4 as having been notorious for a long time and 'hateful to the patron of the said monastery (Alexander) and to the temporal lords of those parts on account of his unhonest life and conversation'. He not only kept a concubine but was leader of a group who violently carried off goods belonging to the monastery. Alexander threatened that he would remove the bones and relics of his ancestors buried there and the precious things which they had given to Iona unless something was done.[62] Probably things in Iona improved, as the work of rebuilding the monastery from its ruinous condition may well have been begun quite soon after this by Donald O'Brolchan — money for such work was being collected as early as 1403 and a considerable drive was made in the 1420s, but the 'goings on' suggest that not much would have been achieved before 1444.[63] In view of all this it is perhaps fitting that Alexander, who died at Dingwall in May 1449, was buried not in Iona with his ancestors but at the Chanonry of Ross.[64] He seems to have died as he had lived as Earl of Ross rather than as Lord of the Isles.

His son John was much more involved with the Isles. He has been described by a clansman as a 'meek, modest man . . . more fit to be a churchman than to command so many irregular tribes of people'.[65] Yet John managed to quarrel with his wife, his son and his king and to lose both his earldom and his lordship. The chronology of the first few years of his rule is very difficult but important enough to look at quite closely. The sources for both national and local history are poor at this time, the chronicles confused and undated, and the main source, the *Exchequer Rolls*, were drawn up for accounting purposes and not designed to be helpful to historians in search of exact dates.

John is said to have succeeded his father in May 1449 at the age of about 15[66] — this in itself presents problems as he appears to have had no tutor or guardian, while the

King at 19 was still officially a minor. National history in the summer of 1449 is involved with the fall of the Livingstons who, until that time had held all the top jobs. John was concerned in this because he married Elizabeth daughter of James, later Lord Livingston, chamberlain of Scotland.[67] The exact timing of events would be of great interest as the marriage came either just before or just after the fall of the family — it was not a success. One theory is that the king arranged the marriage as a favour but against the inclination of the parties themselves — another is that the marriage alliance was a factor in turning the king against the Livingstons, and a third is that the bride's father hoped to gain a powerful ally against the king after his fall. James Livingston escaped execution and joined his son-in-law in the west. In support John seized the royal castles of Inverness, Urquhart and Ruthven. The rebellion must have been fairly short lived as James Livingston seems to have been keeper of Inverness castle on behalf of the king by July 1452 and by 1454 he was even back as chamberlain.[68]

The Livingstons on the whole were allies of the Douglases and the ups and downs of that family had considerable influence on John Lord of the Isles in ways which would last to the end of his life. The Douglas story is not primarily the concern of a highland historian but you will remember that king James clashed with them throughout 1451, and in February 1452 he personally murdered Earl William at Stirling. Chroniclers have stated that the outstanding issue between James and the earl was a bond which Douglas had made with the earls of Crawford and Ross and which the king demanded that he should break.[69] No copy of such a bond exists and no firm date has been attached to it (except by Sir James Balfour who gives 7 March 1445 which is unlikely[70]) and it may not have been formally written. Crawford certainly did rise in 1452 to help Douglas and was defeated by Huntly at Brechin in May. A passage in the Auchinleck chronicle provides a most tantalising clue. Dated 12 May, but without a year, it states that 'James the brother of erll William of Douglas that was slane in the castell of Strivling, come to Knapdale and spak thar with the erll of Ross and lord of the Ilis and maid thaim all richt gret rewardis of wyne clathis silver and silk and ynglis clath and thar gaf thaim mantillis agane and quhat was thar amangis thaim wes counsall . . . .' The May meeting of Douglas and John was evidently followed by a raid on Inverkip, Bute and Arran undertaken in July by Donald Balloch, cousin of John, with a fleet of galleys.[71] The only clue to the year is that it was the same year as the siege of Blackness. There are authorities who claim that these things took place in each of the three years 1452–54 inclusive, and they all base their views upon items in the Exchequer Rolls.[72] I am afraid I am not prepared to pronounce judgment.

On 1 May 1455 Douglas was defeated at Arkinholm and earl James fled to England. The king appears to have dealt lightly with John lord of the Isles, as in 1454 or 55 he was granted Urquhart and Glenmoriston with the Castle of Urquhart for life.[73]

The Douglas manoeuvres, of course, were linked with the wars of the Roses in England, especially after the death of James II in 1460. James had favoured Lancaster while Douglas and John of the Isles backed York. In March 1461 following his victory at Towton, Edward of York became king of England and Henry of Lancaster fled to Scotland. On 22 June 1461 Edward appointed James earl of Douglas and 4 Englishmen to visit John earl of Ross and lord of 'Owteryles' and his cousin Donald Balloch and on 17 July Douglas received money for the journey.[74] On 27 June John was in Bute with the Bishops of St Andrews and Glasgow who were probably trying to gain his support for the policies of the Regency.[75] The English party found the Lord of the Isles at Ardtornish in October and on 19th of the month

John gave a commission to Ronald of the Isles and Duncan archdeacon of the Isles to act as his ambassadors to Edward — using words nearly identical with those used by Edward which would have been available as a 'crib'.[76] Douglas was duly paid for safely escorting them from Morvern to the king's presence at Westminster.[77] There on 13 February 1461/2 a treaty was completed. Its terms[78] were startling and far reaching enough to satisfy the territorial ambitions of the Lord of the Isles and his militant cousin: for John himself, Donald Balloch and Donald's son John, bound themselves with their subjects and followers to become vassals of England, pledged to co-operate with Douglas and the armies of Edward in subduing and dismembering their native land — the part of which lying north of the Forth was to be shared between the three Macdonalds as vassals of the crown of England.

The ambassadors duly returned north with gifts of money and promises of more. John went to work quickly and took over Inverness and acted as king of the north. Although the treaty was still secret, he was summoned before the Scots parliament in the spring of 1462 but the Regent was not strong enough to make him come.[79] In March 1463 King Edward empowered the bishop of Down (Ireland) to take oaths and homages from John, Donald Balloch and his son,[80] but I know of no record that these were in fact given. Meanwhile the Scottish regency was abandoning Lancaster and turning to York and a 15 year truce was signed in June 1464. This presumably left the Lord of the Isles free to make his peace with the Scottish government. Mackenzie of Kintail is said to have got a charter from John at about this time of the lands of Strathgarve to defray his expenses in making peace between the king and the earl of Ross.[81] At any rate John admitted to seizing the burgh customs of Inverness worth £74 (but not of course to the treaty with Edward) and was accepted and forgiven when bishop Kennedy and others visited Inverness and Elgin in August 1464.[82] He did not himself attend parliament in Edinburgh that October but he was officially represented, as he was in 1467 and 1471.[83]

So there was a period of comparative peace and this seems an appropriate moment to consider the internal affairs of the Isles and Ross. Perhaps the most interesting aspect of this is the council which we know advised John on a fair number of occasions. The first reference to the council occurs in 1443/4, when Alexander with the advice of his council granted lands in Lochaber to Mackintosh.[84] In John's time there were a number of similar examples — the most interesting being the first as it is the only record of a sitting. On 28th May 1450 in the earl's chamber within the enclosure of the castle of Dingwall, John Ross of Balnagowan and three others appeared before John earl of Ross and Lord of the Isles and his council for consideration of a dispute over some lands granted by the old earls of Ross. The witnesses to this purely domestic Ross affair were John Stewart of Lorn, Lauchlan Maclean of Duart, John Maclean of Coll, Ranald MacAlistair and William thane of Cawdor.[85] It has been suggested that there might be separate councils for Ross and the Isles but on that evidence and on the whole it does not look like it. After this 1450 example we know of another nine charters granted by John with consent of his council,[86] some concerning island and others concerning Ross lands but all have a substantial number of island personalities as witnesses — also his son Angus made a grant in 1485 with the consent of his father and the council. There are various traditions covering the composition of the council in the isles, said to have met on the council isle in Loch Finlaggan in Islay, but quite evidently in session in Dingwall and elsewhere. These and the household or court which centred on the lords of the isles have been dealt with by Dr Bannerman in his essay in *Scottish Society in the Fifteenth Century*.

John was in trouble with his marriage at least as early as 1463/4 — we have only

Elizabeth's side of the story, but she had petitioned the Pope to admonish John for ejecting her from his lands and adhering to a certain adultress.[87] Twelve years later she says that the bishop of the Isles (Angus, son of the previous bishop and first cousin of John) was ordering her back to her husband and 'she fears lest the said bishop ensnare her with sentences and censures'.[88] Elizabeth had fled to the Scottish court and later got favours from James III for her devoted service to Queen Margaret.[89] Eventually in 1478 the Pope did grant her a separation. It has been assumed that there were no surviving children of the marriage though Elizabeth stated that she had borne children to John, but in 1506/7 'Elizabeth Ylis dochter to umquhile John Lord of the Isles' got a grant of lands in Islay for one year. Her mother was already dead.[90] I cannot help wondering if she was a legitimate daughter and if so what happened to her later. John's heir (officially recognised in 1476) was his illegitimate son Angus, born apparently before his father's marriage as he was old enough to go with Donald Balloch to take Inverness in 1462 — there was another illegitimate son John who apparently died before his father, but was junior to Angus.

Plots such as those hatched by John in 1462 could not remain secret for ever, and the treaty of Ardtornish came to light after Edward of England made peace with James III in 1474. In September 1475 John was ordered to appear before Parliament in Edinburgh in December. In spite of summonses by Unicorn Pursuivant at Dingwall castle and at the market cross of Inverness on 16th October John did *not* appear, and his life and lands were forfeited on 1 December. Four days later commissions against him were issued to Lennox, Huntly, Atholl and Argyll. Dingwall castle must have been taken by 28th March as James III wrote to Huntly on that day to thank him for his 'grete labour and charge in recovering the king's castle of Dingwall'. In parliament in Edinburgh on 1 July 1476 John, still styled '*excellentissimus et illustrissimus princeps*' and apparently at the request of Queen Margaret, was once more received by the king and the estates.[91] John renounced the earldom of Ross, the offices of sheriff of Inverness and Nairn and the lands of Knapdale and Kintyre — sealing the document with a seal now showing only the galley of the isles with no quartering of Ross lions[92] — but he was reinstated in his other lands and created a lord of parliament (surely somewhat of a come-down from the early family title of King?).

The exact progress of events after this is confused, as usual. Angus his son apparently did not support his father's submission — the family MS history says that Angus 'followed his former courses came to Inverness and demolished the castle'. He also made raids against Arran and in Knapdale and it was probably Angus rather than his father, who got the blame, who was in Castle Sween 'art and part of the treasonable stuffing of the said castle with men victuals and armes of weire' and holding it against the king. Once again John was summoned to parliament,[93] once again he submitted and got a renewed charter of his lands on 16 December 1478 when he was certainly present in Edinburgh as he granted a charter there himself six days later to Leslie of Wardis.[94] Among the long list of witnesses to this charter was Colin earl of Argyll and at some period after this Angus was married to Argyll's daughter.

In 1481 John was further humiliated in the eyes of his more hot-headed followers. He was given a charter by James III 'for his faithful service' of parts of his old lands in Kintyre and Knapdale, but for his lifetime only with no succession to Angus, and they are described as lying within the newly created sheriffdom of Tarbert — in other words fully integrated into the kingdom of Scotland. Quite a sizeable chunk of Knapdale including castle Sween had six months earlier been given to the earl of Argyll. John had also been present when the king raised an army intended to fight the English — perhaps this was his faithful service.[95] This attitude may have been the ultimate cause of the great sea battle fought at Bloody Bay north of Tobermory between John, supported by Macleods, Macneills and Macleans, and Angus with good assistance from the clan Donald. Angus emerged the winner and apparently dominated the northern scene until his murder by his harper in Inverness in 1490[96] — certainly when, as master of the Isles, he granted a charter to the abbey of Iona in November 1485 he had as witnesses the *judex* and the *archipoeta*, presumably members of the official household.[97]

After the death of Angus the leader of the hawks, or eagles, was Alexander of Lochalsh, son of John's natural brother Celestine.[98] In August 1492 he granted a charter along with John, though he was given no official position.[99] The Annals of Ulster refer to him as deputy of Macdonald, but the entry is one that records his death in battle.[100] Before that Alexander, with or without John's approval, but along with Farquhar son of the Mackintosh chief, invaded Ross but was defeated at the battle of Blair na Parc probably in 1491. John's last known charter was dated at Aros in Mull on 6 December 1492 and granted the patronage of the church at Kilberry to the bishop of Lismore.[101] After that there is a mysterious silence during which John was quite evidently forfeited yet again, and lost all the lands of the lordship. No mention is made of this in the Acts of Parliament and Sheriff Macphail even went so far as to suggest that it didn't happen — but in late August 1493 the king granted a charter of lands which it was specifically stated were in the king's hands owing to the forfeiture of John, formerly lord of the Isles.[102] The internal discord among the island families probably gave James IV the chance to strike 'sua that the kingis lyegis may lif in quiete and peax'[103] (or something nearer to quiet and peace anyway) which James III had not been strong enough to take against a united front in 1476. John fades from the scene and even the date of his death has been constantly mistaken. In fact he survived for nearly ten years as a pensioner at the court of James IV. Astonishing as it may seem — and an indication of how innocuous he had become — he was even allowed to revisit his former lands, as the Treasurer's Accounts show that in 1502 he got material for a new doublet 'agane his passing to the Ilis' and 28s. 'to his expense to pas to Lochabir'. The following January the king was at Dundee and John of the Isles was reported ill on 10 January and by 5 February he was dead, for money was remitted for his burial.[104]

James IV was at Dunstaffnage and maybe elsewhere in late summer 1493. Alexander of Lochalsh surprisingly appears to have submitted early — he and John Macdonald of Dunnivaig and the Glens, son of Donald Balloch, were knighted and Alexander evidently received some promise from the king for security of tenure for freeholders within the lordship[105] — certainly during the next few years a number of royal charters were granted to John's former vassals on terms similar to those by which they had held before, and these provide valuable evidence on landholding within the lordship in cases where no earlier charter is available. Sir Alexander was killed certainly before August 1498 and according to the Annals of Ulster as early as 1494 by John Cattenach son of Sir John of Dunnivaig, and John MacIan of Ardnamurchan.

The king visited the west regularly during the next few years, based mainly on the royal castle at Tarbert, in April and July 1494, in May 1495 and in March, May and August of 1498. But the lordship was not yet quiet. There were at least seven major risings during the next 50 years[106] — more than the Jacobites staged for the Stuarts in fact. Sir John of Dunnivaig and the Glens and his son John Cattenach were eliminated first; after the rebellion at Dunaverty castle in Kintyre in 1494 they were captured with the help of MacIan of Ardnamurchan and eventually hanged in

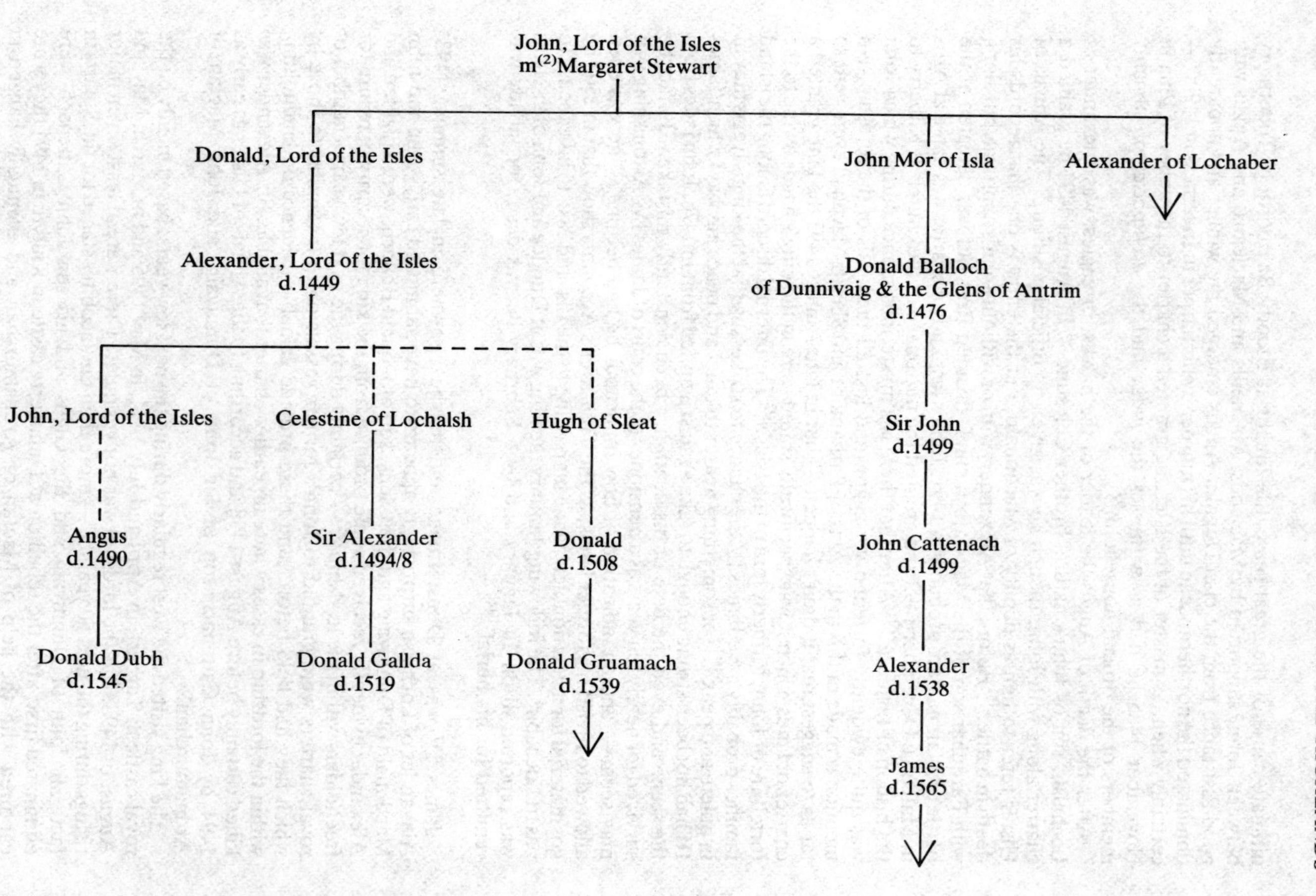
John, Lord of the Isles
m(2)Margaret Stewart
Donald, Lord of the Isles
John Mor of Isla
Alexander of Lochaber
Alexander, Lord of the Isles
d.1449
Donald Balloch
of Dunnivaig & the Glens of Antrim
d.1476
John, Lord of the Isles
Celestine of Lochalsh
Hugh of Sleat
Sir John
d.1499
Angus
d.1490
Sir Alexander
d.1494/8
Donald
d.1508
John Cattenach
d.1499
Donald Dubh
d.1545
Donald Gallda
d.1519
Donald Gruamach
d.1539
Alexander
d.1538
James
d.1565

Edinburgh in 1499.

Donald, son of Alexander of Lochalsh rose twice between Flodden in 1513 and his own death in 1519 — the later rising probably aimed mainly at MacIan of Ardnamurchan. He had been joined by Alexander, son of John Cattenach who tried again himself in 1529. Donald Gruamach grandson of Hugh of Sleat, also had a go at the royal forces in 1539 when he was killed by an arrow at Eilean Donan. But all these were small efforts in terms of men and influence.

All this time there remained one real threat to the throne and he insured that the forfeiture of the lordship was not accepted as final for more than 50 years. Angus, master of the Isles, left a son Donald Dubh, by Argyll's daughter whom the government rightly or wrongly claimed to be illegitimate. Donald was an infant or probably not yet born when his father died and he grew up a prisoner in the castle of Inch Connel in Loch Awe. He escaped in 1501 and was not recaptured for six years and three government campaigns, for he was supported by virtually all the former lordship vassals. The campaign of 1504 was directed by Huntly against the castles of Eilean Donan and Strome regarded as 'rycht necessar for the daunting of the Ilis'.[107] But Donald was retaken and he remained a prisoner until, at the time of the Rough Wooing in 1545, he was once more at liberty — Gregory says 'in what manner Donald Dubh effected his second escape is doubtful; but it is certain that he owed his liberty to the grace of God and not to the goodwill of the government'.[108] Again all the former vassals rose — a council was held on Eilean Carne apparently off the south of Jura on 28 July at which successors of the old councillors appointed two commissioners to treat with the English[109] — shades of Ardtornish in similar circumstances some 85 years before. In August the islesmen crossed the narrow channel to Ireland with a fleet of about 180 galleys. What followed was anti-climax. As Donald waited for the earl of Lennox who was also supporting the English his followers began to quarrel over the distribution of the English money. Lennox eventually gathered an expedition at Dublin of mixed English, Irish and islesmen to capture Dumbarton castle which he had promised the English he would do and had tried without success in 1544. The fleet did not leave until mid November and returned to Ireland having accomplished nothing. Soon afterwards Donald Dubh died of fever at Drogheda while on his way back to Dublin. The islanders tried to carry on under James of Dunnivaig but got no help from England and soon gave up.

Donald died without issue and with him died the last real hope of re-establishing the lordship of the Isles, which had dominated the west highlands for more than 400 years since the time of Somerled.

FOOTNOTES

1. *Scottish Society in the Fifteenth Century*, ed. Jennifer M. Brown (London 1977), 209–40
2. *Scottish Historical Review* (1966), xlv 123–42.
3. K.A. Steer & J.W.M. Bannerman, *Late Medieval Monumental Sculpture in the West Highlands* (RCAHMS 1977), 201–2.
4. Ranald Nicholson, *Scotland: The Later Middle Ages* (Edinburgh 1974), 25. Readers are frequently referred in these notes to this work, in which Highland events are fully discussed and chronicle sources (as well as records) extensively used and cited.
5. Steer & Bannerman, 203–4.
6. Nicholson, 143.
7. *Acts of the Parliaments of Scotland*, xii 6.
8. *Highland Papers*, ed. Macphail (SHS 1914), i 76–78.
9. *Calendar of Papal Letters*, iii 381.
10. *APS*, i 499–501.
11. *APS*, xii 16–17.
12. D. Monro, *Western Isles*, ed. R.W. Munro (1961), 94.
13. Steer & Bannerman, 208.

14. Book of Clanranald, in A. Cameron, *Reliquiae Celticae*, ii 161.
15. *HP*, i 26.
16. I.B. Cowan & D.E. Easson, *Medieval Religious Houses — Scotland*, 77.
17. *Ibid*. 59.
18. *Ibid*. 151.
19. *Ibid*. 93.
20. *Ibid*. 94.
21. D.E.R. Watt, *Fasti Ecclesiae Scoticanae Medii Aevi* (SRS 1969), 28.
22. *Ibid*. 197.
23. *CPL*, iii 279.
24. Watt, *Fasti*, 207.
25. Register of Supplications (Vatican Archives), 289 fo. 253.
26. *Ibid*. 550 fo. 212.
27. *Ibid*. 683 fos . 173–4.
28. *HP* i 27; *Rel. Celt.*, ii 161.
29. *Inchaffray Charters* (SHS 1908), 136 no 142.
30. *Reg. Mag. Sig.*, 1 Jan 1372/3.
31. *APS*, xii 16.
32. *Rotuli Scotiae*, ii 11.
33. *Facsimiles of the National MSS of Scotland*, pt. ii, p 46 & plate lix.
34. *RMS* 13 July 1495.
35. *Inchaffray Charters*, 137 no 143.
36. *RMS* 1 Dec. 1528.
37. *New Statistical Account of Scotland* (Argyle), 384.
38. *APS*, i 537–8.
39. *Book of the Thanes of Cawdor* (Spalding Club 1859), 5.
40. *Calendar of Patent Rolls* (1405–8), 363.
41. Rymer's *Foedera*, iv (1) 131.
42. Dr Bannerman in *Scottish Society* (1977), 214.
43. *APS* i 549.
44. Nicholson, 235.
45. Scottish Record Office, Reg. Ho. charter no 243.
46. *Calendar of Scottish Supplications to Rome* (SHS 1934), i 268–9 &c.
47. *Register of Moray* (Bannatyne Club 1837), 475–6.
48. E.g. *Scots Peerage*, ed. Sir J. Balfour Paul, v 42.
49. *CSSR* (SHS 1956), ii 189; *RMS* 14 Nov 1495.
50. *HP* i 34.
51. *RMS* 14 Nov 1495.
52. Nicholson, 315–16.
53. *APS* ii 19.
54. Nicholson, 316–17.
55. *Familie of Innes* (Spalding Club 1864), 73; *RMS* 4 Aug 1476; C.F. Mackintosh, *Antiquarian Notes*, i 184–5.
56. Charter to Alexander McCulloch, 6 Jan 1436/7, transcript in National Library of Scotland, MS 35.4.12a; *Exchequer Rolls*, v 33-34.
57. W. Fraser, *Earls of Cromartie* (1876), ii 511.
58. Reg. Supp., 289 fo. 253.
59. *HP* i 94–5; *Scrymgeour Inventory* (SRS 1912), no 145.
60. *HP* i 92–3.
61. Watt, *Fasti*, 203.
62. *HP* i 90.
63. Steer & Bannerman, 106–8.
64. *Ane Breve Chronicle of the Earlis of Ross* (1850 edn.), 10.
65. *HP* i 47.
66. *Exch. Rolls*, v preface xcii.
67. *Asloan Manuscript*, ed. Craigie (STS 1923), 235.
68. Nicholson, 362.
69. *Ibid*, 358.
70. *Annales of Scotland* (1824 edn.), i 173.
71. *Asloan MS.*, 221.
72. E.g. Nicholson 362, Bannerman in *Scottish Society* 217, A.I. Dunlop, *Life and Times of Bishop James Kennedy* (1950), 151.
73. *Exch, Rolls*, vi 68, 217.
74. *Foedera*, xi 474; *Calendar of Documents relating to Scotland*, ed. Bain, iv 1317.
75. *RMS* 11 April 1475; Dunlop, *Bishop Kennedy*, 223.
76. *Rot. Scot.*, ii 407.
77. *Cal. Docs. Scot.*, iv 1326.
78. *Rot. Scot.*, ii 405–7.
79. Nicholson, 402.
80. *Foedera*, xi 499.

81. Fraser, *Cromartie*, ii 473.
82. *Exch. Rolls*, vii 296–7; *RMS* 16 & 21 Aug. 1464.
83. *APS* ii 84, 87, 98.
84. Nat. Lib. Scot., MS 2123 fos. 69–70.
85. SRO ref. GD 297/191.
86. Monro, *Western Isles*, 140–3.
87. *CPL* v 671.
88. *CPL* xiii 66–7.
89. *RMS* 14 Dec 1476, 15 Oct 1477.
90. *Reg. Sec. Sig.*, 1 Jan 1506/7; *RMS* 1 Jan 1505/6.
91. *APS* ii 108ff.
92. SRO, ref. RH 6/457.
93. *APS* ii 155.
94. *RMS* 16 Dec 1478, 4 Feb 1478/9.
95. *RMS* 11 Aug 1481; C.M. Macdonald, *History of Argyll*, 254.
96. *Rel. Celt.*, ii 163; *HP* i 52.
97. SRO, ref. RH 6/517.
98. Nicholson, 542–9.
99. SRO, ref. RH 2/1.
100. Steer & Bannerman, 207.
101. *RMS* 26 Dec 1507.
102. *RMS* 29 Aug 1493.
103. *APS* ii 228.
104. *Treasurer Accounts*, ii 301, 344, 354, 357.
105. *RMS* 5 Aug 1498.
106. For a good summary see Steer & Bannerman, 209–13.
107. *APS* ii 240.
108. D. Gregory, *History of the Western Highlands and Isles* (1836), 155.
109. *Cal. State Papers* (Thorpe), i 53; Monro, *Western Isles*, 121–2.

X70 Castle Urquhart.

THE MEDIEVAL ARCHITECTURE OF THE SCOTTISH HIGHLANDS

JOHN DUNBAR

Introduction

Foreseeing the difficulty in defining the boundaries of the Scottish Highlands, your Secretary, in issuing an invitation to prepare this paper, proposed that the area in question should be taken to comprise the present Highland Region together with the District of Argyll and Bute. Accordingly this suggestion has been adopted, although with some modifications, of which the most important are the exclusion of Nairn and the inclusion of the Outer Hebrides and the Island of Arran, as also of the Isle of Man during that period when it was directly subject to Scottish influence i.e. up to about the middle of the 14th century. It follows that in the context of medieval historical studies the area under discussion corresponds almost exactly with the four dioceses of Caithness, Ross, Argyll and the Isles.

To what extent the Highlands as thus defined may be considered to have formed a single historical entity during the Middle Ages must be left for other contributors to consider. So far as architecture is concerned, it is convenient to discuss the region in terms of two major geographical divisions, of which the first comprises the Western Isles together with the western mainland south of a line from Inverness to the Kyle of Lochalsh, while the second embraces the northern mainland. The first of these divisions corresponds broadly with the medieval dioceses of Argyll and the Isles and the second with the dioceses of Caithness and Ross.

Although geography ensured that in both these areas settlement was mainly coastal, it tended to set them apart in certain other important respects. In the West Highlands and Islands prime agricultural land was to be found only in a few favoured localities, such as Bute and parts of Islay and Kintyre, but excellent grazing was available almost everywhere. Whereas communications with central and eastern Scotland were in general difficult, often involving arduous overland journeys through inhospitable country, the Western Highlands and Islands themselves were linked by a network of coastal waterways, which also brought the Clyde Basin, Ireland, the Northern Isles and much of the west coast of England within comparatively easy reach.

The ready availability of water transport was of particular importance to the building industry, because the area as a whole was poorly provided with building materials. The local rocks did not for the most part lend themselves to building, while freestone frequently had to be shipped long distances from the few suitable quarries, notably those at Ardtornish (Morvern), Carsaig (Mull), and at various localities on the Island of Arran. Nor was timber at all plentiful, except in parts of mainland Argyll and Inverness-shire, and there were few islands where major building operations could be undertaken without the import of at least the larger scantlings. Little is known of the organisation of the medieval building industry in the Western Highlands and Islands, but it is clear that the scattered nature of building activity, coupled with remoteness from mainland architectural centres, encouraged the growth of local idiosyncracies, and these grew more pronounced when the area became politically and culturally isolated in the later Middle Ages.

In the northern mainland settlement was concentrated in a narrow coastal belt of good arable land extending from Inverness to Thurso. Communications with eastern and central Scotland were generally good, with Moray and Buchan, in particular, being readily accessible by sea. To the north Orkney lay within a short sailing distance of Caithness, while southwards an important natural route by way of the Great Glen linked the area to adjacent parts of the West Highlands.

Easter Ross and the Dornoch Firth were well provided with freestone, and the excellent sandstone quarries of Moray also lay within easy reach. Local supplies of timber may likewise have been supplemented by imported materials from the same area. In Caithness and much of Sutherland, on the other hand, although the local flagstones were ideal for general building purposes, freestone and timber were hard to come by. The most convenient sources of freestone lay around Dunnet Head and in Orkney, but there is little evidence for the use of material from these areas until towards the end of the period now under review. In these circumstances it is not surprising to find that, whereas south of the Dornoch Firth architecture was responsive to developments in the principal eastern and central mainland centres, in the north local influences predominated.

FROM THE 12TH CENTURY TO THE WARS OF INDEPENDENCE

The West Highlands and Islands

Two main periods of building activity can be identified, the first extending from about the third quarter of the 12th century to the middle of the following century and the second from the last quarter of the 13th century to the first decade or so of the 14th century.

One of the earliest manifestations of the first period of activity can be recognized on the island of Bute, where there are surviving remains of two churches, both possibly of parochial status, together with a major castle, all probably constructed between 1170 and 1200. Both churches were erected on pre-existing ecclesiastical sites, the larger of them within the earlier monastic settlement of Kilblane[1] and the smaller upon the offshore islet of Inchmarnock.[2] Although differing considerably in size, both churches are two-chambered, each comprising an oblong nave and a small square-ended chancel entered by means of a narrow chancel-arch. At St Blane's enough remains to show that the church was richly decorated in the late Romanesque style, while the few surviving mouldings from Inchmarnock closely parallel comparable details at Kilblane. Both in plan-form and decoration these churches belong to the main stream of Scottish Romanesque church architecture as evidenced in the southern and eastern lowlands.

Fig. A

It is less easy, however, to find a convincing architectural context within which to place Rothesay Castle.[3] As first constructed, this comprised a simple castle of enclosure of almost circular plan measuring about 42 m in diameter; no towers projected from the curtain-wall and the two entrances were of the plainest description. Little is known of the early arrangement of the interior, but it is possible that most of the accommodation was contained within lean-to buildings of timber construction surrounding an open central court. In Scotland the closest parallels are to be found among a group of simple rectangular and polygonal castles of enclosure of late 12th- and 13th-century date, some of which are mentioned below. Similar castles of circular and polygonal plan, often termed 'shell-keeps' or 'shell-walls', occur widely in England (e.g. at Restormel), usually being placed on elevated sites.

Fig. E

The plans of many of these castles were dictated by the configuration of earlier defensive earthworks and this may also have been the case at Rothesay, where the castle occupies a strategic albeit low-lying site adjacent to the harbour.

Stylistic considerations indicate that the churches of St Blane and Inchmarnock date from about the third quarter of the 12th century, while similarities between the sandstone ashlar masonry at the former and that employed in the curtain-wall at Rothesay suggest that the castle was erected during the same phase of building activity. It is possible, therefore, that this activity is to be associated with the establishment of the Stewart family in Bute some time in or after the latter part of the reign of Malcolm IV.[4]

The same period witnessed a good deal of church building in the adjacent mainland parts of Argyll, but under different patronage and in a different architectural style. At Saddell, in Kintyre, a Cistercian monastery was founded by Somerled (d. 1164), or his son Reginald, lord of Kintyre.[5] The exact date of establishment is unknown, but apart from the Savigniac (afterwards Cistercian) house of Rushen (1134), in the Isle of Man, of which the existing church seems to have been laid out only in the 1190s, Saddell appears to have been the first medieval monastic foundation in the area under review. Saddell was colonised from Mellifont, Co Louth, and the elementary cruciform plan, with its aisleless nave, conforms to that of *Fig. B* the simplest Irish and Scottish churches, such as Shrule, Co Longford (another daughter-house of Mellifont), Grey, Co Down, and Culross and Balmerino, Fife; the transepts may have incorporated pairs of shallow eastern chapels, but there is no conclusive structural evidence of these. To judge from the character of surviving fragments of Romanesque decoration at Saddell, it seems likely that Irish masons were employed in the construction of the church. Rushen,[6] colonised from Furness, Lancashire, also incorporated an aisleless nave and there is some evidence to suggest that this was not completed until about the middle of the 13th century; little is known of the stylistic character of the church, of which only a few fragments now survive.

The earliest parish churches of Kintyre, which appear to belong to the second half of the 12th century, are more akin to the pre-Romanesque churches of the West Highlands and of Ireland than to contemporary examples in Bute and mainland Scotland. Examples occur at Kilchenzie, Kilcousland and Killean, all of which are *Fig. A* simple unicameral buildings with little or no architectural embellishment.[7] Similar churches were erected in Knapdale, as at Keils and Kilmory Knap, both of which probably commemorate the patronage of the local baronial family of MacSween, whosc adjacent and contemporary stronghold of Castle Sween is described below (p.44). Kilmory is of particular interest on account of its twin-light east wall, perhaps the earliest surviving example of a type which became popular in the 13th century. The keeled roll-moulding of the S nave-doorway suggests, however, that the church was erected not earlier than about the last decade of the 12th century.

Towards the turn of the 12th and 13th centuries the focus of West Highland architectural activity, so far at least as church building was concerned, shifted to Iona, where it was to remain intermittently until the end of the Middle Ages. Already in about the third quarter of the 12th century Somerled, or his son Reginald, had erected a family mortuary chapel within the principal burial-ground of Iona, the Reilig Odhráin. The west doorway of St Oran's Chapel,[8] which may have been constructed after the completion of the main fabric, incorporates carved detail of Irish Romanesque character, as seen for example at Clonkeen, Co. Limerick, and Aghadoe, Co. Kerry. It may therefore be inferred that for their primary building operations at Iona, as at Saddell, the Somerled family found it more convenient to bring masons from Ireland than from the Scottish mainland, and Irish influences continued to play an important, although not exclusive role, in the architecture of the two religious houses subsequently established on the island by Reginald (d. 1192 × 1207).

The Benedictine abbey of Iona[9] was founded in about 1200 and the first church comprised an aisleless choir, transepts with small mural chapels, and a nave having aisles at the east end only; there was no provision for a cloister. The plan is an unusual one, for which there are no obvious antecedents, and close parallels are likewise lacking for the somewhat austere Romanesque ornament, now surviving mainly in the north transept. The occurrence of certain Irish mannerisms, such as the use of continuous string-courses, suggests, however, that Irish masons were employed. Irish influences are also apparent in the second phase of building, commencing about 1220, during which the eastern arm of the church was considerably enlarged upon an undercroft and the construction of claustral buildings was begun. The extensive use of dog-tooth ornament during this phase suggests that masons from eastern Scotland were also present, but these imported styles soon merged to form a distinctive local school, whose character is clearly exemplified at the adjacent Augustinian nunnery. *Fig. B*

The original buildings of Iona Nunnery[10] are executed in the same architectural style as the extended choir and east claustral range of the abbey and are evidently of contemporary date. The church itself was quite small, comprising a nave and choir with a north aisle extending along both; the choir and north choir-chapel were vaulted — a rare feature in Highland medieval architecture. The church is richly decorated in the Transitional style, with an abundance of well-cut mouldings, sculptured capitals and dog-tooth ornament. Some features of the design, such as the framed windows of the west and east gables (the latter being of the twin-light variety) and the external angle-shafts of the choir and east claustral range, are characteristic of the contemporary ecclesiastical architecture of Ireland, while the placing of the nave windows above the arcade piers can be paralleled both in the Cistercian architecture of Ireland — as at Jerpoint, Co. Kilkenny — and in mainland Scotland.[11]

Stylistic influences emanating from Iona are clearly to be discerned in several churches erected on the Argyll mainland during the first half of the 13th century. The ornate chancel that was added to the parish church of Killean[12] incorporates external angle-shafts and a framed double-light window which seem to derive directly from Iona Nunnery, as well as zoomorphic decoration possibly inspired by the west doorway of St Oran's Chapel. The chancel may well have been designed and built by one of the Iona masons, although faults in the setting-out of the east window and uncertainties in the handling of the ornamental vocabulary suggest the work of a craftsman of limited experience. Similar paired windows and angle-shafts occur in the elegant chapel erected by the MacDougalls of Lorn in about the second quarter of the century at Dunstaffnage,[13] in close proximity to their contemporary castle of the same name (p.46).

Dunstaffnage Chapel finds a close parallel, so far as size and plan form are concerned, in the parish church of Inchcailleach,[14] Stirlingshire, situated just outside the limits of the Highlands as defined for the purposes of this paper. The mouldings of the two churches also display similarities, but Inchcailleach has no angle-shafts and its waterleaf capitals are of conventional type. Simple unicameral churches of similar kind were erected in other parts of Scotland during the 13th century and the resemblances noted above are insufficient to establish a direct connection between the two buildings. *Fig. A*

Most of the churches built in Lorn and Mull between about the end of the 12th and the middle of the 13th century, however, were of simpler design. Examples survive at

Kilchattan,[15] Kilvickeon and Pennygowan,[16] as well as on Iona itself, at St Ronan's and the Michael Chapel.[17] Here and elsewhere in the area twin-light east windows were popular and examples can be seen at Inchkenneth (Mull),[18] Southend (Kintyre),[19] Eilean Mòr (Knapdale), Kildalton (Islay), Faslane (Dunbartonshire)[20] and in second-period work at St Blane's (Bute). Few churches of the period can be identified in Skye and the Outer Hebrides, but Kilmaluag (Raasay)[21] appears to be of 13th-century date, while carved fragments of Transitional character at Snizort (Skye) (including a scalloped capital similar to some of those in the cloister arcade of Iona Abbey) bear witness to the existence of a church of some consequence, which may have been associated with a community of clergy such as is known later to have been established there.[22] Teampull na Trionaid,[23] at Carinish on North Uist, may also be of 13th-century date, while Teampull Mholuidh, Eoropie, on Lewis, has been ascribed to the end of the previous century on the strength of its distinctive plan-form and round-arched windows.[24] The plan of St Moluag's Church is certainly unusual, the unicameral church being flanked at its east end by a pair of narrow wings or side-chapels of which the east walls are flush with the east gable of the church. The parallel drawn between this plan and that of certain early Norse churches, such as Gardar Cathedral, Greenland, is not wholly convincing, however, and similar eastern wings occur in a number of Irish and Scottish churches of the later Middle Ages, such as Lismore Cathedral (p.43) and Oronsay Priory (p.52).

Fig. A

Apart from Iona Abbey and Nunnery, the only 13th-century monastic foundation in the area was the Valliscaulian monastery of Ardchattan, established by Duncan MacDougall of Lorn in about 1230.[25] This, with its sister-houses of Beauly, Inverness-shire (p.50), and Pluscarden, Morayshire, was one of three British houses of the Order founded at this time, all of them within or near the Scottish Highlands. Little now remains at Ardchattan of the original monastic church, which appears to have comprised a nave with narrow north aisle, transepts with twin eastern chapels and (presumably) a short aisleless choir, but certain details of its construction reflect local architectural influence. Thus, the transeptal chapels are of unusually shallow projection and can be more closely paralleled at Iona Abbey than in contemporary Cistercian churches, upon which those of the Valliscaulians were most frequently modelled. Other links with the Iona churches, or their derivatives at Killean and Dunstaffnage, are evidenced by the employment of external angle-shafts, fleur-de-lys capitals and copious dog-tooth ornament.

Fig. B

While work was going on at Ardchattan two important churches were under construction on the Isle of Man. As already noted (p.40), little now remains of the nave of Rushen Abbey, which appears to have been completed shortly before 1257, but the cathedral of the Isles at Peel retains the imposing chancel erected by Bishop Simon before his death in 1247.[26] Simon was an Argyll man, but the architecture of St German's Cathedral has more in common with that of Anglo-Norman Ulster than of the West Highlands. The building of the cathedral is thought to have been promoted by King Godred II's daughter Affreca, wife of John de Courcy, lord of Ulster, and foundress of the Cistercian abbey of Grey, Co. Down, and the design of the chancel, with its prominent lancet windows, certainly recalls that of the east limb of Grey, while some of the light brown sandstone used for the cathedral dressings is said to derive from an Ulster quarry.[27] At the beginning of the 14th century the level of the chancel floor was raised to accommodate an enlarged crypt (thus inaugurating an arrangement similar to that previously introduced at Iona Abbey), while later in the same century the nave and crossing of the cathedral were rebuilt in the Decorated style.

Fig. C

Following an apparent lull during the third quarter of the 13th century, a second and much shorter phase of church building began in about 1270 with an ambitious proposal to erect a new and very large south transept at Iona Abbey (p.41). This transept, of which only the footings were laid before work was abandoned, was designed to incorporate an eastern aisle of three vaulted bays, communication with the adjacent two-level monastic choir of the early 13th century being contrived by means of an extruded stair-tower. It is not clear what purpose the transept was intended to serve, but it is possible that, like the somewhat similar annexe-transepts of Irish friary churches, the extension was designed to provide additional accommodation for the laity, perhaps in this case being undertaken in response to a demonstrated or anticipated increase in pilgrimage traffic. There is nothing recognizably Irish about the surviving Iona mouldings, however, and the layout of the eastern aisle finds its closest parallel in the transepts of St Andrews Cathedral.

The most important undertaking of the period was the erection of the cathedral church of the diocese of Argyll on the island of Lismore, where the see had been established for more than a century. Not surprisingly, in view of the poverty of the see, the cathedral[28] was of simpler design than any other of its period in Scotland, the plan comprising an aisleless nave and choir, from the north wall of which there projected a small sacristy; a tower of modest dimensions was subsequently added to the west end of the nave. In general the layout recalls that of some of the minor Irish cathedrals, such as Tuam,[29] but the curious mouldings of the presbytery bear little relationship to surviving work either in the West Highlands or in Ireland; indeed, the closest parallels so far discovered are with certain details in the south aisle of Fortrose Cathedral (p.55). In these circumstances it is difficult to postulate a date for the erection of Lismore Cathedral but, since most of the architectural detail apears to be of early 14th-century character, it is likely that the greater part of the building belongs to this period.

Fig. C

Finally, mention should be made of Kilbrannan Chapel, Skipness,[30] probably erected at about the turn of the 13th and 14th centuries in consequence of the contemporary reconstruction of Skipness Castle (p.45). There is nothing distinctively Highland in the design of this church, for the plan can be paralleled not only at Dunstaffnage (p.91), but elsewhere in Scotland, as at Barevan and Altyre[31] in Nairn, while the mouldings are of conventional Anglo-Scottish First Pointed type.

Fig. A

Returning now to secular architecture, it may be noted that virtually the only type of building that falls to be considered is the stone castle. Buildings of other types and materials there undoubtedly were — it is recorded, for example, that a timber hall was constructed at Abertarff, Loch Ness, in the early 13th century[32] — but, since few survive in recognizable form, little can usefully be said about them here. Except in parts of Cowal, mottes and other earthwork castles of the period are uncommon in the area[33] and their absence can satisfactorily be accounted for partly by the known imperviousness of the Highlands to the spread of royal authority and feudalisation, and partly by the nature of the terrain, which made motte-building largely supererogatory. On the other hand, many natural rock-summits were no doubt crowned by defences of dry-stone masonry, timber and other perishable materials and the well-known poetic description of Somerled's castle in Galloway probably gives us a very good idea of the contemprary Highland stronghold:

'Upon a great dark-coloured rock
He had his house right nobly set,
Built all about with wattle-work.
Upon the summit was a tower
That was not made of stone and lime
Of earth the wall was builded, high,
And crenellated, battlemented,'[34]

As already noted, however, churches of stone and lime were being erected in the Highlands by about the end of Somerled's reign (d. 1164) and it was not long before the greater barons, at least, began to apply these materials to the construction of castles. One of the first to do so was Suibhne, lord of Knapdale, a member of a powerful local family having influential connections throughout the West Highlands and Ireland.[35] The dates of Suibhne's rule are not recorded, but traditional genealogies indicate that he flourished in about the last quarter of the 12th century and, although earlier dates have been proposed, there is no reason to doubt that the castle that bears his name was erected at that time.

Although Castle Sween[36] is sometimes described as a keep, all the evidence suggests that it was originally conceived as a simple castle of enclosure in which lean-to buildings, probably of timber-frame construction, were ranged round a small internal courtyard and light-well. Thus, the general conception resembles that of the contemporary castle of Rothesay (p.39), except that Castle Sween is smaller (21 m by 15 m internally) and its plan rectangular. The most remarkable feature of the castle, however, is the distinctly Romanesque character of the external elevations, which display angle- and mid-buttresses of flat pilaster type, one of which incorporates the semicircular-headed entrance doorway. *Fig. D* The origin of this design must remain a matter for speculation. The Irish affinities of the neighbouring churches (p.40), no less than the family relationships of the MacSweens, suggest the probability of an Irish derivation, but no convincing models are to be found among the surviving castles of that country. All that can safely be said is that the design of Castle Sween was probably formulated by a mason familiar either with the major Romanesque churches of Ireland or Lowland Scotland or with the Norman keeps of the Anglo-Scottish border.

The only true keep known to have been built within the area under review is Castle Rushen,[37] in the Isle of Man, the erection of which is usually attributed to Godred II, King of Man (d. 1187). As first built this was a plain square keep with a forebuilding, having neither plinths nor clasping buttresses. Simple unbuttressed keeps are comparatively uncommon in England and the surviving examples are a good deal smaller than Castle Rushen (about 13 m square internally), for which a closer parallel, in terms of overall size and plan-form, is presented by Carrickfergus,[38] Co. Antrim (about 11 m square internally), which appears to have been erected, or at least commenced, by John de Courcy, lord of Ulster, some time before his death in 1204. As already noted (p.42), de Courcy was closely related to the Manx royal family and his brother-in-law, King Reginald (1187-1226), was one of his chief supporters in his struggle against King John of England. In the light of these circumstances it is possible that Castle Rushen, like the chancel of St German's Cathedral (p.42), may have been built by masons brought from Anglo-Norman Ulster and that it dates, not from Godred's reign but from that of Reginald. Another Irish castle, Trim, Co. Meath, is generally believed to have served as a model during a second and not long subsequent phase of building operations at Castle Rushen in which small central towers were added to two sides of the keep. Some two centuries later the castle was even more drastically remodelled by an incoming English lord of Man, Sir William Montacute, who added a gatehouse to the keep, within the interior of which he also formed a small courtyard or light-well bearing a remarkable, but no doubt entirely fortuitous, resemblance to that at Castle Sween.

During the course of the 13th century a number of simple rectangular castles of enclosure similar in conception to Castle Sween were erected in the West Highlands, but few can be closely dated. The earliest is probably Innis Chonnell,[39] Loch Awe, which is about the same size as Castle Sween and, although partially reconstructed during the later Middle Ages, shows evidence of similar buttresses, as well as of fish-tailed arrow-slits of a type introduced into Britain about the turn of the 12th and 13th centuries. Innis Chonnell was a seat of the Campbells of Loch Awe and Argyll and despite the fact that the family does not come on record until towards the end of the 13th century, credible tradition holds that they acquired the lands of Loch Awe at a considerably earlier date.[40] It seems likely, therefore, that the castle was erected by a founder member of the Campbell family in about the first quarter of the 13th century.

Other castles of this group are to be found at Duart, on the island of Mull, at Castle Roy, on Speyside, and at Achadun, on the island of Lismore. At Duart,[41] which probably belonged to the MacDougalls of Lorn, little 13th-century work now remains, but Castle Roy[42] retains much of its enclosure wall, which incorporates an arch-pointed gateway, similar in style to one at Duart, and traces of lean-to timber buildings; the solitary angle-tower appears to be of secondary construction. Castle Roy was a stronghold of the powerful Comyn lords of Badenoch who had another castle, now vanished, at Ruthven, on Upper Speyside, as well as one at Inverlochy. This last probably belongs to about the third quarter of the 13th century (pp.46-7) and is more advanced in conception than Castle Roy, which seems likely to be of somewhat earlier date. Achadun[43] was an episcopal castle, the property having been granted to Bishop William of Argyll in 1240. One side of the courtyard was occupied by a substantial range of stone buildings, which probably incorporated a first-floor hall. Recent excavations have produced evidence indicating that the castle was erected at about the end of the 13th century and some of the masons' marks found there occur also in the neighbouring cathedral of Lismore (p.43).

To this period also may be ascribed the remodelling of the original stronghold of Skipness[44] (p.48) to form a quadrangular castle of similar layout to Achadun. Skipness is bigger and better equipped, however, the hall block being partially extruded from the main enclosure in the interests of greater length, the gatehouse being furnished with both portcullis and machicolation, and the curtain-wall in part being provided with well-placed arrow-slits of distinctive type. The mouldings and other dressings are of the highest quality and all are executed in the characteristic Edwardian style found in certain major Scottish buildings of the late 13th and early 14th centuries. Similar work occurs at the neighbouring chapel of Skipness (p.43) and elsewhere in the Clyde Basin at the castles of Brodick (p.47), Lochranza (p.49) and, to a lesser extent, Ardrossan Castle, Ayrshire.[45] At this period Skipness formed part of Knapdale,[46] which had been acquired from the MacSween family by Walter Stewart, Earl of Menteith, in the 1260s, and the rebuilding of the castle may probably be attributed to one of the Stewart Earls or to Sir John Menteith, on whose behalf Knapdale was being held in 1301.[47]

Fig. D

Larger by far (38 m by 33 m internally) than any of the simpler rectangular castles of enclosure so far described, and occupying a position of much greater strategic importance than its neighbour at Skipness, was the royal castle of Tarbert,[48] Loch Fyne, which guarded a vital porterage between the Clyde Estuary and the western seaboard. Only footings of walls now remain, but these show that the castle incorporated four ranges of stone buildings surrounding a square court entered by means of a central gateway. Tarbert Castle has no recorded history before the reign of Robert I, but in view of its close resemblance in size and plan to the royal castles of Kincardine, Kincardineshire, and Kinclaven, Perthshire, which appear to have been erected during the reign of William the Lion or Alexander II, there need be no hesitation in provisionally assigning it to the same period. In 1222 Alexander II made an expedition to Argyll which may have secured control of Cowal, Knapdale and perhaps Kintyre, and it is possible that the construction of Tarbert Castle was thereafter undertaken to consolidate the authority of the Crown in that area.[49]

Another group of simple castles of enclosure, probably broadly contemporary with those described above, is characterised by plans of polygonal shape. In general, these castles stand upon irregular and steep-sided rock summits and their distinctive outline probably reflects the practical difficulties of construction rather than any particular concept of military engineering. In such circumstances it was no doubt easiest to build the wall of enclosure in short straight stretches, varying the angle of intersection as the site dictated and frequently rounding off the external corners so as to economise in the use of freestone dressings. Several castles of similar form exist in Ulster,[50] as in the first phases of Dundrum, Co. Down and Carrickfergus, Co. Antrim, while Loch Doon, Ayrshire[51] represents a more sophisticated version of the same type.

The only West Highland example to retain datable features is Mingary Castle, Ardnamurchan,[52] which incorporates a few lancet windows of 13th-century character. The original wall of enclosure is also well preserved and, like that of Rothesay, preserves much of its early parapet and wall-walk sealed beneath later medieval work. The early history of the castle is obscure, but it may have been built by one of the MacDonald lords of Islay, who were certainly in possession during the first half of the 14th century. Another branch of the Somerled family, the Macruarie lords of Garmoran, were presumably responsible for the erection of the neighbouring castle of Tioram,[53] in Moidart, which in its first phase was so similar to Mingary as to suggest that the two buildings are contemporary. Smaller than either of these, but probably of similar date is Duntroon Castle,[54] Mid Argyll, which may have been another stronghold of the Campbells of Lochawe, while the fragmentary remains of the royal castle of Dunoon,[55] in Cowal, first recorded in the early 13th century, may also belong to this group.

Fig. E

In addition to the simple enclosure-castles already described, there were a number of more elaborately designed castles of enclosure of a type found throughout the British Isles during the 13th and early 14th centuries. These incorporated not only high curtain-walls, but strong gateways and well-defended flanking-towers, one of which often served as a keep or donjon.

Of the four castles of this category that can be identified within the area under review, the earliest is Dunstaffnage,[56] which displays architectural detail similar in character to that seen at the adjacent chapel (p.41) and at the neighbouring priory of Ardchattan (p.42), both of which evidently date from about the second quarter of the 13th century. The castle can therefore be ascribed either to Duncan MacDougall, lord of Lorn, or to his son Ewen, one of the most powerful magnates of the western seaboard, who succeeded to the lordship in about the late 1230s.[57] Among Scottish castles, at least, the design is advanced for its period, the irregular quadrangular enclosure incorporating two cylindrical angle-towers, as well as a half-cylindrical tower flanking the entrance, which was also defended by a drawbridge. Towers and curtain-wall incorporated long fish-tailed archers' slits, similar to those noted at Innis Chonnel (pp.44-5), while the larger of the angle-towers, placed *en suite* with a spacious stone-built hall, probably served as a keep. Nevertheless, the designer, who must have been a man of more than local experience, failed to exploit the full defensive potentiality of the angle-tower, those at Dunstaffnage being of too shallow projection to provide effective flanking defence for the curtain-wall.[58]

This deficiency, however, was amply remedied at Inverlochy, Lochaber,[59] erected by the MacDougalls' northern neighbours and allies, the mighty Comyn lords of Badenoch and Lochaber, to secure the southern sea-outlet of the Great Glen and the scarcely less important overland route to the Upper Spey by way of Glen Spean. Here the ground was open and low-lying and the castle was laid out as a regular quadrangle with boldly projecting angle-towers of circular plan. As at Dunstaffnage, one of these towers served as a lord's residence and keep, while the fish-tailed slits that so effectively flank the curtain-wall are likewise of the type employed at Dunstaffnage; they also occur in the 13th-century Comyn castle of Lochindorb, Morayshire, situated just outside the area now under review. Inverlochy seems originally to have been surrounded by a moat and the principal entrance may have been defended by a drawbridge, as both entrances certainly were by portcullises, but neither here nor at Lochindorb was there a strong gatehouse of the kind that became fashionable in major castles throughout the British Isles in early Edwardian times and which is found in notable Scottish castles of this period such as Caerlaverock and Kildrummy. The Comyns were in possession of Lochaber by the 1230s and, although documentary evidence relating to the construction of Inverlochy Castle is lacking, a date in the third quarter of the century seems appropriate on architectural grounds. Moreover, the family is known to have built at least one other castle at this period, for in 1269 the Earl of Atholl quarrelled with John Comyn of Badenoch about a castle that the latter had started to build at Blair Atholl.[60]

The two other developed castles of enclosure of which account must be taken here lay in the Stewart territory of Arran and Bute. Both present considerable problems of interpretation. At Brodick Castle, Arran, recent investigations by the Royal Commission on the Ancient and Historical Monuments of Scotland[61] have revealed part of a substantial drum-tower and an adjacent arch-pointed entrance, incorporated in the fabric of the eastern portion of the existing main block. Planted against the front of the entrance there is a forework or barbican containing an entrance passage and an upper chamber, traditionally known as Bruce's Room. The tower is equipped with archers' slits of fish-tailed crosslet type, similar to those at Skipness Castle (p.45). When considered in the light of the general character and layout of the present building, this evidence suggests that a strong castle of enclosure, provided with cylindrical flanking-towers, was erected at Brodick at about the turn of the 13th and 14th centuries, and was shortly thereafter strengthened by the construction of a barbican. The history of Arran at this period is obscure, but it seems to have formed part of the earldom of Menteith. According to Barbour there was 'a stith castell of stane' at Brodick by 1307 and, on the assumption that there would have been little opportunity to carry out extensive building-operations during the turbulent years of the interregnum of 1296-1306, it may be surmised that the initial erection of the castle was undertaken by Walter Stewart, Earl of Menteith (died c. 1292-3) or by his son Earl Alexander, who is not heard of as earl after 1297.[62]

Fig. E

The neighbouring island of Bute had for long been in the possession of the senior branch of the Stewart family and it is not surprising to find that here, too, efforts were made to strengthen the principal local castle. Already during the early decades of the 13th century the main entrance of the original castle of Rothesay (p.39) had been strengthened by the erection of a forework. Subsequently, four great drum-towers, comparable to those at Inverlochy, were added to the curtain-wall,[63] their effectiveness for flanking defence, however, being considerably diminished by the circularity of the enclosure. The date at which these towers were erected is uncertain. They contain archers' slits having deeply-plunged spade-shaped terminations characteristic of late 13th- and early 14th-century work, but all the slits appear to have been restored to a greater or lesser extent and it has been plausibly suggested that their spade-shaped terminations are modern imitations of a genuine slit of this type at Caerlaverock Castle,[64] Dumfriesshire. No early drawings of the slits are known and no detailed description of them is given in William Burges's penetrating report of 1872.[65] Moreover, there is preserved within the castle as a detached fragment the base of a fish-tailed archer's slit which may well derive from one of the flanking-towers. In the present context, bases of fish-tailed type in association with plain slits, such as occur at Inverlochy, are suggestive of a date in the second half of the 13th century, and in association with crosslet slits, such as occur at Skipness and Brodick, of a date about 1300. The Rothesay slits appear to have been plain, but it is difficult to be certain on this point. All that can safely be said, therefore, is that towers were added to Rothesay Castle before or during the first War of Independence.

The West Highland hall-houses form a fairly well-defined family group for which the closest parallels are to be found in Ireland.[66] None can be closely dated, but the hall-house constituting the original nucleus of Skipness Castle (p.45) is probably among the earliest to survive. As first constructed this was a freestanding building with a detached chapel, the whole possibly having been enclosed within a fenced rampart.[67] The hall-house comprised two main storeys, namely a cellar and a first-floor hall, together with an upper room, presumably a solar, which may or may not have extended the full length of the building. The principal doorway appears to have been situated at first-floor level and approached by means of a forestair rising against one of the side-walls. The hall itself was well lit, the principal surviving window being a double lancet set within a round-headed outer arch wrought with a plain edge-roll between single fillets; a mural latrine opened off one corner of the hall. The heating arrangements cannot now be ascertained. The architectural style of the window just described is indicative of a date within the first half of the 13th century and, since Skipness was owned by the MacSweens of Knapdale during that period, the builder may tentatively be identified as Dugald, son of Suibhne (the builder of Castle Sween, p.44), who is on record as lord of Skipness at various dates up to 1262.[68]

Fig. F

In four of the remaining hall-houses there was a ground-floor doorway in the centre of one of the end-walls, leading by means of a mural stair to the hall above; some of these buildings, however, may also have had first-floor doorways and forestairs of which no traces now remain. Of these four, Fincharn, Loch Awe, the lands of which are on record in 1240, was a small hall-house possibly associated with the MacGilchrist lords of Glassary,[69] while Castle Coeffin, in the island of Lismore, may have belonged to the MacDougall lords of Lorn.[70] Larger than either of these, and considerably better preserved, is Fraoch Eilean, Loch Awe, which is probably the castle mentioned in a charter grant of 1267 to Gillechrist MacNaughtan.[71] This incorporated an unusually spacious hall, of which the floor was supported upon an axial beam carried on timber posts within the undercroft; heating was probably supplied by means of an open hearth ventilating through a louver. Both in plan and overall dimensions Fraoch Eilean bears a close, although no doubt largely coincidental, resemblance to the English royal castle of Greencastle, Co. Down, erected in about the middle of the 13th century.[72] A closer parallel, so far as geography is concerned, is provided by the much ruined hall-house of Ardtornish, in Morvern, which probably belonged to the MacDonalds of Islay.[73] This, too, was similar in size and layout to Fraoch Eilean, even to the extent of incorporating, at one corner of the hall, a mural garderobe partially contained within an external buttress. The very wide span of the hall, identical to that of Fraoch Eilean, suggests that here, too, the floor was supported by central posts.

In two other hall-houses the buttressed corner-chamber was extended to form a small wing comparable to those found in the more elaborately planned eastern mainland hall-houses of Rait, Nairnshire, and Tulliallan, Fife. At Aros,[74] on the island of Mull, the wing probably incorporated a latrine opening off a solar which, together with the large adjacent hall, occupied the first floor. The hall itself appears to have risen to an open timber roof, but there seems to have been a chamber or loft above the solar. The scanty surviving architectural detail suggests a date of erection in the late 13th or early 14th century. As already noted (p.45), Lochranza Castle,[75] in the island of Arran, belongs to the same period. The original hall-house has been much overlaid by later work and analysis is difficult, but it is clear that the entrance arrangements were quite elaborate, the ground-floor doorway having been provided with outer, middle and inner doors, as well as with a machicolation. The wing appears to have incorporated a ground-floor prison (an arrangement found also at Fraoch Eilean), with a latrine above, opening directly from the hall.

Finally, mention should perhaps be made of the fragmentary remains of the castle of Camus, or Knock,[76] on the island of Skye, which may have been a hall-house. If so it is the only structure of this class so far to have been identified in Skye and the Outer Hebrides.

Ross, Sutherland and Caithness

In contrast to the large numbers of buildings of this period that survive in the Western Highlands and Islands, the architectural remains of the mainland area north of Inverness make a decidedly poor showing. Secular architecture is almost entirely lacking and the only ecclesiastical buildings of any consequences are those stemming from a short period of building activity during the first half of the 13th century.

The earliest churches that can be identified, some of which may be as old as the 12th century, are situated in Caithness. The best preserved of these is St Mary's Chapel, Lybster,[77] which is a small two-chambered building comprising a square-ended chancel together with a nave having a west doorway. The footings of two or three other chancelled chapels also exist, although recent excavation at one of these has shown that the nave was added to an original unicameral building.[78] St Peter's Church, Thurso, a cruciform structure of mainly 17th-century date, incorporates at its east end a small apsidal-ended cell which may be a relic of an early chancelled building.[79] *Fig. H*

The evidence is too scrappy to allow any firm conclusions to be drawn, but the presence of small chancelled churches deserves comment since buildings of this type are, as already noted, almost unknown in the Western Highlands at this period. Such churches are, however, a familiar feature of the 12th- and 13th-century architecture of the Northern Isles and in view of the close political links then existing between Orkney and Caithness it seems likely that the design of these mainland churches was derived from Orkney.

The major ecclesiastical foundations of the first half of the 13th century were all made in the area between the Moray Firth and the Dornoch Firth within a few years of one another, and bear witness to the success of the Scottish Crown in pushing the frontier of royal authority thus far northwards at that period. Caithness itself, however, had still to be fully integrated within the Scottish realm and it was no doubt for this reason that, following his appointment as bishop in 1223, Gilbert de Moravia moved the episcopal centre from its original site at Halkirk (where his predecessor had recently been murdered) to Dornoch, at the southern extremity of the diocese, where he and others of his family were major landholders.[80]

Of the first cathedral of Caithness, which presumably stood at Halkirk, nothing now remains, but enough survives of its successor at Dornoch to enable the main features of the design to be grasped.[81] The church comprised an unaisled choir lit by a series of tall single-light windows, an aisled nave of four bays, a crossing with central tower, and short transepts; on the north side of the choir there was a chapter-house or sacristy. The architectural evidence suggests that building commenced soon after Bishop Gilbert's appointment, and work was sufficiently advanced by 1239 to allow the remains of the murdered Bishop Adam to be translated thither from Halkirk. 18th-century descriptions and drawings of the now-vanished nave indicate, however, that this was rebuilt during the later Middle Ages.

As might be expected in view of the relative poverty of the see, Dornoch is one of the smallest Scottish cathedrals. The design belongs to the main stream of early Gothic architecture in Scotland and alike in plan, dimensions and architectural style the building bears a close resemblance to the cathedral of Brechin, erected during the early decades of the 13th century. At Brechin, however, the tower stands at the north-west corner of the nave, while the general treatment, as seen for example in the decoration of the choir, is richer than at Dornoch.

Although the cathedral of Fortrose seems to have been begun about the same time as that of Dornoch, little work of this period survives. Here, too, building was commenced on a new site, for the early cathedral of the diocese of Ross stood at Rosemarkie and it was only during the episcopate of Bishop Robert (1214-49), when the cathedral chapter was considerably enlarged, that the see appears to have been moved a short distance southwards to Fortrose.[82]

Fig. C

To judge from the foundations exposed by excavation in about 1873, the cathedral laid out in Bishop Robert's time comprised a long aisleless choir, having a sacristy (perhaps with a chapter-house above) on the north side, together with an aisleless nave with a north-west tower; there were no transepts. Apart from the sacristy, which has evidently been extensively remodelled during the later Middle Ages and again in post-Reformation times, nothing of this building remains, but clearly it was conceived on an ambitious scale, the overall length of 64 m being very much greater than that of Dornoch and Brechin and only a little less than that of Dunblane. The closest parallel, so far as overall plan-form is concerned, is the much smaller cathedral of Lismore (p.43), but the long aisleless choir is evidently the product of similar thinking to those at Dunkeld and Dunblane. Nothing is known about the progress of building operations, but it may be conjectured that at the onset of the Wars of Independence work came to a halt with the nave still incomplete. What is certain, however, is that, when operations were resumed some time during the second half of the 14th century, the design was amended to incorporate the remarkable south nave-aisle that today forms the most conspicuous feature of the remains (p.55).

Both major monastic foundations of the period were made by local magnates associated with the expansionist policies of Alexander II. Some time during the 1220s Ferquhard, Earl of Ross, brought Premonstratensian canons from Whithorn to Fearn, in Easter Ross, whence the foundation was transferred to a new site in the parish of Tarbat in about 1238.[83] Nothing now remains, however, of the first church of New Fearn, as the abbey came to be called, and the existing buildings are mainly of 14th-century date (p.56).

Beauly, at the upper limit of the Beauly Firth, appears to have been founded by John Byset in or shortly before 1230 and colonized by Valliscaulian monks brought directly from France.[84] Although the church was considerably altered and rebuilt during the later Middle Ages, the original plan in large measure survives. This is of simple cruciform type with a long aisleless nave of similar proportions to that at Saddell (p.40). The choir, too, was aisleless and, in contrast to the arrangements at the sister-houses of Ardchattan (p.42) and Pluscarden, no separate structural

Fig. B

provision was made for eastern chapels in the transepts; nor was there any crossing-tower.

Although the foundation of cathedrals and monasteries in the area to the south of the Dornoch Firth is likely to have been accompanied by the building of parish churches, scarcely any examples survive. Indeed, apart from the former parish church of Tain (situated immediately to the south east of Tain Collegiate Church), which may incorporate the shell of a 13th-century building, the only church of the period that can be identified is that of Allangrange,[85] in the Black Isle, of which the parochial status is in doubt. Whatever its precise function may have been, however, this elegant little church is of interest, not only in demonstrating that the First Pointed style of eastern and southern Scotland had been thoroughly assimilated by local masons, but also in providing a possible stylistic clue to the appearance of the vanished 13th-century cathedral of Fortrose (p.50).

Fig. H

So far as secular architecture is concerned, the principal surviving structure that can be ascribed with any degree of confidence to the period under review is Skelbo Castle, which may first have been erected following a grant of the lands of Skelbo to Gilbert de Moravia, afterwards Bishop of Caithness (p.49), in about 1211.[86] The first castle at Skelbo seems to have been an earthwork structure of motte-and-bailey type, but as at Duffus Castle, Morayshire, which in many respects it resembles, the earthwork defences were afterwards renewed in stone and lime. Whether any portion of the existing curtain-wall is of 13th-century date is uncertain, but the stone keep or hall that crowns the summit of the site may well belong to the period of the Wars of Independence. This building, now sadly ruinous, is of similar proportions to the slightly larger keep at Duffus and seems likewise to have housed a large first-floor hall having a timber floor supported on a central row of posts.

Fig. J

Another possible stone castle of the period is to be found at Dun Lagaidh, Loch Broom, in Wester Ross. Here, recent excavations have shown that some time during the late 12th or 13th century an abandoned prehistoric hill-fort and associated dun was converted into something akin to a small keep-and-bailey castle by the construction of additional walls of lime-mortared masonry. The minor local baron to whom the re-fortification of Dun Lagaidh can presumably be attributed is unlikely to have been the only member of his class to have made use of earlier defensive sites at this period and evidence for the medieval re-occupation of forts, duns and crannogs in various parts of the Highlands is now coming to light.[87]

Some early castles were of earthwork construction and several of these can be identified, including Ring of Castlehill, Caithness,[88] and Dunscaith, Easter Ross.[89] This last was probably erected during the northern campaigns of William the Lion, which also saw the destruction of some native fortifications, such as that of Earl Harald of Caithness at Thurso.[90] Other major castles on record in the area include Beaufort, Lovat, Avoch, Dingwall, Buchollie and Scrabster, but little if any early work can now be identified at these sites.[91]

FROM THE WARS OF INDEPENDENCE TO THE REIGN OF JAMES IV

The West Highlands and Islands

There appears to have been little architectural activity in the area between about the death of Robert I and the last quarter of the 14th century. Building was resumed towards the end of the 14th century, however, and operations of one kind or another appear to have been carried out throughout the remainder of the period, the main volume of activity probably occurring during the second half of the 15th century.

Turning first to ecclesiastical architecture, the earliest major building to be considered is the Augustinian priory of Oronsay, founded by John, 1st Lord of the Isles, some time before 1353.[92] Some portions of the existing remains may belong to the period of foundation, but the church itself seems to date from about the end of the 14th century. As first laid out this was a very small aisleless building of unicameral plan having a narrow lateral projection, perhaps a sacristy, on the north side of the sanctuary. The architectural detail is of the simplest kind, the east window being of three lights with plain intersecting tracery, and the remaining windows of a single light with cusped trefoiled heads; the cloister arcades, which may be a little earlier than the church, are completely unadorned and comprise narrow round-arched openings of rubble masonry.

Fig. B

A few parish churches and chapels may also belong to this period. These include the chapels at Orsay and Finlaggan, Islay, both traditionally ascribed to John, 1st Lord of the Isles,[93] the parish church and adjacent chapel at Kirkapoll, Tiree,[94] and perhaps also the chapel of Kilnave, Islay. These are all small single-chambered buildings of the type familiar in this area since the 12th century (p.40) and they are remarkable chiefly for their extreme plainness, which arises largely from the fact that little if any use is made of freestone dressings in their construction. As already noted, the Oronsay cloister arcade displays a similar absence of freestone, although there is no shortage of this material in the church itself.

By far the most important centre of building activity during the later Middle Ages was Iona, where major schemes of reconstruction were carried out under the patronage of the Lords of the Isles both at the Abbey and the Nunnery.[95] At the former the two-level choir of the 13th century (p.41) was replaced by a lofty new choir having a south aisle linked to an enlarged south transept, while the nave was considerably widened; at the same time a substantial tower was erected over the crossing. The alterations made to the Nunnery church were less fundamental, but two of the adjacent claustral ranges were rebuilt round a larger cloister garth. Building seems to have been in progress at both monasteries simultaneously, the bulk of it being completed within the period c.1450-90.

The late medieval buildings of Iona display a highly idiosyncratic style indicative of a local school of craftsmen. Some of these, like the master-mason Donald Ó Brolchán, whose signature appears on one of the capitals of the Abbey choir-arcade, were evidently of Irish extraction, but although their work is generally reminiscent of late Irish Gothic it incorporated important independent elements. Thus, the ornamental vocabulary, as seen for example in the rich carvings of the Abbey choir and Nunnery cloister-arcade, is closely related to that employed in local monumental sculpture (p.53), while certain features of design, such as cylindrical piers, appear to be modelled upon earlier work at Iona itself.

In view of the highly localized character of the Iona school of architecture it is perhaps not surprising that few examples of the direct influence of Iona are identifiable elsewhere. Obvious similarities between the tracery of one of the Abbey windows and a tomb-canopy at Dungiven Priory, Co. Londonderry,[96] however, suggest that the latter was the work of an Iona mason. There is also a close stylistic relationship between Iona Abbey and St Clement's Church, Rodel, Harris,[97] which appears to have been erected in about the 1520s and thus falls just outside the period now under review. Many of the features of this handsome church, such as the arches opening into the transepts, have evidently been copied from Iona, but in view of the difference in date it is unlikely that the same hands were at work.

Apart from the collegiate church of Kilmun, in Cowal, of which only a fragment now survives, the only other considerable remains of ecclesiastical architecture are to be found at the priories of Ardchattan and Oronsay. At Ardchattan the modest 13th-century choir (p.42) gave way to a much grander one, while parts of the crossing and of the claustral buildings were likewise remodelled, all these operations presumably being financially suported by the local lay patrons, the MacDougalls of Dunollie.[98] Although work seems to have been in progress concurrently with that at Iona Abbey and Nunnery, there is no close stylistic resemblance between these buildings and Ardchattan. Indeed, the Ardchattan masons produced their own brand of local antiquarianism, modelling the external angle-shafts of the new choir upon those of its demolished predecessor and employing similarly archaic mouldings in the construction of the refectory pulpit. In certain other respects, however, the late medieval buildings of Ardchattan show a close correspondence with Irish architecture of the period and it seems likely that some, at least, of the craftsmen had obtained training or experience in Ireland.

The same is no doubt true of much of the later 15th- and early 16th-century work at Oronsay (p.52), although here the new buildings, which include the west tower of the priory church and most of the cloister-arcades, are much plainer in character. Building-inscriptions within the cloister-arcade attribute the work to the master-mason Mael-Sechlainn Ó Cuinn, whose name also appears on the nearby MacDuffie Cross of c. 1500 and who probably belonged to the Ó Cuinn family of the Glens of Antrim.[99]

The MacDuffie Cross is a particularly fine example of a distinctive series of monumental crosses, effigies and grave-slabs produced in the West Highlands between the 14th century and the Reformation.[100] Most of these monuments were designed to stand out of doors and, since the local sandstone rocks have poor weathering qualities, the carvers sought out more durable media, notably the chlorite-schist rocks of the Loch Sween area of Knapdale. Local schools of craftsmen were established at various centres in Argyll, including Iona and Oronsay, where from time to time their talents were harnessed to the production of architectural ornament as well as monumental sculpture. The profuse and varied decoration of these works, in which naturalistic and abstract designs are handled with great vigour and inventiveness, affords a unique insight into the art and society of the West Highlands during the later Middle Ages.

The late medieval secular architecture of the West Highlands, like that of Scotland as a whole, was dominated by the tower-house, of which numerous examples were erected throughout the area. In general these towers correspond to their counterparts elsewhere, but they also display certain distinctive features of regional significance.

Thus, a considerable number of West Highland tower-houses were constructed without vaults or mural fireplaces.[101] Dunvegan Castle, Skye, for example, although of particularly massive construction, appears originally to have been unvaulted, while Moy, Mull, although vaulted at several levels had no mural fireplaces; Kisimul, Barra, and Breachacha, Coll, had neither vaults nor chimneyed fireplaces. These peculiarities, although by no means unparalleled in eastern and southern Scotland, probably resulted from the unfamiliarity of local masons with large-scale building enterprises and it is interesting to observe that the equally remote tower-houses of Caithness display similar characteristics (p.56). Moreover, some of the vaults that were built were constructed not upon plank centering, as was customary in most parts of Scotland, but after the Irish fashion, in which use was made of wickerwork mats. A good example of this type of construction is to be found at Dunollie Castle, Lorn.[102]

Fig. G

Many of the tower-houses of the region were constructed with a minimum of freestone dressings and mouldings and this makes them difficult to date with any degree of precision. Despite their often primitive appearance, however, there is no reason to believe that any of these towers are of earlier date than their counterparts elsewhere in Scotland, the oldest surviving examples of which belong, in the present writer's view, to about the middle of the 14th century.

Thus, the very massive tower-house at Duart, Mull, is likely to have been added to the early castle of enclosure (p.45) not long after the property came into the hands of the MacLeans in about 1390, while the somewhat similar tower at Dunvegan, Skye,[103] probably belongs to about the same period. Another dozen or so relatively well-preserved tower-houses that for one reason or another can be attributed to the 15th and early 16th centuries are illustrated in Fig. G and it is noticeable that these vary greatly in size, Carrick, Cowal,[104] being (like Duart) among the largest buildings of its class in Scotland and Castle Sinclair, Barra,[105] among the smallest. Saddell Castle, Kintyre,[106] built by the Bishop of Argyll between about 1508 and 1512 provides a closely dated example of a tower-house erected towards the end of the period under review and its well conceived domestic arrangements and elaborate wall-head defences foreshadow architectural fashions of the later 16th century.

Although it is convenient for analytical and chronological purposes to distinguish between the castles described in this paper as hall-houses and attributed mainly to the period before the Wars of Independence (p.48) and those described as tower-houses and attributed to the period after the Wars of Independence, this distinction should not be pressed too far. Both types of structure fulfilled a similar function for the same class of society and both were designed as freestanding defensive residences in which all or most of the accommodation requirements of their owners were housed beneath a single roof. Given also that in tower-houses, as in hall-houses, the principal room was invariably a first-floor hall, it is evident that the differences between the two types of structure are those of degree and proportion rather than of kind.

Fig. G

The point is well illustrated by Chleit Castle, Jura, and Ǵlensanda Castle, Morvern,[107] which correspond closely, both in layout and proportion, with a number of the earlier hall-houses of the area. The tower-like building that was added to the north-east corner of Castle Sween (p.44), on the other hand, seems to have had a different function. In all probability Castle Sween already possessed a hall and the additional tower was no doubt intended to provide extra private accommodation, thus constitituting what can perhaps best be described as a chamber-block.

Halls were also erected within castles of enclosure, a type of structure which, as Castle Sween itself demonstrates, remained in use throughout the later Middle Ages. When Innis Chonnell (pp.44-5) was remodelled in about the middle of the 15th century a handsome first-floor hall was constructed, linked to a private chamber-block similar to that at Sween. At Urquhart Castle, Inverness-shire,[108] extensive rebuilding operations were undertaken towards the end of the 14th century, including the erection of what must have been a very fine range of domestic buildings, comprising a first-floor hall, great chamber and solar, as well as of a strong residential tower separated from the remainder of the enclosure by a ditch. At Kilchurn, Kisimul and Breachacha, ground-flooor halls were erected within courtyard enclosures which had grown up round originally free-standing tower-houses.

Perhaps the most remarkably situated of the late medieval halls of the West Highlands is that on Finlaggan Island, Islay,[109] a principal residence of the MacDonald Lords of the Isles. Described by the late 14th-century chronicler John of Fordun as a 'dwelling-house' (*mansio*) rather than a castle, Finlaggan is unusual in that, apart from a small chapel, all its buildings are entirely domestic in character and the site is unenclosed, except by water. The hall itself, now represented by footings, was freestanding and comprised a fair-sized ground-floor hall and screens, the cooking evidently having been done in a separate structure; an adjacent group of buildings probably housed the private residential quarters of MacDonald and his household. What role this hall played in the inaugural ceremonies of the Lords of the Isles and the meetings of the celebrated Council of the Isles is by no means clear, but its unfortified situation bears witness to the fact that, on Islay at any rate, the power of the MacDonalds was considered unchallengeable.

Although there are no close parallels for the Finlaggan complex as a whole, a smaller freestanding hall of similar plan stood within the MacKinnon castle of Dun Ara, on the island of Mull.[110]

Finally, in this discussion of late medieval secular architecture, some mention should be made of castle gatehouses, of which good examples survive at Dunstaffnage, Rothesay and Urquhart. That at Dunstaffnage (p.46) replaced an earlier gateway of simple form and seems to have incorporated a drawbridge operated from a first-floor chamber; the upper floors of the gatehouse were probably residential. The Rothesay gatehouse, too, replaced a simpler entrance, but here the residential character of the building is even more pronounced, the upper floors incorporating a large hall and screens as well as a handsome solar. This building, which was begun by James IV and completed by his successor, was no doubt intended to supplement the existing accommodation within the early castle of enclosure (p.38) by providing for the monarch a separate private suite of rooms of the kind that was being introduced into royal palaces at that time. Although the gatehouse at Urquhart (p.54) appears to be approximately contemporary with that at Rothesay, its planning is comparatively old-fashioned, the entrance passage being flanked by drum towers designed primarily for defence; both gatehouses were equipped with drawbridges, that at Urquhart being separated from the main building by a causeway.

Ross, Sutherland and Caithness

Although there is evidence of a greater volume of building activity during the later Middle Ages than during the 12th and 13th centuries, the architecture of the northern mainland, with one or two notable exceptions, again compares unfavourably both in quantity and quality with that of the West Highlands and Islands. Few of the secular buildings can be closely dated, but the principal churches appear to have been erected during the late 14th and early 15th centuries.

Outstanding among these is the south nave-aisle of Fortrose Cathedral, which ranks as one of the most original and distinguished examples of late medieval ecclesiastical architecture in Scotland. As already explained (p.50), the aisle appears to have been an afterthought and certain features of the building suggest that one of its main purposes was to provide dignified accommodation for the tombs of the cathedral's patrons, the Earls of Ross. The design is elegant and well-detailed, with richly-traceried windows (now fragmentary), multi-rib vaults and canopied tombs set between the arcade piers. The foundation of the aisle is usually attributed to Euphemia, Countess of Ross (d.1394) or her son, Alexander, Earl of Ross (d.1402), and heraldic evidence indicates that the building was not vaulted until after 1420.[111] Apart from some probably derivative work at Tain (p.56), there are no close stylistic parallels for the architecture of Fortrose. Some of the details, such as the buttresses and eaves corbel-course, are of late First Pointed character, as found, for example in the late 13th-century choir of Elgin Cathedral. It seems likely, therefore, that in adopting this rather archaic style for the nave-aisle the Fortrose masons were seeking

Fig. C

to bring their work into harmony with that of the cathedral as a whole, and it is interesting to find the same vocabulary contemporaneously employed in the choir of Pluscarden Priory in similar circumstances.

Whatever the stylistic antecedents of Fortrose, it is clear that building operations were handsomely financed. At Fearn (p.50), where the abbey church is said to have been rebuilt between 1338 and 1372 under the patronage of William, Earl of Ross, it is no less evident that funds were signally lacking.[112] Although the church attained a respectable length (c. 38 m), neither nave nor choir was aisled while transepts, if planned, seem not to have been completed. There is an almost complete absence of mouldings and carved detail, and all the windows, including a conspicuous group of four in the east gable, are plain lancets.

Fig. B

The only surviving church in the area to reflect the influence of Fortrose Cathedral is the collegiate chapel of Tain.[113] Although small in size, the building is well conceived and executed, much of the detail bearing a close correspondence to that at Fortrose. The fenestration is unusually varied, the windows on the north side being simple lancets, while those in the other three walls (now considerably restored) show large expanses both of intersecting and of geometric tracery. The plan, like that of certain other small collegiate establishments such as Maybole and Fowlis Easter, is of simple unicameral form. As in the case of the south nave-aisle at Fortrose, certain features of the building are of First Pointed character, but it seems unlikely that the church as a whole was completed before the beginning of the 15th century. It is difficult to believe, however, that any substantial portions of the fabric post-date an allegedly destructive fire of 1427.[114]

Other remains of late medieval ecclesiastical architecture in the area are at best fragmentary. At Dornoch Cathedral (pp.49-50) the nave was rebuilt with cylindrical piers and plain pointed arches similar to those of c. 1424-40 at St Machar's Cathedral, Aberdeen, but nearly all remains of this work were swept away during a 'restoration' in 1835-7.[115] At Beauly (p.50) various repairs and alterations were made during the course of the 15th century, including the remodelling of the north transept and the insertion of a large traceried window at the east end of the choir. Beauly also retains a number of late Gothic canopied tombs similar to those already noted at Fortrose Cathedral (p.55) and of which a further example occurs at Fearn Abbey (*supra*), where it forms the principal feature of the late 15th-century Michael aisle; two smaller aisles were added to the church after the period covered in this review.

So far as secular architecture is concerned, the only standing buildings of the period that survive are a handful of tower-houses situated mainly in Caithness and Sutherland. A number of castles of enclosure that can be identified on coastal promontories, such as Scrabster and Berriedale, Caithness, may also belong to this period, but none are sufficiently well preserved to require assessment here. Larger than any of these, but little less ruinous, is Avoch Castle in the Black Isle, Easter Ross, which comes on record as early as the 12th century, but of which the existing remains probably belong mainly to the later Middle Ages.[116]

Fig. J

Most of the tower-houses are small in size and primitive in appearance. Thus, apart from Eilean Donan and Ackergill, none measures more than about 16m square externally and all are noticeably thick-walled. Wick, Forse, Dirlot and Braal[117] are built without freestone dressings and are unvaulted; of these only Braal shows evidence of internal stairs or chimneyed fireplaces. Windows and doorways are in general of the plainest description, the windows, even at upper levels, being mere slits in the walls. At Dirlot the masonry appears to be laid in clay mortar, a feature also observable in the outbuildings at Forse. Two other small towers, too ruinous to admit of illustration but of similar character to those just described, occur at Caisteal na Coire and Proncy, Sutherland.[118]

Because of their rudimentary character a number of these tower-houses, and others in Caithness and Orkney, are sometimes ascribed to the 12th and 13th centuries, when similar castles are known to have been erected in various parts of Northern Europe outside Scotland, but no conclusive literary or archaeological evidence in support of such an early date has yet been furnished for any of the buildings in question.[119] Until such evidence is forthcoming, the apparent primitiveness of the Caithness towers, like that of certain of the West Highland castles, described above (pp.53-4), can best be explained by their remoteness and by the intractable nature of the materials employed in their construction. The Caithness flagstones, although more than adequate for general building purposes, did not lend themselves to the fashioning of quoins and dressings and it is only with the introduction of imported sandstone on a considerable scale in the late 15th and 16th centuries, as for example at Ackergill and Girnigoe,[120] that mouldings and carved detail seem to have been generally employed in this area.

Moreover, some of these castles are a good deal less primitive in design than they are in construction. Braal, with its well-planned disposition of chimneyed rooms, mural chambers, latrines, aumbries and intramural stairs, corresponds closely to some of the smaller 15th-century towers of southern and central Scotland and can probably be ascribed to the same period. The Earls of Caithness had for long had an important seat in this neighbourhood, however, and it is likely that the existing tower stands on or near the site of an earlier castle.[121]

Fig. J

Another example of fairly sophisticated planning is provided by the defensive arrangements at Forse. Here the original first-floor entrance in the east wall was evidently reached by means of a drawbridge linking the tower to a forebuilding; the approach path to the forebuilding was so contrived as to pass directly beneath this bridge, while the doorway of the tower was further protected by a stone porch. Like the castle of Wick, which in many respects it resembles, Forse was held during the 14th century by the Cheyne family and it is possible that both towers were erected at that time or early in the following century.

Of the two larger towers, Ackergill,[122] although somewhat restored, is a typical example of a late 15th- or early 16th-century tower-house and is associated with the Keith family. Eilean Donan, one of the very few castles on the western seaboard, is on record in the 14th century and the existing building, although almost entirely reconstructed during the present century, may first have been erected at that time; it belonged to the Earls of Ross, but passed to the Mackenzies of Kintail in the early 16th century.[123]

Conclusions

Any attempt to assess the nature and volume of building activity within a given area and period on the evidence of surviving remains alone must be to some extent speculative. Certainly this is the case where the medieval architecture of the Highlands is concerned, for there is reason to believe that 12th- and 13th-century buildings may have a higher survival rate there than in the Lowlands. Nevertheless, the material presented in this paper suggests that during the period before the Wars of Independence, the progress of architecture in the Highlands showed a much closer correspondence to developments elsewhere in Scotland than is often assumed. Several monasteries and cathedrals were founded, parish churches and chapels appeared in considerable numbers and stone castles of various kinds were introduced as early — and in some localities as densely — as anywhere else in the country.

This activity, however, was by no means uniformly distributed throughout the

Highlands. While the Argyll mainland and southern islands, together with Easter Ross, saw a good deal of building, there was little activity in the northern Hebrides or in the mainland north of the Dornoch Firth. It is also noteworthy that Islay, despite its obvious advantages for settlement, failed to attract either a major religious foundation or an early castle of note.

Although the principal categories of building found in the Highlands during this period had their counterparts elsewhere in Scotland, certain regional pecularities are apparent. Highland parishes tended to comprise extensive areas with scattered populations and it comes as no surprise to find a pattern of church building in which a relatively small number of parish churches, usually of the plainest description, were supplemented by a correspondingly large number of dependent chapels. The concentration of hall-houses in the West Highlands also requires explanation. The Scottish and Irish hall-house was more domestic in character than most other types of contemporary castle, corresponding closely in this respect to the English fortified manor-house. The presence of numerous buildings of this class in Argyll is indicative of a high degree of local stability and prosperity and it is perhaps not too fanciful to see the West Highland hall-house as an embodiment of the continuing power of the Somerled family.

Architectural style varied mainly in accordance with local geography. The early churches of Caithness had affinities with those of Orkney, while those of the Dornoch Firth and Easter Ross showed influences emanating from eastern Scotland. In the West Highlands Irish and eastern Scottish elements mingled to form a distinctive style most clearly manifested in the ecclesiastical architecture of Iona and its hinterland, but in Bute and Arran Scottish mainstream influences predominated. Although Iona and the other Western Isles lay within the Norwegian archdiocese of Trondheim, the buildings of this area show no recognisable Scandinavian characteristics.

The Highlands shared in the general decline of architectural activity that is apparent in Scotland following the Wars of Independence, but after the resumption of building operations towards the end of the 14th century Highland and Lowland building patterns diverged. Although a few large-scale enterprises were undertaken in the Highlands during the later Middle Ages, as for example at Iona and Fortrose, the range and volume of activity was for the most part very limited. There were no counterparts in the Highlands to the prosperous burghs of eastern and southern Scotland, with their handsome kirks and occasional stone-built houses, nor were more than a handful of friaries, hospitals and collegiate churches to be found. The elaborate residence of the Lords of the Isles at Finlaggan, however impressive to the local inhabitants, was scarcely a match for the royal palaces of Linlithgow and Stirling, while among baronial castles only Urquhart and perhaps Avoch could bear comparison with the great fortresses of the Lowlands. Considerable numbers of tower-houses were, it is true, built in the West Highlands, but there were few in Caithness and Sutherland and, surprisingly, almost none in Easter Ross.

So far as style is concerned, the architecture of the West Highlands became even more localised and idiosyncratic than in the period before the Wars of Independence. These tendencies are particularly noticeable in the fields of carving and monumental sculpture, where no less than four local schools developed during the 14th and 15th centuries. Both in building and sculpture Irish influence remained strong and there is evidence to suggest that traffic in craftsmen and ideas flowed westwards as well as eastwards across the North Channel.

The emergence of regional styles during the later Middle Ages can be recognised in other parts of Scotland than the West Highlands, however, and the northern mainland proved no exception in this respect. But while the tower-houses of Caithness were in some respects as localised as those of the Hebrides, Fortrose Cathedral, unlike Iona Abbey, achieved distinction within the main stream of the European Gothic style. Finally, it may be noted that whatever degree of political unity may from time to time have been created by the amalgamation of the Earldom of Ross with the Lordship of the Isles, the architecture of each territory always retained its own identity.

FOOTNOTES

The following abbreviations are used:

Barrow, *Kingdom of Scots* Barrow, G W S, *The Kingdom of the Scots* (1973)

Barrow, *Robert Bruce* Barrow, G W S, *Robert Bruce and the Community of the Realm of Scotland* (1976)

Cast. and Dom. Arch. MacGibbon, D and Ross, T, *The Castellated and Domestic Architecture of Scotland* (1887–92).

DES Discovery and Excavation, Scotland Annual publication of Scottish Regional Group, Council for British Archaeology.

Eccles. Arch. MacGibbon, D and Ross, T, *The Ecclesiastical Architecture of Scotland* (1896–7).

Inventory of Royal Commission on the Ancient and Historical Monuments of Scotland: *Inventory of the Ancient and Historical Monuments in* [the county stated].

NMRS National Monuments Record of Scotland.

Origines Parochiales Origines Parochiales Scotiae, Bannatyne Club, (1851–5).

PSAS Proceedings of the Society of Antiquaries of Scotland.

SHR Scottish Historical Review

Steer and Bannerman, *Monumental Sculpture* Steer, K A, and Bannerman, J W M, *Late Medieval Monumental Sculpture in the West Highlands* (1977).

TGAS Transactions of the Glasgow Archaeological Society.

Watt, *Fasti* Watt, D E R, *Fasti Ecclesiae Scoticanae Medii Aevi ad annum 1638*, Second draft (1969).

References

1. Harrison, J K, *The Isle of Bute in the Olden Time* (1893–5), i, 167–85; *Eccles. Arch.*, i, 292–8.
2. Cowan, Ian B, *The Parishes of Medieval Scotland* (1967), 85–6; NMRS drawing BUD/M/1.
3. Simpson, W D, 'The Architectural History of Rothesay Castle', *TGAS*, ix (1937–40), 152–84; Cruden, S, *The Scottish Castle* (1960), 29–36.
4. Duncan, A A M and Brown, A L, 'Argyll and the Isles in the Earlier Middle Ages', *PSAS*, xc (1956–7), 203; Duncan, AAM, *Scotland. The Making of the Kingdom* (1978), 136.
5. *Inventory of Argyll*, i (1971), 21–2, 140–5.
6. Butler, Lawrence, *A Guide to Rushen Abbey* (1978); *Medieval Archaeology*, xxiii (1979), 254–5. I am grateful to Dr Butler for discussing the results of his current excavations at Rushen with me and for allowing me to reproduce the simplified plan illustrated in Fig. B.
7. *Inventory of Argyll*, i (1971), 22.
8. Ibid., iv (forthcoming).
9. Ibid., iv (forthcoming).
10. Ibid., iv (forthcoming).
11. Leask, H G, *Irish Churches and Monastic Buildings*, ii (1958), 58–76; Honeyman, H L, 'Trefoil rear-arches', *Archaeologia Aeliana*, 4th series, viii (1931), 127; Stalley, R, 'Mellifont Abbey: Some Observations on its Architectural History', *Studies, An Irish Quarterly Review*, lxiv, No. 256 (Winter 1975), 358.
12. *Inventory of Argyll*, i (1971), 129–36.
13. Ibid., ii (1975), 124–9.
14. NMRS, STR/1/1; STD/103/2–5.
15. *Inventory of Argyll*, ii (1975), 144.
16. Ibid., iii (1980), 152, 160–1.
17. Ibid., iv (forthcoming).
18. Ibid., iii (1980), 138–40.
19. Ibid., i (1971), 23.
20. *Eccles. Arch.*, ii (557–9).
21. *Inventory of Outer Hebrides* (1928), 178.
22. Ibid., 192; Watt, *Fasti*, 207.
23. *Inventory of Outer Hebrides* (1928), 47–9.
24. Ibid., 2–3; Simpson, W D, *The Castle of Bergen and the Bishop's Palace at Kirkwall* (1961), 7–10.
25. *Inventory of Argyll*, ii (1975), 99–115.
26. Craine, David, *Peel Castle, Isle of Man* (1958), 5, 11–15. The plan reproduced in Fig. C is based upon the one incorporated in this booklet.
27. Ibid., 11.

28. *Inventory of Argyll*, ii (1975), 156–63.
29. Clapham, Alfred, 'Some Minor Irish Cathedrals', *Archaeological Journal*, cvi (1952), 16–20.
30. *Inventory of Argyll*, i (1971), 112–20.
31. Simpson, W D, 'Rait Castle and Barevan Church, Nairnshire', *PSAS*, lxxi (1936–7), 98–115; *Eccles. Arch.*, ii, 290–2.
32. Barrow, *Kingdom of Scots*, 376.
33. Simpson, G G, and Webster, B, 'Charter evidence and the distribution of mottes in Scotland', *Chateau Gaillard, Etudes de Castellologie Médiévale*, Caen, 5 (1972), 175–92; Talbot, Eric, 'Early Scottish Castles of Earth and Timber — Recent Field-Work and Excavation', *Scottish Archaeological Forum*, 6 (1974), 54–6.
34. *Roman de Fergus*, quoted in Ritchie, R L G, *The Normans in Scotland* (1954), 307–8.
35. Sellar, W D H, 'Family Origins in Cowal and Knapdale', *Scottish Studies*, 15 (1971), 21–37.
36. Simpson, W D, 'Castle Sween', *TGAS*, xv (1960), 3–14; Cruden, Stewart, *The Scottish Castle* (1960), 22–5.
37. O'Neil, B H St. J, 'Castle Rushen, Isle of Man', *Archaeologia*, xciv (1951), 1–26.
38. Jope, E M, *A Guide to Carrick Fergus Castle* (1957). I am grateful to Mr B R S Megaw for putting information about Rushen Castle and Rushen Abbey at my disposal.
39. *Inventory of Argyll*, ii (1975), 223–31.
40. Sellar, W D H, 'The Earliest Campbells — Norman, Briton or Gael?', *Scottish Studies*, 17 (1973), 109–25.
41. *Inventory of Argyll*, iii (1980), 191–200.
42. *Cast. and Dom. Arch.*, i, 65–7.
43. *Inventory of Argyll*, ii (1975), 168–71.
44. Ibid., i (1971), 165–78; Simpson, W D, 'Skipness Castle', *TGAS*, xv (1966), 87–109.
45. Caldwell, David H, 'Ardrossan Castle, Ayrshire; a preliminary account', *PSAS*, 104 (1971–2), 201–21.
46. Dunbar, J G, and Duncan, A A M, 'Tarbert Castle', *SHR*, 1 (1971), 6–7.
47. Barrow, *Robert Bruce*, 261; Barrow, *Kingdom of Scots*, 373.
48. *Inventory of Argyll*, i (1971), 179–84.
49. Dunbar, J G and Duncan, A A M, 'Tarbert Castle', *SHR*, 1 (1971), 1–17; Duncan, AAM, *Scotland. The Making of the Kingdom* (1978), 439.
50. Jope, E M, 'The Scottish Castle', *SHR* xlii (1963), 149–50; MacNeill, T E, 'The History and Archaeology of the Anglo-Norman Earldom of Ulster' (Ph.D. thesis, Queen's University of Belfast, (1973), 83–149).
51. *Cast. and Dom. Arch.*, iii, 96–105.
52. *Inventory of Argyll*, iii (1980), 209–17.
53. Simpson, W D, 'Castle Tioram, Inverness-shire and Mingary Castle, Ardnamurchan, Argyllshire', *TGAS*, xiii (1954), 70–90.
54. *Cast. and Dom. Arch.*, iii, 85–7.
55. Plan and report in NMRS.
56. *Inventory of Argyll*, ii (1975), 198–211.
57. Duncan, A A M, *Scotland. The Making of the Kingdom* (1978), 549.
58. He also made a mistake in the construction of the west angle-tower by providing more arrow-slits in the outer wall at first-floor level than the chamber within could accommodate.
59. Cruden, S, *The Scottish Castle* (1960), 58–61.
60. Barrow, *Kingdom of Scots*, 377–8; Barrow, *Robert Bruce*, 105.
61. Plan and report in NMRS.
62. Barrow, *Robert Bruce*, 261; Barbour J, *The Bruce*, Book IV, lines 347, 388. I am grateful to Professor Barrow for putting the available information about the contemporary history of Brodick at my disposal and for identifying various possible builders.
63. Investigations made in 1966 confirmed Mr Stewart Cruden's view (*The Scottish Castle* (1960), 34–5) that the towers were secondary.
64. Simpson, W D, 'The Architectural History of Rothesay Castle', *TGAS*, ix (1937–40), 161.
65. Harrison, J K, *The Isle of Bute in the Olden Time* (1893–5), ii, 107–32.
66. E.g. Cargin, Co. Galway; Grenan, Co. Kilkenny and Kindlestown, Co. Wicklow. I am grateful to the late Mr Dudley Waterman for information about these and other Irish hall-houses.
67. *Inventory of Argyll*, i (1971), 165–78.
68. *Origines Parochiales*, ii, part i, 29.
69. Sellar, W D H, 'Family Origins in Cowal and Knapdale', *Scottish Studies*, 15 (1971), 29.
70. *Inventory of Argyll*, ii (1975), 184–7.
71. Ibid., 212–7.
72. *An Archaeological Survey of County Down* (1966), 211–9.
73. *Inventory of Argyll*, iii (1980), 170–4; Barrow, *Robert Bruce*, 409.
74. *Inventory of Argyll*, iii (1980), 174–7.
75. Cruden, S, *The Scottish Castle* (1960), 95.
76. *Inventory of Outer Hebrides* (1928), 188.
77. *Inventory of Caithness* (1911), 89–90.
78. Ibid., 27, No. 81; 28–9, No. 91; 126, No. 460; *DES* (1977), 11.
79. *Inventory of Caithness* (1911), 110–3.
80. Crawford, Barbara E, 'The Earldom of Caithness and the Kingdom of Scotland, 1150–1266', *Northern Scotland*, 2 (1974–5), 97–117.
81. Bentinck, Charles D, *Dornoch Cathedral and Parish* (1926), 377–412.
82. *Eccles. Arch.*, ii, 394–402; Watt, *Fasti*, 266; Cowan, Ian B and Easson, David E, *Medieval Religious Houses, Scotland* (1976), 207.

83. Cowan, Ian B and Easson, David E, *Medieval Religious Houses, Scotland* (1976), 101–2.
84. Ibid., 84; Simpson, W D, *Beauly Priory, Inverness-shire* (1954), passim. The plan reproduced in Fig. B is based on the Ministry of Works drawing incorporated in this booklet.
85. *The Archaeological Sites and Monuments of the Black Isle, Ross and Cromarty District, Highland Region* (Royal Commission on the Ancient and Historical Monuments of Scotland, October 1979), No. 108; according to local tradition the church was a private chapel of the Bishops of Ross (Craven, J B, *Journals of the Episcopal Visitations of the Right Rev. Robert Forbes . . . 1762 and 1770* (1923), 273).
86. Simpson, W D, 'Skelbo Castle, Dornoch, Sutherland', *Scottish Notes and Queries*, Vol. ii, 3rd series, No. 10 (October 1924), 149–52.
87. 'Dun Lagaidh', *Current Archaeology*, 2 (1969–70), 8–13; Morrison, A, 'Some Prehistoric Sites in Scotland with Medieval Occupation', *Scottish Archaeological Forum*, 6 (1974); Laing, Lloyd R, *Settlement Types in Post-Roman Scotland* (1975), 23–36.
88. Talbot, Eric, 'The Ring of Castlehill, Caithness — a Viking fortification', *PSAS*, 108 (1976–7), 378–9.
89. *The Archaeological Sites and Monuments of Easter Ross, Ross and Cromarty District, Highland Region* (Royal Commission on the Ancient and Historical Monuments of Scotland, February 1979), No. 247.
90. Duncan, A A M, *Scotland. The Making of the Kingdom* (1978), 193–6; Crawford, Barbara M, 'The Earldom of Caithness and the Kingdom of Scotland, 1150–1266', *Northern Scotland*, 2 (1974–5), 106.
91. Some of the problems of identification are discussed in Talbot, Eric, 'Scandinavian Fortification in the British Isles', *Scottish Archaeological Forum*, 6 (1974), 37–45.
92. Steer and Bannerman, *Monumental Sculpture*, 215; *Eccles. Arch.*, iii, 372–81.
93. Skene, W F, *Celtic Scotland* (1886–90), iii, 402.
94. *Inventory of Argyll*, iii (1980), 153–8.
95. Ibid., iv (forthcoming).
96. Steer and Bannerman, *Monumental Sculpture*, 43, note 3 and plate 17E.
97. *Inventory of Outer Hebrides* (1928), 32–7.
98. *Inventory of Argyll*, ii (1975), 99–115.
99. Steer and Bannerman, *Monumental Sculpture*, 120.
100. A definitive study of these monuments may be found in Steer and Bannerman, *Monumental Sculpture*.
101. This topic is discussed by J G Dunbar, 'Kisimul Castle, Isle of Barra', *Glasgow Archaeological Journal*, 5 (1978), 41–3.
102. *Inventory of Argyll*, ii (1975), 194–8.
103. MacLeod, R C, *The Book of Dunvegan* (1938–9), vol. i, xx-xlvi, vol. ii, xxxi.
104. *Cast. and Dom. Arch.*, iii, 186–92.
105. *Inventory of Outer Hebrides* (1928), 129.
106. *Inventory of Argyll*, i (1971), 161–5.
107. Ibid., iii (1980), 202–5.
108. Simpson, W D, *Urquhart Castle* (1964).
109. Munro, R W, *Monro's Western Isles of Scotland and Genealogies of the Clans 1549* (1961), 96–100.
110. *Inventory of Argyll*, iii (1980), 199–202.
111. Batten, E C, *The Charters of the Priory of Beauly* (1877), 194–9; Paul, J Balfour, *The Scots Peerage* (1904–14), vii, 239–42; Scott, A R, *Illustrations of Fortrose Cathedral* (1873).
112. *Origines Parochiales*, ii, part ii, 435–6, quoting *Ane Breve Cronicle of the Earlis of Ross* (1850), 6–8; *Eccles. Arch.*, ii, 542–7.
113. *Eccles. Arch.*, ii, 537–42.
114. Cowan, Ian B and Easson, David E, *Medieval Religious Houses, Scotland* (1976), 227–8.
115. Bentinck, Charles D, *Dornoch Cathedral and Parish* (1926), 396.
116. Beaton, J, 'Notes on Ormond or Avoch Castle . . .', *PSAS*, xix (1884–5), 400–5.
117. *Inventory of Caithness* (1911), 137–9, 48–9, 30, 30–1.
118. *Inventory of Sutherland* (1911), 18, 52.
119. Cruden, S, *The Scottish Castle* (1960), 20–2; Talbot, Eric, 'Scandinavian Fortifications in the British Isles', *Scottish Archaeological Forum*, 6 (1974), 39–41; Omand, D, *The Caithness Book* (1973), 153–9; Lamb, R G, *Iron Age Promontory Forts in the Northern Isles*, (British Archaeological Reports, British Series 79), 90–6.
120. *Inventory of Caithness* (1911), 136–7, 139–43.
121. Crawford, Barbara E, 'The Earldom of Caithness and the Kingdom of Scotland, 1150–1266', *Northern Scotland*, 2 (1974–5), 100.
122. *Inventory of Caithness* (1911), 136–7.
123. *Origines Parochiales*, ii, part ii, 394; the plan reproduced in Fig. J is a conflation of an 18th century Board of Ordnance drawing (National Library of Scotland MS 1648 Z 3/26) and that illustrated by MacGibbon and Ross (*Cast. and Dom. Arch.*, iii, 82–5).

Acknowledgements

The research for this paper was conducted on behalf of the Royal Commission on the Ancient and Historical Monuments of Scotland and this account is published by courtesy of the Commissioners. I am grateful to Professor G W S Barrow and to my colleagues Mr Ian Fisher and Mr Geoffrey Stell for discussing various aspects of the paper with me, and to Mr Duncan Peet for making the drawings. Except as noted in the text, these are Crown Copyright. The paper is published with the aid of a grant from the Civil Service Department.

ILLUSTRATIONS

The plans of buildings illustrated in Figs A–J have been simplified in various ways to facilitate comparison. Original walls are shown in black, inferred walls in dotted line and later walls in continuous line.

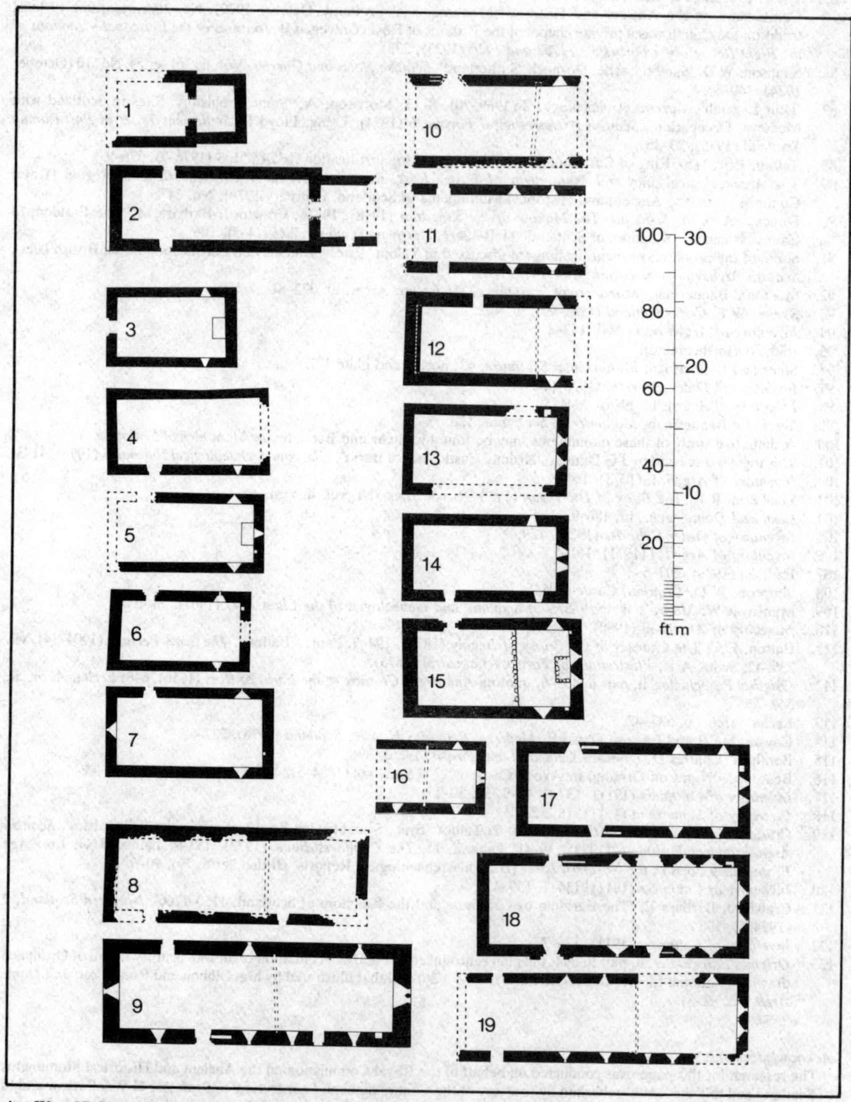

A. **West Highland Churches of the 12th and 13th centuries.**
1. Inchmarnock, Bute; 2. St Blane's, Bute; 3. St Oran's, Iona; 4. Kilchenzie, Kintyre; 5. St Ronan's, Iona; 6. Michael Chapel, Iona; 7. Pennygowan, Mull; 8. Inchcailleach, Stirlingshire; 9. Kilbrannan, Kintyre; 10. Kilvickeon, Mull; 11. Killean I, Kintyre; 12. Kilchattan, Lorn; 13. Faslane, Dunbartonshire; 14. Kilmory, Knapdale; 15. Inchkenneth, Mull; 16. Southend, Kintyre; 17. Kildalton, Islay; 18. Dunstaffnage, Lorn; 19. Killean II, Kintyre.

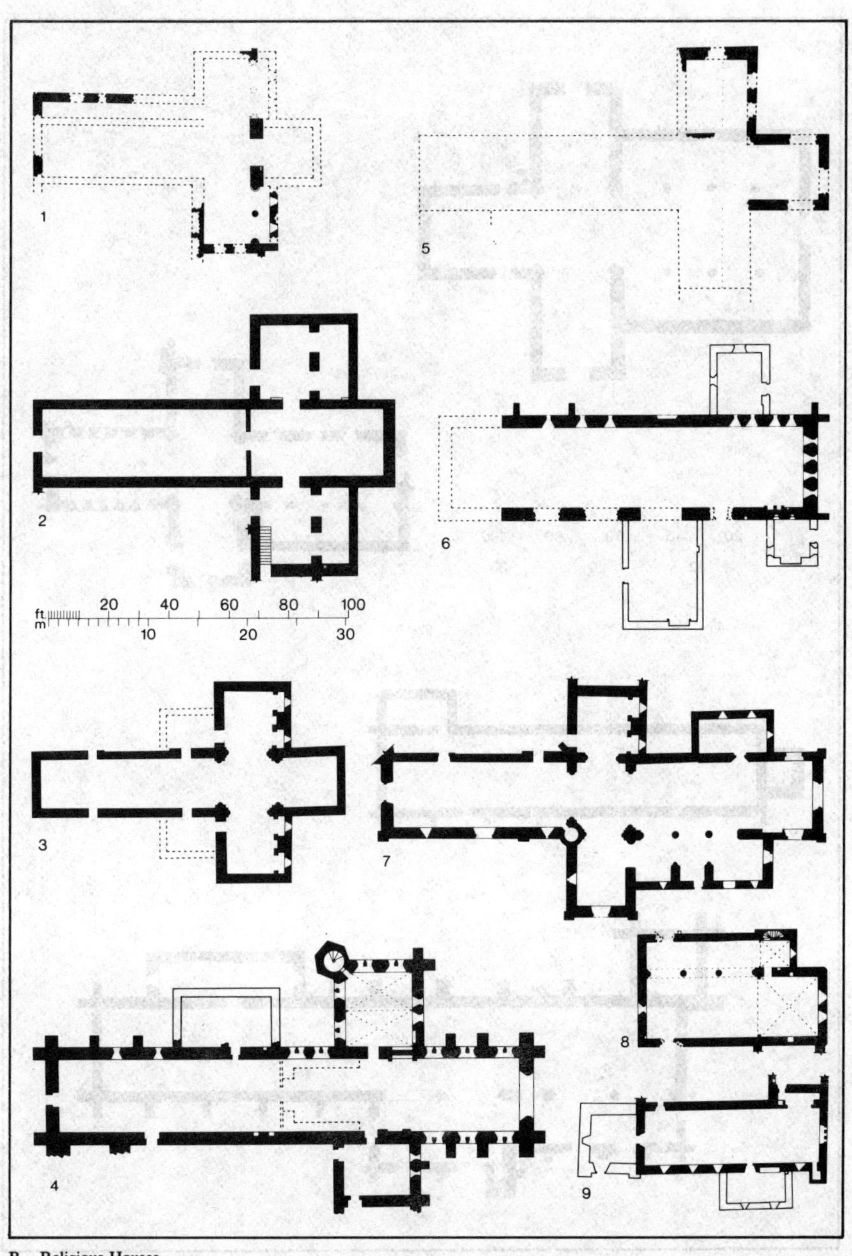

B. Religious Houses.
1. Ardchattan Priory, Lorn; 2. Rushen Abbey, Man; 3. Iona Abbey I; 4. Beauly Priory, Inverness; 5. Saddell Abbey, Kintyre; 6. Fearn Abbey, Ross; 7. Iona Abbey II; 8. Iona Nunnery; 9. Oronsay Priory.

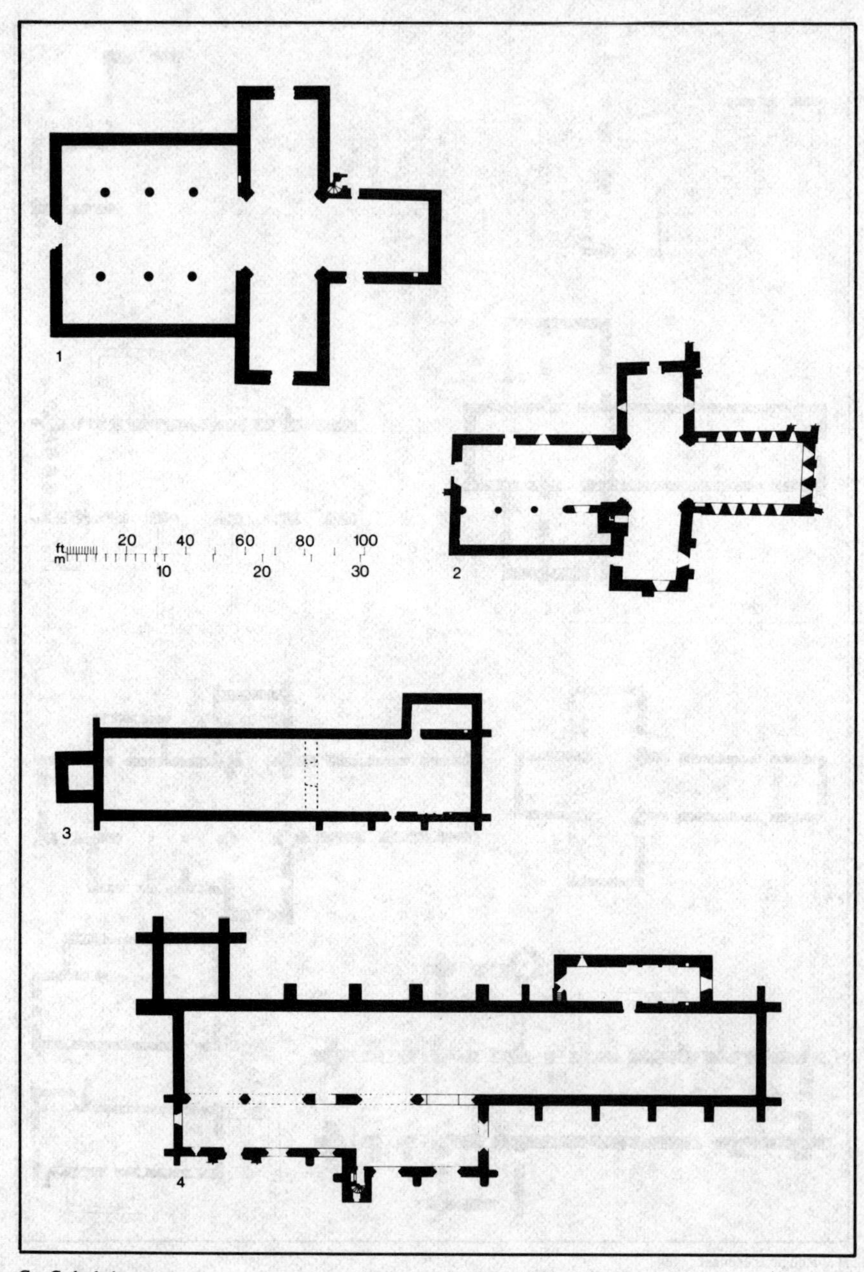

C. Cathedrals.
1. Dornoch, Sutherland; 2. St German's, Peel, The Isles; 3. Lismore, Argyll; 4. Fortrose, Ross.

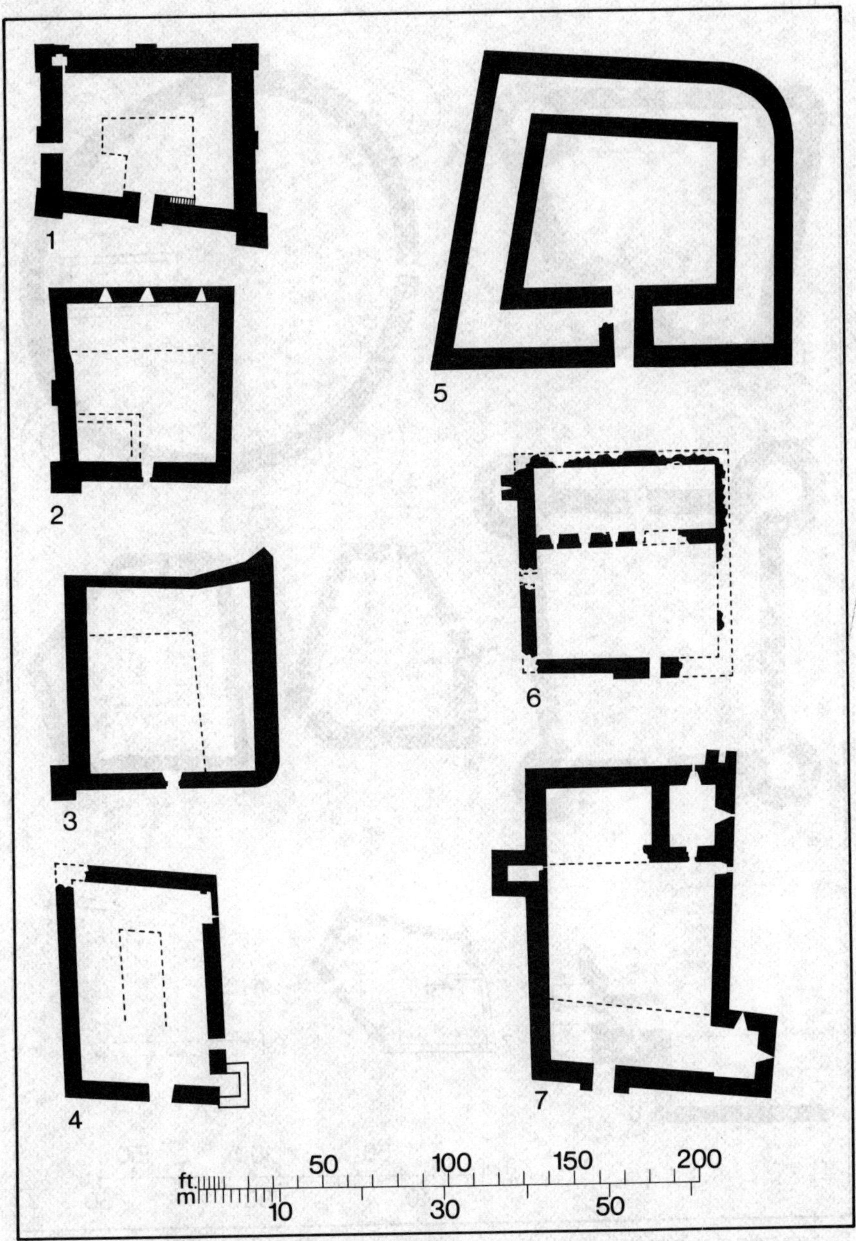

D. Early rectangular castles of enclosure in the West Highlands.
1. Sween, Knapdale; 2. Innis Chonnell, Lorn; 3. Duart, Mull; 4. Castle Roy, Badenoch; 5. Tarbert, Knapdale; 6. Achadun, Lismore; 7. Skipness, Kintyre.

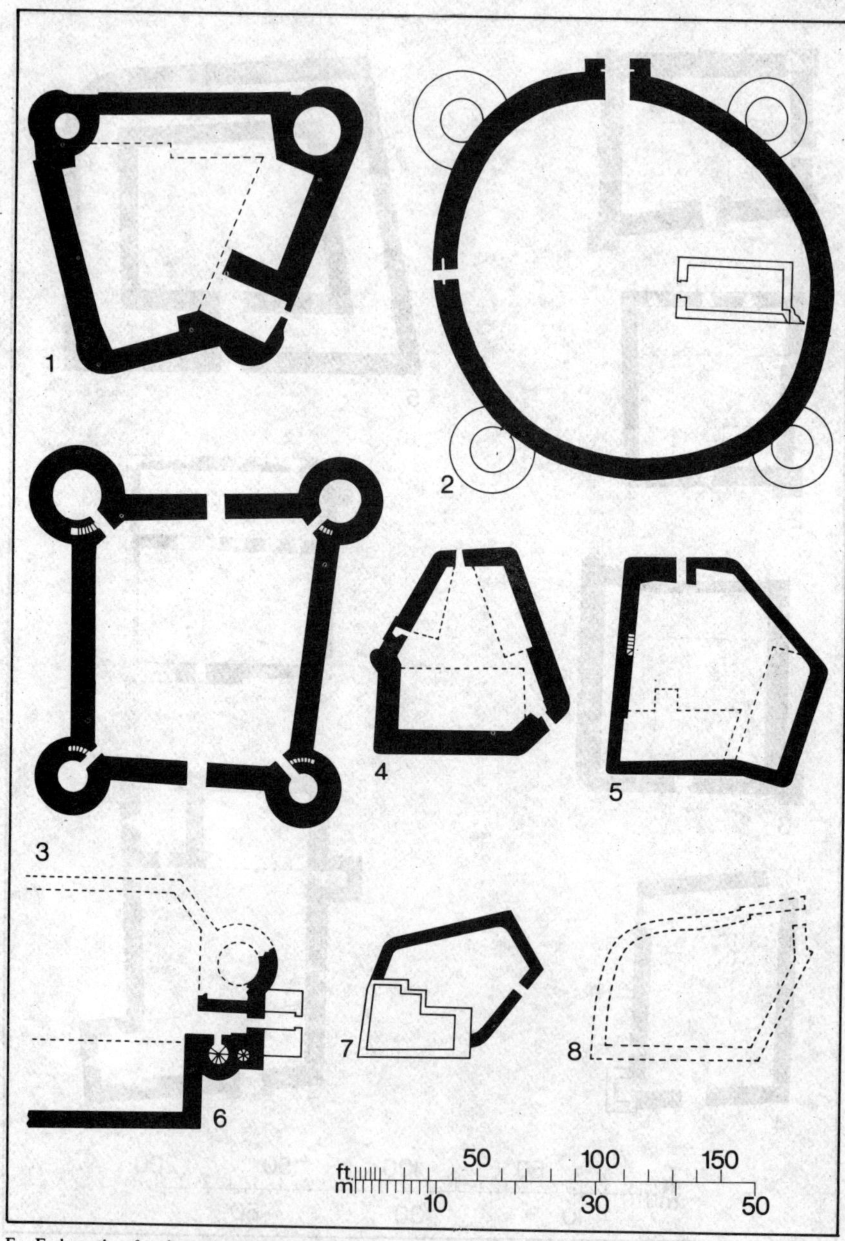

E. Early castles of enclosure in the West Highlands.
1. Dunstaffnage, Lorn; 2. Rothesay, Bute; 3. Inverlochy, Lochaber; 4. Mingary, Ardnamurchan; 5. Tioram, Moidart; 6. Brodick, Arran; 7. Duntroon, Mid Argyll; 8. Dunoon, Cowal.

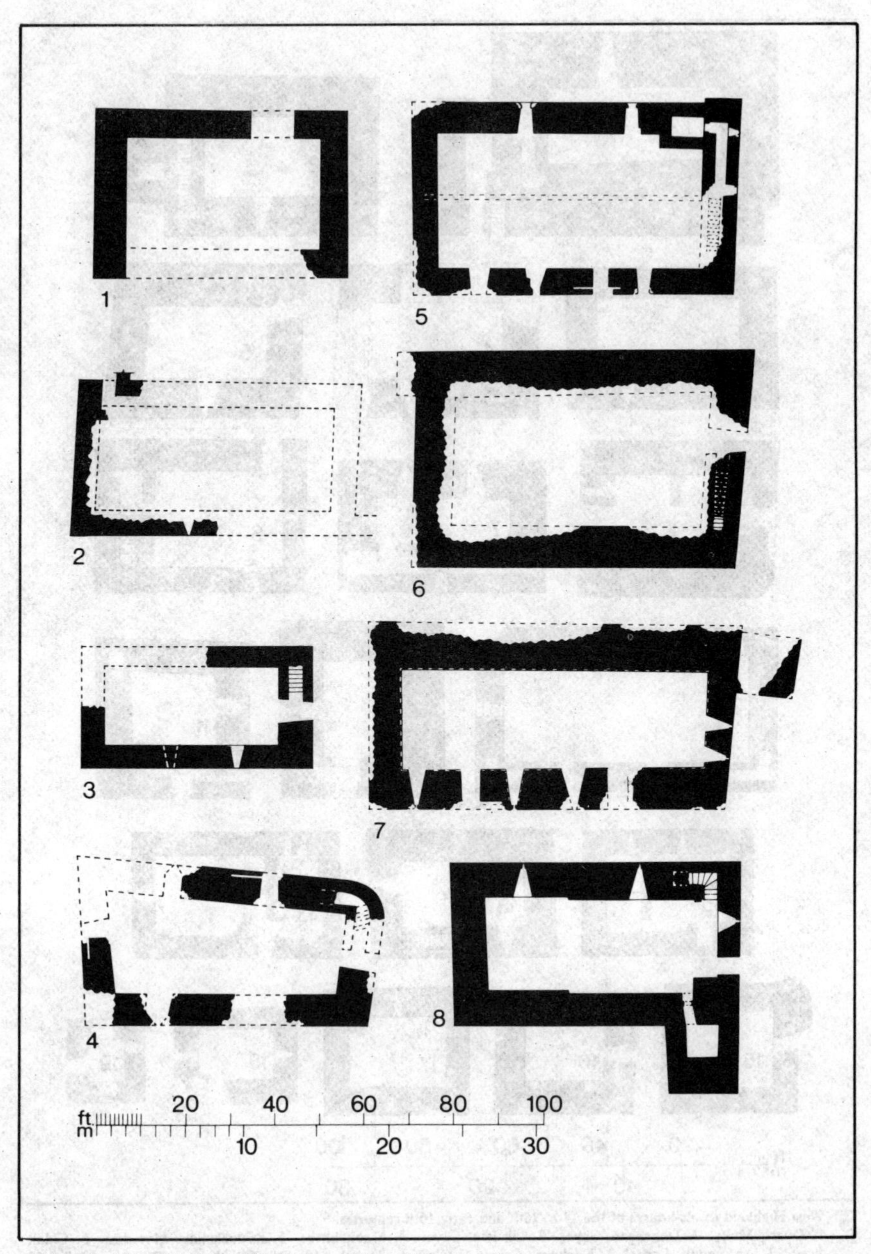

F. West Highland hall-houses of the 13th and 14th centuries.
1. Skipness, Kintyre; 2. Camus, Skye; 3. Fincharn, Mid Argyll; 4. Coeffin, Lismore; 5. Fraoch Eilean, Lorn; 6. Ardtornish, Morvern; 7. Aros, Mull; 8. Lochranza, Arran.

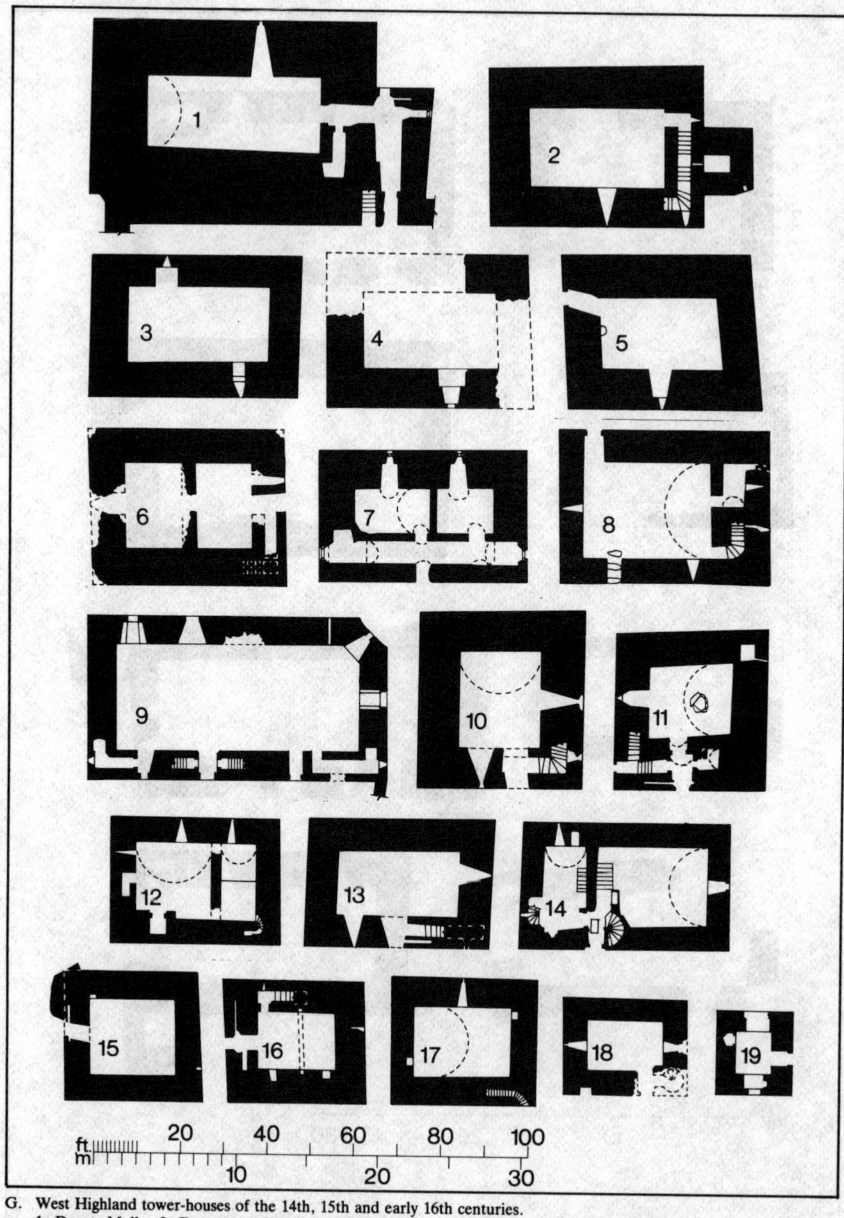

G. West Highland tower-houses of the 14th, 15th and early 16th centuries.
1. Duart, Mull; 2. Dunvegan, Skye; 3. Uisdein, Skye; 4. Maol, Skye; 5. Kinlochaline, Morvern; 6. Chleit, Jura; 7. Ardmaddy, Lorn; 8. Kilchurn, Lorn; 9. Carrick, Cowal; 10. Dunollie, Lorn; 11. Moy, Mull; 12. Toward, Cowal; 13. Glensanda, Morvern; 14. Saddell, Kintyre; 15. Kisimul, Barra; 16. Breachacha, Coll; 17. Loch an Eilean, Badenoch; 18. Kildonan, Bute; 19. Castle Sinclair, Barra.

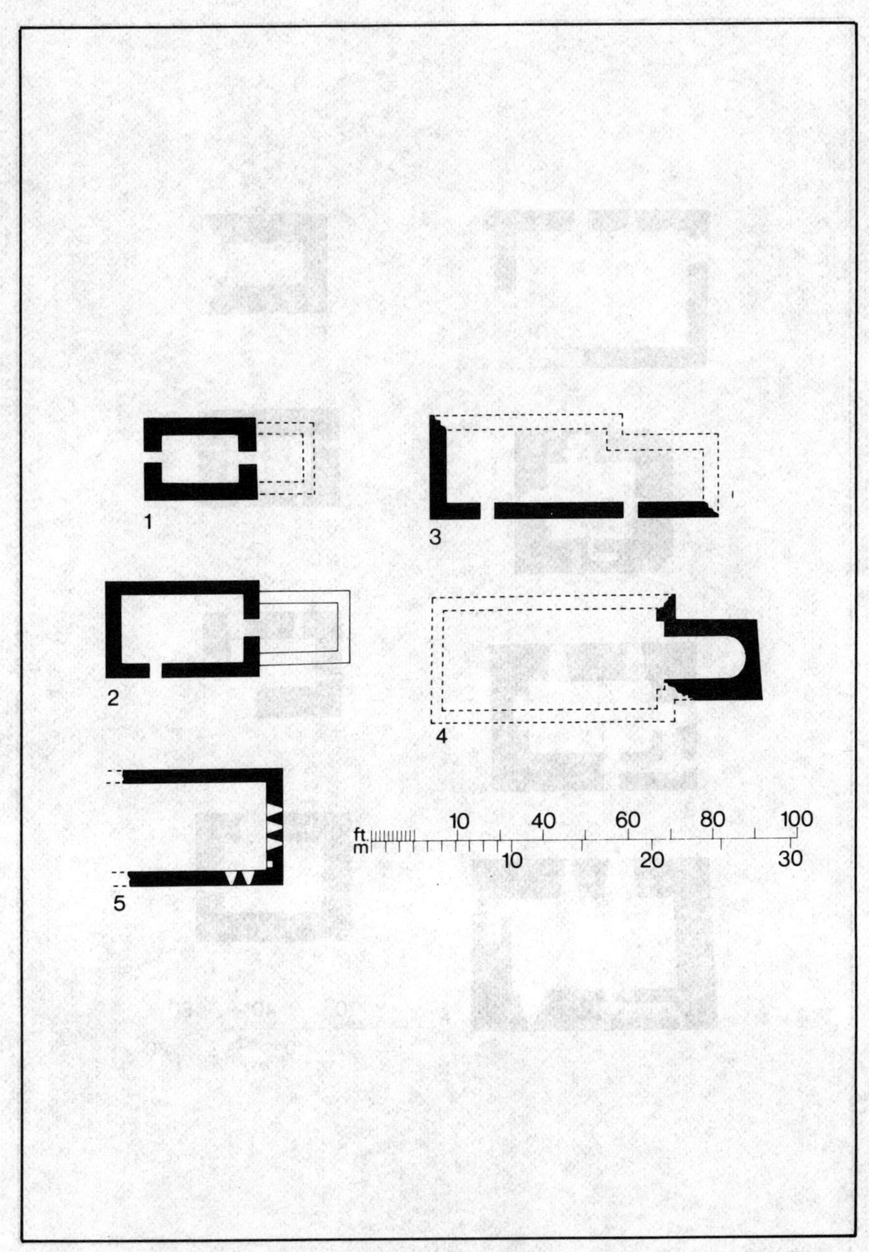

H. Early churches in Caithness and Ross.
1. St Mary's, Lybster; 2. Clour, Watten; 3. St Thomas's, Skinnet; 4. St Peter's, Thurso; 5. Allangrange, Black Isle.

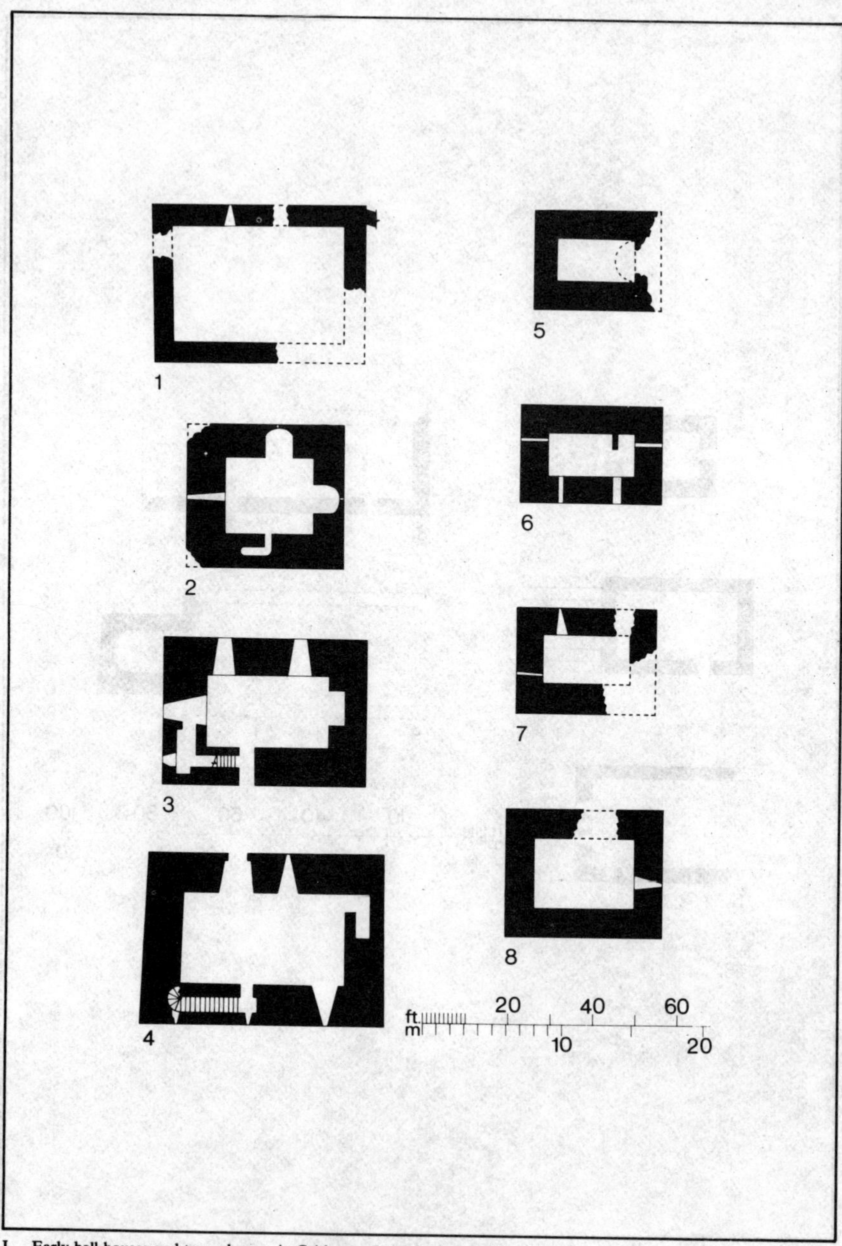

J. Early hall-houses and tower-houses in Caithness, Sutherland and Ross.
1. Skibo, Sutherland; 2. Braal, Caithness; 3. Ackergill, Caithness; 4. Eilean Donan, Ross; 5. Dunrobin, Sutherland; 6. Dirlot, Caithness; 7. Forse, Caithness; 8. Wick, Caithness.

THE ARCHAEOLOGICAL INVESTIGATION OF MEDIEVAL INVERNESS

JONATHAN WORDSWORTH

For the prehistoric periods of Scotland's past, archaeology is the only source of information; for the medieval period there are documents which give a picture of medieval society without any excavation. It is for this reason that medieval archaeology, particularly in towns, started much later than its prehistoric counterpart. In England urban archaeological investigation was a post-war phenomenon which began on City of London bomb sites, the main interest being the Roman remains beneath the medieval layers. In Scotland the first urban excavations took place in 1969 in St Andrews under the direction of Nicholas Brooks and it was not until 1973 that excavations occurred elsewhere with work in Broad Street, Aberdeen and High Street, Edinburgh. The results of these and later investigations are only now being published so that any general interpretations of medieval life, as revealed by excavation, must remain tentative.

One of the most serious problems for the urban archaeologist has been the destruction of medieval deposits by later development in all the towns of Scotland. Medieval burghs such as Edinburgh and Lanark have lost their deposits because the medieval town was built on a natural ridge of rock. This has meant that the construction of later buildings has removed earlier deposits. Destruction has been compounded by the depth of foundations required for 19th and 20th century developments, so that many leading burghs, including Dundee, Glasgow and Leith, have produced little or no information.

The result of these post-medieval building developments is that only Perth, Aberdeen, Inverness and Elgin have so far contributed significant information towards our understanding of life in and the development of the medieval burgh. Of these, Perth with medieval deposits averaging 2-3m has produced the most interesting material. The survival of organic material such as wood, leather and seeds, due to abnormal soil conditions, has meant that the various sites excavated around the town have given a detailed and comparative picture of Perth life. The early medieval buildings found in Perth, and elsewhere in Scotland, are of timber construction, usually of woven wattles with a mud and dung daubing to weatherproof them; there were also timber buildings which used sill beams to hold either wattle fences or were grooved to take a plank wall.

There has been more excavation in Inverness than in most Scottish burghs and this has produced greater information on the survival of deposits within Inverness. The first excavation, to the east of Hamilton Street (see Fig. 1), was undertaken in 1976 by George Duncan and his team. This revealed what was interpreted as part of the town ditch or fosse, later known as the Foul Pool because of the waste thrown into it. The presence of leather offcuts within the fill of the ditch, and dated to a late medieval context, points to the use of this fosse as a dumping ground. It also suggests that the defensive purpose of the ditch was not thought important in the late middle ages.

In 1977 Robert Gourlay, as part of his work on the Burgh Survey Report on

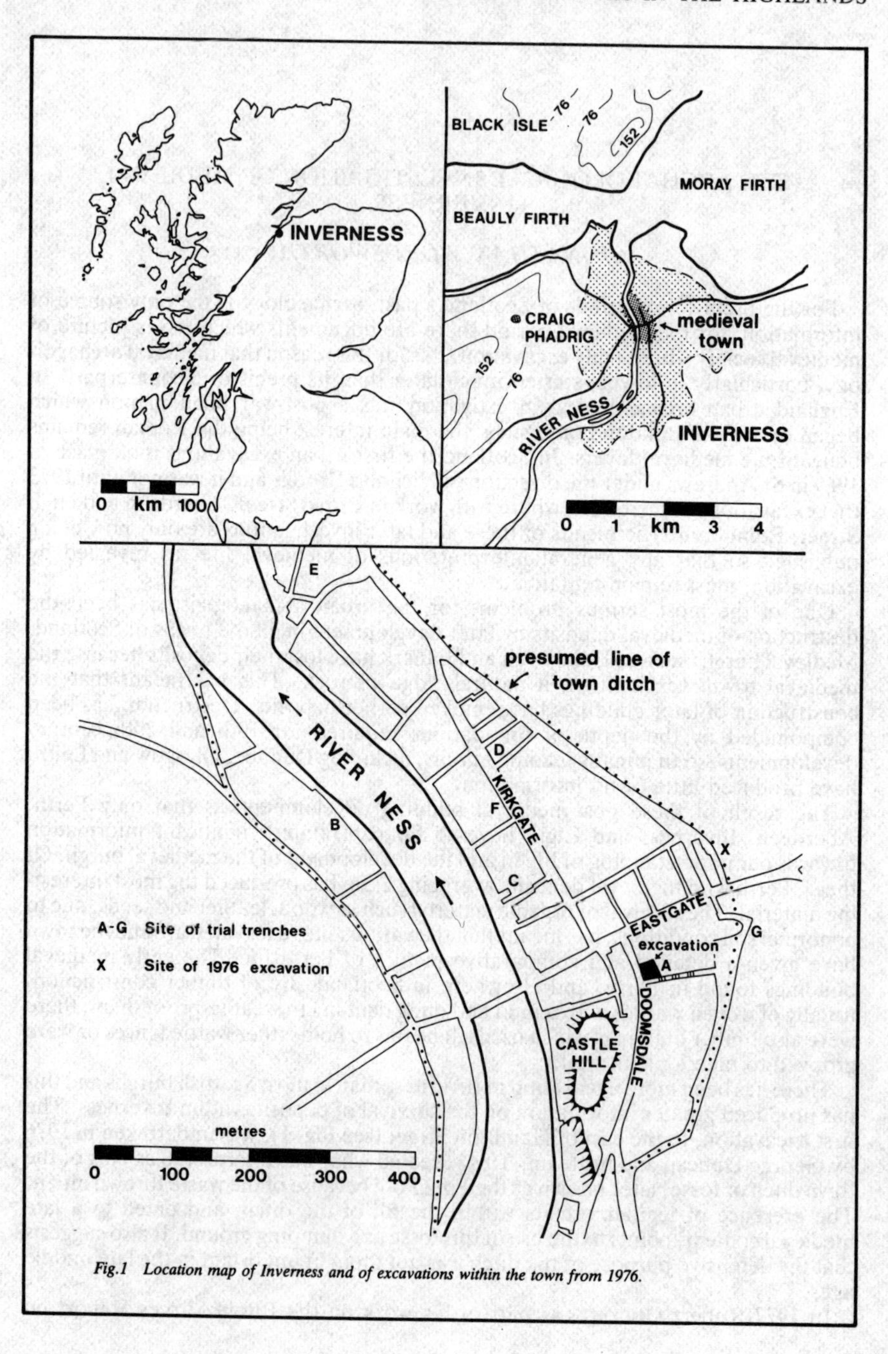

Fig.1 Location map of Inverness and of excavations within the town from 1976.

Inverness, noted that the clearance of High Street for the construction of John Menzies shop was directly on to natural gravel suggesting that medieval deposits had not survived on that side of the High Street. It is reported locally that no trace of occupation material was noted during the construction of Inverness District Museum, the Highlands and Islands Development Board offices and the shops adjacent to them, fronting the north and south of Bridge Street respectively but this may be a failure of detailed observation.

In 1978 an industrious team led by Gordon Ewart spent six weeks digging seven trial holes within the medieval town. These are marked on Fig.1 by the letters A-G. I am grateful to Gordon Ewart for permission to use his unpublished information on these sites.

Trench A, located between Raining Stairs and Castle Street, revealed over 2m of stratified medieval deposits and this was the reason for the author's undertaking the excavation in 1979.

Trench B was excavated in the ground of Balnain House in an attempt to investigate a site on the west bank of the Ness but within the presumed line of the fosse. No deposits were found that were earlier than the 18th century Balnain House.

Trench C was situated behind 43-47 Church Street and produced three large medieval pits, the deepest being 4.5m. All three contained material suggesting they were once used as rubbish pits. Two pits were clay lined, which suggests some industrial use — perhaps connected with either woollen or leather trade. These pits were not related to any surface occupation and, though dating to the 14th century, did not suggest that further excavation there would be useful.

Trench D was dug behind Dunbar's Hospital and contained massive intrusions of modern rubble. As with Trench C, soil accumulation on top of the natural gravels was only 40-60cm which suggests that, even without the modern disturbances, there would have been little medieval occupation material.

Trench E, to the rear of the swimming baths, laid down in what is presumed to have been the harbour area of Inverness, revealed that 19th century construction had destroyed whatever earlier deposits may have been there.

Trench F, south of Abertarff House, was, as were Trenches C and D, located on Church Street. Unlike C and D, Trench F produced 70cm of stratified medieval deposit with the earliest material dating to the 13th century.

Trench G, on the site of 10 Market Brae, was the only Trench excavated outside the presumed line of the town fosse. It produced a series of tipped deposits dating to not earlier than the 17th century.

From Gordon Ewart's survey and previous work, it became clear that the survival of medieval deposits within Inverness was not general. Only two areas, the west side of Church Street and the east side of Castle Street, promised to give further information.

The expansion of the proposed development in Castle Street together with the evidence found by Gordon Ewart led to further work being carried out by the author and his excavators in 1979 (Fig.1). This was initially intended as a salvage excavation to record the vertical relationship of the medieval deposits. However, sufficient material was found to justify a major excavation that lasted for fourteen weeks.

Castle Street, known as Doomsdale, the name reflecting its proximity to the Castle and the valley origin of the street, was thought to have been an early focus for settlement. It was formerly the main route south and, therefore, of some importance.

The earliest reference found to property on Castle Street is in *Invernessiana*, C. Fraser Mackintosh, p.110:

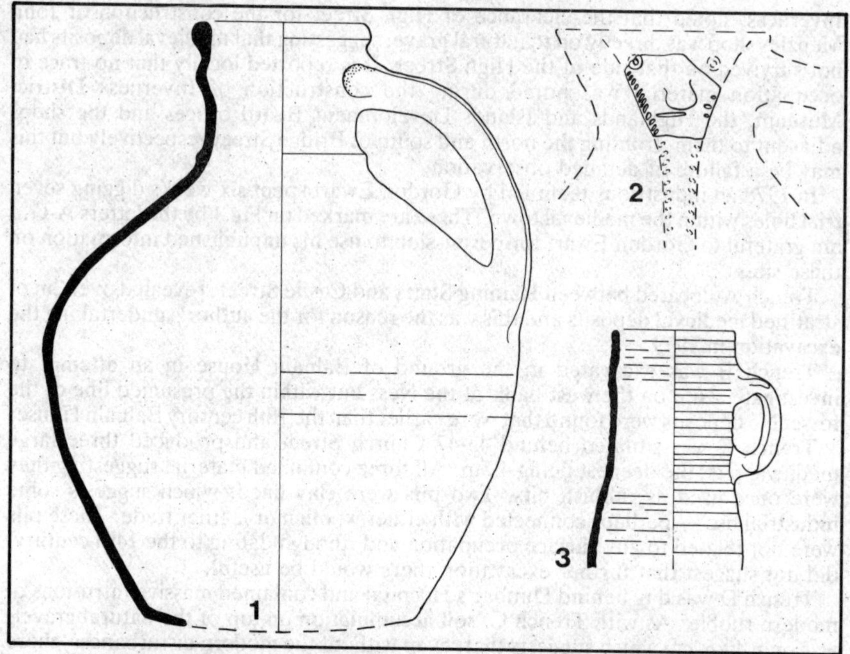

Fig.2 Pottery finds from the excavation. 1. a jug made from local clays and dating to the early 15th century. 2. a bearded face fragment, decoration for a distinctive type of jug made exclusively in East Yorkshire in the late 13th/early 14th centuries. 3. part of a fine stoneware mug, probably imported from Siegburg in Germany at the end of the 14th century.

> 'In 1440 the name of Waus, so long and honourably connected with Inverness, appears for the first time in a deed by John Bathane, heir of the late Thomas Bathane, burgess of Inverness, who sells to his cousin, Alexander Waus and Janet, his spouse, and their heirs and assignees, an annual rent of 3s of the usual money of Scotland, of one particate of land lying in the Dymisdale Street, on the west side thereof, which lies between the land of the late Magnus Sartor at the south on one part and the common vennel at the north on the other, whose front extends to the King's common highway towards the east, and the back to the ridge of the Castlehill towards the west.'

From this and later references it is clear that the Doomsdale was, in the middle of the 15th century, an integral part of the burgh of Inverness.

The excavation revealed no trace of settlement earlier than the 13th century and this is supported by Gordon Ewart's work. There were tilled soils at the lowest medieval level and these may stretch back into the 11th century, or earlier, but no artefacts from such periods were found. Early 13th century occupation included a cobbled area and a large pit more than 2m deep. This pit may have been a ditch, as only one side of it could be excavated and it was at least 5m long. It is possible that this represents part of the fosse for a burgh which would have been much smaller than that suggested for the 16th century by the frontispiece of the Records of Inverness.

There was no evidence of buildings being erected on the site until the middle of the 13th century when a plank and clay walled house was constructed. Enough of this house was uncovered to show that it ran under the present pavement. This would suggest that the Doomsdale road was further west and that the west side of Doomsdale was not feued out at this time.

This house, and the whole site, was covered by a dump of midden material which can be dated by imported English pottery to the late 13th and early 14th centuries. A fragment of a face mask jug brought from Scarborough, Yorkshire is illustrated in Fig.2. It is only in the 14th century that a high proportion of local pottery fabrics was noted relative to those from England and the rest of Scotland. For this late 13th, early 14th century period it was the imported wares that predominated.

There were no structures within the midden save for a few decayed wattle fences which may have acted as boundary markers to delimit the midden. Large numbers of animal bones were found in the midden, as well as in the layers filling four pits. Two of these pits were clearly cess pits as they contained rich organic material with seeds and fish bones. Together with the animal bones, presently being examined, these should give a good picture of the diet in 13th/14th century Inverness.

In the early to mid fourteenth century substantial timber buildings were erected on the site with their frontages set 2.5m east of the present street line. This suggests that the Doomsdale was expanded, rather than shifting eastward, and this enlargement may have been to create a larger market area than was available in Bridge Street alone.

There were three properties averaging 8m in width. The southernmost, lettered A on Fig.3, was the only one which had evidence of internal divisions within the main building. The building was substantial, had timber sill beams, probably to take a plank wall, and was nearly 8m long. The floor consisted of a deposit of yellow sand and the earliest deposit trampled on the floor showed evidence of bronze working. The surviving posts were set over 0.5m into the ground and such a depth suggests that this might have been a two-storey building. Less information was recovered on properties B and C; they were timber buildings but it is not clear what form of walling they had. Both of the buildings fronting the street were less substantial than the main building on property A.

The buildings stood for 50-80 years and one, perhaps two, major rebuildings took place resulting in the plan shown in Fig.3. This phase is ascribed to the late 14th/early 15th century by the finding of several sherds of the German stoneware jug illustrated in Fig.2. The subsequent fire affecting all three properties has preserved information at one distinct period, perhaps contemporary with one of the several historic burnings of Inverness.

In Fig.3 it can be seen that property A is shown as two properties (A1 and A2). The walls of the original building on Property A had been replaced and a timber sill beam inserted down the centre of Property A. The sill beam may only have been a room division as another division made of wattle fencing was recorded further to the south. In a later phase, in the middle of the 15th century, there were two parallel sill beams on this east-west line, clearly delineating two separate structures. Part of the west wall on Property A1 had fallen inwards during the fire and had been carbonised, showing that it had been made of horizontal planks pegged into an upright timber.

Property B, unlike A and C, had walls made of wattles with clay daub. All the structures had clay or sand floors, save for one building in the middle of the 15th century which might have had a timber floor. To the east of Property A2 was a slight structure, probably using the end wall of the main building to support its roof. This was one of only two buildings recovered in the backlands, though this may only reflect the limited excavation that took place in these areas.

The burning of this phase on property A1 preserved fragments of grasses associ-

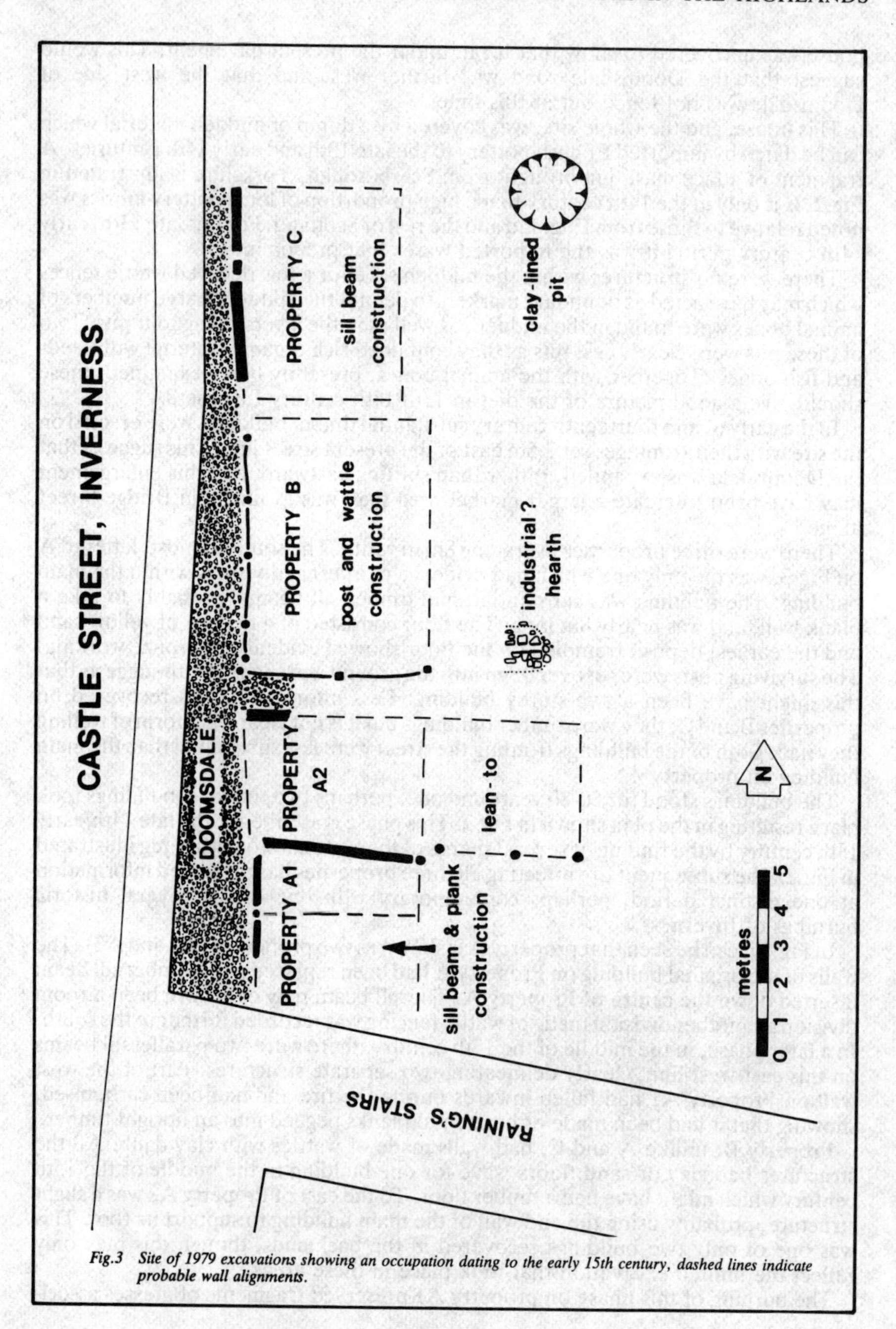

Fig.3 Site of 1979 excavations showing an occupation dating to the early 15th century, dashed lines indicate probable wall alignments.

ated with a burnt clay/silt and these may be turfs, perhaps fallen from the roof. Similar material was preserved in the later burning, although it also contained heather fragments which indicate a thatched rather than a turfed roof.

After the fire of the early 15th century, all three sites were cleared and new buildings erected respecting the same property lines. There was no evidence of decline or abandonment. The buildings constructed on all four properties had sill beam type walling. There was a clay hearth within Property A1. Two other hearths were noted in the backlands area, perhaps indicating some small-scale industrial activity; alternatively, they were the remains of cooking ovens, being sited outside the combustible timber buildings. A similar hearth, dating to the end of the 15th century, was found to have been used for smelting lead. The second, mid 15th century, burning also produced evidence of roofing materials and within Property A a carbonised wooden barrel and small paddle were found. It has been suggested that this paddle was used to stir milk in the barrel to make butter.

Even with the good preservation by fire the function of these buildings is not clear. As with post-medieval structures, it is probable that they had more than one purpose, being used as workshops, shops and dwelling houses.

After the second fire a new road surface was put down but the buildings fronting it appear to be less substantial than previously, with wattle rather than sill beam walls. This decline is succeeded by a re-organisation with buildings once again extending under the modern pavement. Such encroachments on to the street line are paralleled elsewhere in Britain during the 15th/16th centuries. After the 15th century the only features found were too isolated to interpret.

While the fragmented nature of the area examined has restricted the information gained and the interpretation of this information still continues, much more has already been learnt about Castle Street in particular, and medieval Inverness, in general.

It is now clear that this side of Castle Street was not developed until the middle of the 13th century and it is likely that the west side of the street was kept clear for the defence of the castle. If this was so, it seems plausible that the town fosse did not extend along the Barnhill as earlier commentators have suggested. As Professor Barrow pointed out, this would leave the east end of the town overlooked by the Barnhill; however, if the 12th century town was restricted to Kirkgate and particularly the west side of that street, the defensive weakness resulting from siting a fosse below the Barnhill would be minimal. The extent of the fosse as drawn by James Fraser (*Records of Inverness, Vol. 1*) is surely larger than the 12th century burgh limit. There would have been no point establishing a bridgehead on the west side of the river Ness until a bridge was erected. This is not recorded until the 13th century.

The gradual evolution of the burgh, rather than its growth into fixed limits defined during the reign of William the Lion, is shown by the developments in Castle Street. It was not until the mid 14th century that fixed property lines were established on the area excavated and they were part of a definite plan of urban development. Prior to this, the area had been used as gardens and a midden with perhaps some iron working being carried out. After the burgh expanded it became part of the heart of medieval Inverness.

The construction of substantial structures using timber sill beams, suggests relatively expensive buildings and this is supported by their orientation which lay parallel rather than at right angles to the street. This gave a rig width of 8m, some 3m wider than excavated examples from Perth. The restricted lengths of the rigs, due to the Barnhill behind, may be partly the cause of these wide frontages and yet rates were paid by the length of the frontages.

It is true that some of these properties were divided as shown on Fig.3. However, the laying of gravel floors after both fires respected the original property boundaries, suggesting that these later divisions were sub-divisions.

Fresh work on the documentary sources may clear some of the points raised, but for others, in particular the physical aspect of life in medieval Inverness, further archaeological investigation is essential. As has been shown, much of this archaeological record has been removed and it is vital to gather what remains before it, too, is destroyed. Further work will have to be concentrated on Castle Street and the west side of Church Street where deposits are known to survive. Also work could usefully be done establishing the developing extent of the town, as the fosse was a dug feature and thus more likely to have survived.

Acknowledgements

This paper differs substantially from the lecture given in Inverness as the work of interpretation continues. The author would like to thank all those who have assisted him in producing this paper in particular Gillian Harden, Norman MacAskill and Fiona Wilson. Finance for the excavation was provided by the Scottish Development Department (Ancient Monuments Branch).

Bibliography

Barron, E.M., 1906. *Inverness in the Fifteenth Century*, Inverness.

Barron, E.M., 1907. *Inverness in the Middle Ages*, Inverness.

Brooks, N.P. and Whittington, G., 'Planning and growth in the medieval Scottish burgh: the example of St Andrews', *Transactions (New series 1977) Inst. Brit. Geog.*, Vol.2, No.2.

Ewart, G., *Inverness Archaeological Survey 6 Feb.–3 Mar. 1978* (unpublished).

Gourlay, R. and Turner, A., 1977. *Historic Inverness: the archaeological implications of development*, Glasgow.

Fraser MacIntosh, C., 1875. *Invernessiana 1160–1599*, Inverness.

Mackay, W. and Boyd, H.C. (Ed.), 1911. *Records of Inverness*, Vol 1, (New Spalding Club), Aberdeen.

Rait Castle - Nairn

EDUCATION IN THE HIGHLANDS IN THE MIDDLE AGES

D.E.R. WATT

It is well known that the customary modern distinction between Lowlands and Highlands was not one which was in use in the earlier centuries of the Middle Ages; and when from the later fourteenth century onwards we do find Lowland writers beginning to make the distinction, it is expressed either in terms of difference in vernacular language (with those living in the coastal and low-lying regions speaking a version of English and those in the mountains and outlying islands speaking Gaelic), or it was expressed in terms of a general contrast between those who were domesticated, cultured, trustworthy, law-abiding and devout, and those who were wild and untamed, rough and unbending, if handsome and easy-going.[1] We cannot, however, attach any specific geographical area to contemporary definitions of this kind, which are presumably at best prejudiced half-truths. In any case the intention here is to concentrate mainly on the thirteenth and fourteenth centuries before such distinctions between Lowlands and Highlands had much currency; and so we should bear in mind simply the area north and west of the Highland Boundary Fault from Dumbarton to Stonehaven wherever the physical nature of the country dictates that the population lives in scattered communities because the natural resources are unevenly kind to man.

We may begin with the assumption that every established society has an elaborate and subtle set of educational customs acceptable to that society. It is just our misfortune and inadequacy as historians if we cannot now reconstruct the whole picture. This is true of mediaeval Scotland as a whole, and especially true of the Highlands: indeed Dr Durkan has said of rural schools in Scotland in the Middle Ages: 'As to the Highlands proper we know nothing at all!'[2] We therefore have to work with analogies from other areas and countries where the evidence is better, and also from general principles. One of these is particularly important as we focus on a period very different from our own: Professor Lawrence Stone has made the demographic observation that in pre-industrial conditions when only about half the children born could expect to live to manhood, it was a very risky speculation to invest capital in a prolonged and expensive education.[3] We can compare that situation with the fact that today the country as a whole spends a high proportion of the national income on an educational system, and some parents at least choose to go further and make considerable sacrifices for the education of their children in the way which they think most advantageous. We should be prepared therefore to find in the Middle Ages an educational system that was much less institutionalised than we accept as normal today. Indeed it will not be surprising if we find that at some levels it was scarcely institutionalised at all.

It is also a basic general principle that we should not expect to find any single educational system in the Highlands as a whole. This is connected with the fact that in the central Middle Ages no less than five languages were current in the area: Gaelic, Norse, French, Northern English/Scots, and Latin. On the vernacular level it was essential to the situation that the area was the meeting place of four languages with their associated literatures and cultures. In the thirteenth century Gaelic was still spoken in many Lowland areas north of the Forth-Clyde line as well as in the Highlands — even as far away probably as Fife.[4] Professor Derek Thomson has splendidly illumined for us the continuing tradition of the Gaelic learned and literary orders in the Middle Ages in Scotland (the lawyers, doctors, scribes, musicians, historians, genealogists and poets), with emphasis on an educational system based on hereditary professional families who maintained a connection with schools in Ireland.[5] Then there was the Norse tradition in the Hebrides from the ninth century onwards: this has been studied by modern scholars much less in that area than in Orkney and Shetland (where of course it survived much longer); but we need to bear in mind that it was not until 1266 that the Islands were handed back to the Scottish kingdom after more than four centuries of forming part of the Norwegian overseas empire. On the mainland a French-speaking aristocracy arrived from the twelfth century onwards to complicate matters, with the settlement of the Comyns, Bissets, Frasers, Grants, Sinclairs, Morays and many other families with a place in an international chivalric culture that stretched from Scotland through England and France to the Crusading States of Palestine. Lastly the Northern English or Scots tongue spread gradually up the east coast from Lothian from about the same time. Initially it seems to have been the favoured language of an expanding class of people who earned their living as craftsmen and traders rather than by working the land, and who were encouraged in their activities more and more by governmental action in the form of the grant of burgh privileges to their communities. This happened at Elgin, Forres, Nairn and Inverness in the twelfth century, Dingwall, Cromarty and Rosemarkie in the thirteenth century, and Wick in the fourteenth.[6] As sizeable built-up areas developed in connection with at least some of these burghs (though at this period we must think of populations in terms of hundreds rather than thousands), so did the use of Scots as a vernacular language spread in the neighbouring countryside. This kind of development is hard to date; but I have noted one casual reference to the fact that as late as 1366 the people of Dornoch spoke a different language from those of Moray.[7]

All of these vernacular languages must have had some kind of educational system associated with them, however informal and however much based on oral instruction. And presumably in all four cases at least a few members of every generation must have been able to read and write for knowledge of the literature and culture of each vernacular to be handed on. So much we may assume from general principles. But this is not the side of education in the Highlands with which we are concerned here: instead let us look at the position of the fifth language which has been mentioned, Latin, the *lingua franca* used over the whole Highland area. What was its position?

It was the language of the liturgy and the administration of the Christian Church throughout the Highlands in the centuries we are considering (and, of course, for long before). Through knowledge of Latin some Highlanders at least in successive generations became learned men, in contact with the thinking and literature of the classical past and with the developing contemporary culture of Europe as a whole. We can be sure of this, since it is clear that some Highlanders were able to study at schools and universities abroad from the late twelfth century onwards, and then more conveniently at universities in Scotland from the early fifteeenth century onwards.[8] These select few will be considered in more detail later; here the point is to emphasise how through an education in Latin a much wider cultural experience was possible than was offered by an education in any of the four vernacular languages. It is the scale of Latin education that is so impressive compared with the others, and this is the justification for concentrating on it here after this preliminary nod towards vernacular education.

The great bulk of those who acquired Latin learning were *clerici* (i.e. clergy) of one kind or another. (Here it may be suggested that Professor Thomson is misleading when he claims the mediaeval clergy in the Highlands for the Gaelic learned orders:[9] clearly some members of important Highland families whose vernacular tongue was Gaelic did regularly become Christian clergy, often (as elsewhere) on an hereditary basis; but it was through competence in Latin, not Gaelic, that they served as clergy, and if they did pursue Gaelic learned interests sometimes, this was surely more on the level of a side-interest or even a hobby than as the interest which gave them professional standing. It may be argued, indeed, that the clergy were the 'Latin learned order' of the Highlands in the Middle Ages!) The Church seems to have been organised in the Highlands from at least the twelfth century onwards on the standard pattern found in the many provinces of the Church elsewhere in Europe: local clergy were settled in territorial parishes throughout the whole area, and these were organised into a number of dioceses under bishops based on headquarters in cathedral cities sited in a semi-circle around the mountainous area of the country at Glasgow, Dunblane, Dunkeld, Aberdeen, Elgin, Fortrose and Dornoch.[10] In each case the diocese had a Lowland element in geographical terms and more or less of a Highland hinterland. That this balance of Lowland and Highland was a necessary recipe for success is apparently proved by the comparative weakness of the later diocese of Argyll, based on the island of Lismore in the Firth of Lorn, which was detached from Dunkeld diocese at the end of the twelfth century, but which remained with such limited resources that its institutions were only pale shadows of those in other dioceses.[11] The system demanded its strongpoints as centres of leadership, and here we may stress particularly the influence of the clerical leaders of thirteenth- and fourteenth-century Caithness, Ross and Moray at Dornoch, Fortrose and Elgin,[12] for they were as ambitious and active as any other church leaders in Scotland.

Part of this activity was directed towards the production and support of a clerical class capable of communicating in Latin. Note the phrase 'clerical class', for the *clerici* of the Middle Ages comprised not only the 'clergy' with liturgical and pastoral duties: they included also the 'clerks', the men who were masters of the skills of reading and writing in Latin. When we consider the many activities of the 'Church' as the organised community of clerks in this sense, we become aware of the wide variety of services which it offered in the legal and administrative fields, with Latin as the universally-used medium which in a very real sense held an area like the Highlands together. There was the work of notaries providing legal services for all kinds of people; work in estate management for the larger landholders; work in the hierarchy of courts provided by the Church to deal with matters like family law, disputes over contracts, matters of defamation and other moral offences; work in the administration of the Church itself (including regular communication with dioceses in other parts of Scotland and, above all, with Rome, where international standards of procedure had to be matched); and work in civil local government, particularly in the financial, administrative and judicial duties of justiciars, sheriffs and burgh officers, including correspondence with central government.[13] All these kinds of work involved the skill of writing in Latin, sometimes at what may be called the 'tradesman' level (involving training locally on the job), and sometimes at the 'professional' level (involving years of training at distant universities). What then can we learn about the ways in which this literacy and even learning in Latin was acquired in the Highlands in the thirteenth and fourteenth centuries?

Local Schooling

Most of the analysis at this level must be just from general principles, since hard evidence is very scrappy indeed. One such principle which needs to be grasped at the outset is that schools of any size are usually urban institutions in any society.[14] It follows from the paucity of burghs in the Highlands that elementary education in most areas is unlikely to have been conducted in recognisable 'schools' at all. We should not expect to find formal institutions for passing on the basic skills of Latin literacy any more than we should expect to find schools for other trades such as joiners or butchers. Instead it is likely that most children destined to follow the clerical trade learned their reading skills in Latin from a local priest or other clerk; and in a proportion of cases they would learn writing skills also, though in these days reading and writing were not necessarily taught together as they are today. It is clear that, despite the official Church rules at this time about the celibacy of the clergy, clerical skills were often handed on from father to son like those of other trades. In any case the local priest or clerk needed to train up occasional assistants and eventual successors: the system demanded apprentices. In addition most landholders of any substance kept a clerical chaplain among their household servants, who would be involved also in training the next generation in Latin literacy. Children began by mastering the alphabet, and then practised reading Latin words (though with little attention to meaning at this stage). The main teaching material used was the liturgy of the Church, and children were at the same time taught the mysteries of chanting in plainsong. Thus did reading and 'song' go together; and many priests qualified for ordination by their bishop with no further Latin learning than that.[15]

In places where there was a large church staffed by a community of clergy, a more elaborate organisation can be traced. This is true certainly of the cathedral cities, where an officer called the precentor or chanter had responsibility for finding choirboys and organising a Song School to train them in their functions. This was what happened at Elgin and the other cathedral cities to the east and south,[16] and though it cannot be proved, the situation at Dornoch, Fortrose and Lismore is likely to have been the same. We have here therefore an example of the setting aside of some of the Church's endowment for educational purposes, albeit with the direct motive of serving the daily needs of a community who maintained a complicated liturgical round of services. The collegiate church at Tain which was to emerge in the fifteenth century is known to have had a school attached to it which was probably a Song School,[17] and the contemporary collegiate church of Kilmun in Cowal[18] is likely to have had one too.

Monasteries also are known in general to have used their resources to support what are called Almonry Schools within their precincts. These offered instruction that was usually separate from the training given to monastic novices, and were commonly just Song Schools for boys who were required to assist in the services of the community, though sometimes they may have taken their pupils a little further. Nothing is specifically known about the activities of the monasteries in the Highlands in this direction; but a school of this kind is known at Kelso in the thirteenth century,[19] and Almonry Schools are likely enough on a small scale at Kinloss, Urquhart, Pluscarden and Beauly in Moray diocese, Fearn in Ross, and Saddell and Ardchattan in Argyll. We must be on our guard, however, against assertions that these monasteries held a central place in the mediaeval educational system of the Highlands, for the scale of their operations in this sphere (if any) would have been very small in the thirteenth and fourteenth centuries.

After reading and song came grammar. This has recently been described as follows: 'Students learnt how words were inflected and tried to memorise their meanings. They practised prose and verse composition and were taught how to speak the language boldly and fluently. They studied literary texts and were introduced to the principles of literary criticism.'[20] Here is something much more elaborate than reading and song: it could presumably be taught by some of the more literate parish clergy or in private households, but it more commonly demanded the teaching skills of a specialist grammar master in a school. The full course usually took about seven years of study before a boy was fit to proceed to university, and certainly from the thirteenth century onwards it was not uncommon for the grammar master to be himself a man who had been a student for a time.

In most dioceses by this date it was the responsibility of the officer of the cathedral called the chancellor to supervise schools at this level and to appoint or at least license the teachers, certainly within the cathedral city itself and arguably throughout the whole diocese.[21] Within the Highlands we know that this responsibility was exercised by the chancellor at Elgin,[22] as it probably was at Dornoch, Fortrose and Lismore. This does not however mean that Grammar Schools were necessarily in continuous existence at these cathedral cities, for the financial arrangements were at first too uncertain to guarantee that. A school would emerge when there was a master available to offer his services. He would have to charge fees for his teaching until there was a will locally to find other means of remunerating him. The most permanent arrangement was the creation of an endowment whereby a benefice under church law was established, to which a succession of masters might be appointed. Or arrangements might be made for an annual money income for a school master, either from church or burgh funds, though in this case there was less guarantee that the payment would continue when the master died or moved away. No buildings were at first thought necessary, for the master would just use rented or borrowed accommodation; but then gradually buildings of a simple kind came to be provided by Church or Burgh to facilitate more permanent arrangements. Of course the scale is likely to have been tiny by modern standards: a school of twenty to thirty pupils is probably the maximum that we should envisage, taught by one master, assisted perhaps by one or two helpers with lesser qualifications.

There is evidence for a Grammar School of this kind at Elgin just before the Reformation in the sixteenth century. By that time there was a school building and the master was being paid. The evidence about the source of his salary is, however, contradictory: some income from the parish benefice of Kincardine in Strathspey is mentioned in this connection, as are some of the revenues of the bishopric and some funds at the disposal of the burgh council,[23] but we cannot be sure whether he was paid from all these sources at once or whether they were alternatives tapped at different times. The school was clearly an important facility in the community, and efforts were made by the burgh council to strengthen it by forcing a teacher who was running a small private school to come and contribute to the work of the 'principal' or 'common' school of the burgh.[24] But how far back from the sixteenth century we should trace a Grammar School at Elgin is anybody's guess. All that we can reasonably say is that it is the kind of place where grammar teaching as a supplement to more elementary teaching throughout the diocese and as a preparation for higher study at university is very likely to have been regularly provided from the early thirteenth century onwards.

Then there is Inverness, the only other place within the Highlands where the existence of a Grammar School can be proved in our period. As at Elgin a building existed just before the Reformation, and by this time the burgh council was responsible for raising the money for the master's salary.[25] In this way Inverness was like other leading burghs which were not cathedral cities in having its own school, e.g. (New) Aberdeen, Ayr, Dumbarton, Dumfries, Edinburgh, Montrose, Perth.[26] Like some of those too (and unlike Elgin) the existence of a school at Inverness can be traced further back than the mid-sixteenth century — to 1316 indeed, when a certain 'Master Felan' happens to be casually recorded as 'rector of the schools of Inverness'.[27] This style is paralleled elsewhere, as in Aberdeen, where in 1263 Master Thomas de Bennum is found as 'rector of the schools of Aberdeen', and a Master Thomas de Kingorn held the same office in 1386;[28] and it is reasonably clear that in the thirteenth and fourteenth centuries this style indicates the headship of a Grammar School with more than one classroom which had the status of an ecclesiastical benefice. In Aberdeen this benefice (which was probably connected with a school sited near the cathedral in Old Aberdeen) was certainly in the gift of the chancellor of the cathedral in the thirteenth century,[29] though the burgh council of New Aberdeen are found to be in effective control of the patronage of a school there by the early fifteenth century.[30] In Inverness there is likely to have been a similar development from ecclesiastical to burgh responsibility, and with the existence of a benefice there is at least the presumption of continuity, even if we know the name of only one master in 1316 and there follows a gap of 250 years until the next mention of the school! We should not be surprised at the growing burgh involvement in Latin education towards the end of the Middle Ages, for in Inverness as elsewhere this is one way by which we can mark the fact that a different historical era was coming, when laity as well as clerks were to combine in educational enterprises.

With only two Grammar Schools which we can now identify in the whole of the Highlands in the Middle Ages, we are left wondering what was the whole picture of what we may call secondary education in the area. Possibly there were one or two similar schools in other places which have left no record because they had no endowment or other arrangements to support a master regularly, and so were episodic institutions as masters happened to be available and parents were willing to pay fees. It is also likely that grammar schooling was available for some of the time at Dornoch, Fortrose and Lismore. But since there were so few urban settlements in the area, it is unlikely that there were ever many schools around. Of course young clerks from the Highland parts of Glasgow, Dunblane, Dunkeld and Aberdeen dioceses could secure a grammar education in the schools of their cathedral cities in the Lowlands; and perhaps some Highlanders from further afield also chose to travel to these distant schools. But however they did it, there can be no doubt that a sizeable number of Highlanders in every generation in the thirteenth and fourteenth centuries acquired sufficient facility in Latin to staff the tradesmanlike offices, and a few regularly proceeded to professional training at universities. This requires acceptance of the view that Grammar School education was available somewhere.

As a tailpiece to this consideration of secondary education we need to examine again the place of the religious orders. There is no evidence that any of the local monasteries offered instruction at this level to anyone outside their own membership in the period, though by the early fifteenth century at any rate some of the monastic superiors (such as the Benedictine Priors of Urquhart[31]) were to be regularly men with university degrees. But the Dominican Order of Friars Preachers or Black Friars calls for attention since it had small convents from the mid-thirteenth century in both Elgin and Inverness.[32] This order encouraged the regular study of arts and theology by every friar as a preparation for effective preaching. Each house was supposed to have a *lector* to direct these studies. In addition various houses were designated as centres for grammar study and others for more advanced study at the equivalent of university level, with a very few (such as those at Oxford and Paris) designated for the study of theology at the most advanced level. The dozen Scottish convents shared in this general system as a Vicariate (or subordinate section) of the English Province of the order, and seem regularly to have sent friars after suitable preparation for advanced study abroad.[33] But, though the order took in young boys sometimes and trained them in basic grammar, this was normally with a view to their joining the order when they grew up. And only certain convents would specialise in study at this level: there was no need for all of them to do so, since friars were recruited to the order as a whole and were moved around from convent to convent as their training progressed and then as the work-opportunities for fully-trained friars developed.[34] In most houses therefore the studies were devised for mature men who had already experience of learned work at university level. It appears that on occasion they were willing to admit equally learned men from among the local clergy to join in some of these studies.[35] This may well have been the situation at both Elgin and Inverness, where the Dominican convents are likely to have been regarded as places of intellectual stimulus as well as bases from which the friars went about their main business of preaching tours at the behest of the bishop.[36] There is certainly no evidence, however, that these small convents ever ran schools for the young clerks of the neighbourhood at grammar school level, and it is out of character to suggest (as has sometimes been done[37]) that they did. Certainly Master Felan of Inverness in 1316 is unlikely to have had any connection with the Dominicans; and if it happens that a school building had by the later sixteenth century been erected beside a piece of property belonging to them,[38] this is just as much a coincidence as the fact that the town school of Aberdeen happened also to be developed on the edge of a Dominican site.[39] In neither case is it valid to suggest that the friars themselves departed from their usual purpose and practice to open schools for local children.

The University Elite

From the very beginning of universities on the continent and in England in the later twelfth century, Scotland as a whole benefited from the new and exciting opportunities for higher education which were developed thenceforward.[40] Clerks bearing the title of 'Master' (indicating graduate status of some kind) are found in the Highlands from about 1200 onwards, not in large numbers certainly, and largely concentrated around the cathedral communities; but it was an increasing phenomenon, so that by the fourteenth century it was rare for any bishop or holder of other senior office in the church not to be a graduate. Whether these men holding positions of influence in the Highlands were natives to the area or appointees from other parts of Scotland is immaterial for the first main point that has to be made about them: they brought to the Highlands continuously up-to-date knowledge of affairs overseas, and by their very presence ensured that the Latin culture of the Highlands was neither backward nor stultified.

The sources are not sufficiently specific at first to tell us what a graduate had studied or where, though we can find out much more about these things by the later fourteenth century. There is enough, however, to tell us that graduates in all the faculties of the mediaeval universities were represented in the Highlands at one time or another, with the greatest number qualified in arts or law, and a comparative handful in medicine and theology.[41] The pattern of university-going favoured by Scots in general was a changing one over the centuries: in the thirteenth century they certainly went to Oxford, Paris, Bologna, and probably Padua; at the turn of the century the son of an Earl of Ross is found at Cambridge with a Bruce and a Comyn;[42] in the fourteenth century the Italian universities fell out of favour during the long period when the papal court was north of the Alps at Avignon, Oxford was only intermittently accessible in periods of truce in the Hundred Years' War, and

Paris led in popularity, with lesser numbers going to Orleans and Avignon;[43] with the fifteenth century came a new situation once St Andrews became available in 1410 and Glasgow in 1451, though many Scots still chose to go additionally or alternatively to a new selection of universities abroad as well.

It is pertinent to enquire into the resources which made it possible for young clerks from the Highlands to go abroad for periods of years as university students. Some came from well-to-do landholding families, such as that of the Earl of Ross or the Lord of the Isles, or the Macdougalls of Lorn, or the Aird, Bosco, Brodie, Innes and Urquhart families based around the Moray Firth, or the Macleods of Dunvegan.[44] Sons of such families were probably able to pay their way, as may members of prosperous burgess families such as the Trebruns of Elgin.[45] But family influence could be used to obtain a benefice as a means of support for one of its student members e.g. Alexander de Brodie was vicar of Dyke in Moray in the 1380s while a student at Orleans, and John de Innes held the archdeaconry of Caithness in the 1390s whilst a student at Paris.[46] Others belonging to less prominent families would seek out the patronage of some lord who was not a relative in order to obtain similar support, as in the case of Bean MacIan of Argyll diocese, who had served Donald Lord of the Isles as a chaplain before being presented by him to the church of Kilmonivaig in Lochaber in the 1380s and going off to study at Paris.[47] The general practice of using an ecclesiastical benefice as a means of subsistence whilst a student was a well-established and widely-accepted one, as can be seen already in the mid-thirteenth century when a dean of Moray who was already a master of arts was allowed to leave his benefice for further study of theology or canon law;[48] and we know that it was to be a continuing practice in the fifteenth century when beneficed clerks from the dioceses of Argyll, Moray, Ross and the Isles at any rate can be found as students at St Andrews and Glasgow.[49] It was the practice of centuries to allow benefices to be used in this way. Church law, indeed, encouraged bishops to grant leave of absence to benefice-holders to become students (though they usually had to pay a vicar or other substitute if cure of souls was attached to the benefice), and it was common enough for such men to be allowed to delay their ordination as priests during their years of study without the normal penalty of the forfeiture of their benefices.[50] In addition some bishops themselves made it their business to assist favoured clerks to become students: Bishop Fyvin of Ross was apparently active in this field in the 1270s with regard to a student at Bologna, and Bishop Bur of Moray certainly was in the 1390s, when he augmented out of the bishopric revenues the income which John de Innes drew from the archdeaconry of Caithness to enable him to return for a further spell of study at Paris.[51] Furthermore the bishops of Moray had a bursary fund at their disposal from 1326 onwards to support students from their diocese at Paris in particular. It was called the Grisy Bursary after the name of a farm property in the district of Brie near Paris which was bought on the instructions of Bishop David de Moray to provide an endowment income. At first four students were supported by this fund (one in theology and three in arts); but by the 1380s at any rate and later it was being given to just one student at a time and not always to a Moray man.[52] Nevertheless the existence of such a bursary fund demonstrates the assumption of permanence in the practice then current that some Highland students went to study in the university of Paris.

This assumption had presumably been cultivated already for up to 100 years by the earlier generations of university graduates who can be traced in influential positions in the Highland dioceses. Moray, Ross and Caithness all had at least some graduate bishops in the thirteenth century, and regularly had them in the fourteenth:[53] Argyll was rather different, with an interesting series of three learned Dominican bishops (who may have been the only men willing to take on so difficult a diocese) for over 100 years from 1264, followed by two graduate bishops from local families.[54] Such men can be shown to have often made it their business to appoint other graduate clerks to their administrative staffs (particularly as archdeacons and officials) or to their cathedral chapters. Often the policy clearly was to encourage clerks educated to high professional standards to come and live for at least part of their careers in the Highland cathedral cities. The evidence for this policy is clearest at Elgin, where Bishop Andrew de Moray, for example, assembled a highly qualified community to establish his new cathedral and enlarged chapter as early as the 1220s and 1230s;[55] and the fourteenth century Bishops David de Moray, John de Pilmor, Alexander Bur and William de Spynie all had a high proportion of graduate clerks in their chapters.[56] By this time, it is true, most of these appointments were being made centrally by the pope rather than by the bishop himself, and as the more ambitious clergy were increasingly being allowed to hold more than one benefice as a reward for their professional eminence we notice that quite a number of members of the Highland chapters came to be non-resident for long periods while making their careers elsewhere. Some, indeed, by the later fourteenth century may never have even visited the area from which they drew part of their substantial incomes. This does modify the earlier picture, for the stimulus towards Latin education to university level offered then by a visible resident community of graduates was now to some extent removed. But it became all the clearer in the fourteenth century that the top appointments in the church were open to talent rather than just to local connections and influence, and that the only way to earn papal patronage was to proceed beyond grammar school education to several years of study at a university abroad. This was the way for a young clerk from the Highlands as elsewhere to qualify as a member of an élite professional group educated to international standards, whom the pope recognised as worthy of promotion.[57]

We cannot quantify the numbers of young clerks from the Highlands who sought university education in the thirteenth and fourteenth centuries, for the boundaries of the area are too indefinite and the evidence for a known graduate's place of origin is all too often lacking. Certainly we are not talking about a large number. On a rough calculation there were in all Scotland on average about 200 graduates around in any one year of the two centuries, forming a professional élite in a clerical population of between 3000 and 4000, in a general population of perhaps half a million. Of course this graduate population was to grow quite fast to perhaps three-times the size by the end of the fifteenth century once local universities were available in Scotland; but before that development we must think of just a handful of ambitious young clerks each year who found it possible to leave Scotland and travel to seek a university training abroad: and only a proportion of this handful came from the Highlands. A total of perhaps fifty to sixty over two centuries is all that can be identified today as going to university from the dioceses of Caithness, Ross, Moray and Argyll, though of course there is also a number of others whose place of origin is unknown but who may have gone from the Highlands. Yet even if the size of this élite of professional men is small, we can still find a great deal of interest in considering their quality, since they represent the best that the education system in the Highlands in the Middle Ages could produce. The following selection of examples of the careers followed by Highlanders in the period who did become graduates is offered so that we may form some idea of the variety of opportunities in life which came their way as a result:

The Trebrun family group in the second half of the fourteenth century.[58] Five of this family were graduates in the same generation, apparently all kin of an older Henry de

Trebrun, himself a Master, who later in life settled in Elgin as a merchant and died in the early 1360s. All five in this case chose to make their careers away from the Highlands.

John After studying arts, civil and canon law at Paris and Oxford, he was beneficed in Glasgow, Dunkeld and St Andrews dioceses and made his career at the papal court in Italy and at Avignon. He died c.1379.

Andrew Perhaps John's brother, he was a student of arts, civil and canon law at Paris and elsewhere. He was beneficed in St Andrews and Brechin dioceses, failing in his efforts to obtain a canonry of Elgin. After residing at the papal court at Avignon for a time, he returned to Scotland apparently to his parish benefice of Kinnoull near Perth, and was employed in the royal administration in a minor way. He died between 1410 and 1415.

William Certainly a brother of Andrew, he studied arts and theology at Paris, spending 20 years there as student and teacher, eventually becoming one of the few doctors of theology. A steady stream of Scots took their arts degrees under his supervision. He was beneficed in Glasgow diocese, and died apparently at Paris c.1385.

David He studied civil and canon law at Orleans and Oxford, and then practised as a notary back in Scotland, at least in Melrose and Edinburgh, dying after 1400.

Peter He studied arts at Paris and perhaps theology. Apparently beneficed in St Andrews diocese, he seems to have returned to live in the south of Scotland, dying after 1378.

It would appear that the Highlands did not gain from the effort and expense put into the education of the five members of this burgess family.

William and John de Spynie[59]

William He was certainly a Moray man, presumably from Spynie near Elgin, but began his career in the service of Bishop Laundels of St Andrews c.1350. Then he studied arts and canon law to bachelor level at Paris before returning to Scotland in the 1360s, probably to practise as a lawyer in the church courts at Elgin, where he now held a canonry among his benefices. He returned abroad for further study of civil and canon law, perhaps at Oxford and certainly again at Paris, qualifying as doctor of canon law; and then was active back in Scotland again for twenty years as a skilled lawyer practising in the courts at Elgin and Aberdeen, becoming dean of Aberdeen in 1387. He is thought to have been a consultant on tricky points of law; and as an experienced lawyer with local knowledge he was a particularly active bishop of Moray for nine years at the end of his life until 1406 (when he was in his eighties), as he picked up the pieces after the disastrous burning of Elgin Cathedral by the Wolf of Badenoch in 1390. This man brought back much to his native heath as a result of his education abroad.

John Probably William's son, he held among his benefices the vicarage of Duffus which was in William's gift as bishop of Moray. For long a student at Paris in arts, canon law and then medicine, he is known to have revisited Moray once in 1413 after his father's death, by which time he was precentor of Moray; but he then returned abroad to make his career at the court of Pope Benedict XIII in Spain, where he was employed as a clerk in the Department of the Penitentiary. He left the papal court, however, before he died between 1415 and 1417. Unlike his father he is basically another example of the Highland Scot Abroad.

An Inverness Trio[60]

Lastly we may consider the careers of three clerks who took their surname from the burgh of Inverness and who may be presumed to have grown up there and have been products of its Grammar School.

Roger He studied sufficiently at the university level to earn the style of Master and probably his degree was in canon law, for from the early 1290s he is found back in the Highlands as official of the bishop of Moray (i.e. president of the bishop's court) and member of the cathedral chapter, being successively a canon, succentor, chancellor and precentor, until his death forty years later in the early 1330s. He also played a part in government service under King Robert I, helping at least with the negotiations leading to the Treaty of Inverness with Norway in 1312, and was rewarded with a substantial land-grant and a pension for his pains. University education for him opened the door to a varied professional life back in his home diocese.

John He had a similar career, again as an undifferentiated Master who in the 1340s appeared as Roger's next-known successor both as chancellor of Moray and bishop's official. He too made his career as a member of the Elgin cathedral chapter.

Eustace He is found more specifically as a student of law by 1350, qualifying eventually as a licentiate in civil law and bachelor in canon law, though we do not know where he studied. Whilst a student he was helped both by Bishop Pilmor of Moray and the pope to secure appointment by the abbey of Arbroath as patrons to the vicarage in his home burgh of Inverness. After using the income of this benefice for about eight years to support him in his studies abroad, he returned to Inverness in the early 1360s to live there for more than twenty years, seeing to an increase in the number of chaplains who staffed his church, defying strong-arm methods used by agents of Arbroath abbey in a dispute over the abbey's share of the benefice, taking his share in burgh administration by acting as customs official for a time, and adding to his local status by securing appointment as canon in the cathedral chapters at both Fortrose and Elgin. Not many Highlanders who had gone so far with Latin education as to achieve two university degrees can be shown on the surviving evidence to have returned home to serve their own communitties as parish priest in this way; but his career shows that it could happen. He was certainly not a typical figure, for most parish clergy were tradesman-clerks rather than professionals; but we may learn from his case that the intelligent well-educated priest was at least sometimes a notable figure in the society of the Highlands in the Middle Ages.

FOOTNOTES

1. *Johannis de Fordun Chronica Gentis Scotorum*, ed. W.F. Skene (Edinburgh, 1871–2), i, 42; see also G.W.S. Barrow, *The Kingdom of the Scots* (London, 1973), 362.
2. J. Durkan, 'Education in the century of the Reformation', *Innes Review*, x (1959), 85. (This article was reprinted in *Essays on the Scottish Reformation 1513–1625*, ed. D. McRoberts [Glasgow, 1962], 145–68, but is cited here in its original form.)
3. L. Stone, 'Literacy and education in England 1640–1900', *Past and Present*, xlii (1969), 92.
4. Cf. Barrow, *Kingdom*, 363.
5. D.S. Thomson, 'Gaelic learned orders and literati in medieval Scotland', *Scottish Studies*, xii (1968), 57–78.
6. G.S. Pryde, *The Burghs of Scotland* (Oxford, 1965), nos. 8, 13, 20, 25, 34, 36, 98, 129.
7. *Calendar of Entries in the Papal Registers relating to Great Britain and Ireland: Petitions to the Pope*, ed. W.H. Bliss (London, 1896), i, 528.
8. Pre-15th-cent. names are to be found in D.E.R. Watt, *A Biographical Dictionary of Scottish Graduates to A.D. 1410* (Oxford, 1975); St Andrews names in *Acta Facultatis Artium Universitatis Sancti Andree* (Edinburgh and Scottish History Society, 1964); Glasgow names in *Munimenta Alme Universitatis Glasguensis* (Maitland Club, 1854).
9. Thomson, 'Gaelic learned orders', 65–68.
10. For situation as at c.1274 see *An Historical Atlas of Scotland c.400–c.1600*, ed. P. McNeill and R. Nicholson (St Andrews, 1975), 35–37, 136.
11. D.E.R. Watt, *Fasti Ecclesiae Scoticanae Medii Aevi ad annum 1638*, 2nd draft (St Andrews, 1969), 26, 28–29; I.B.

Cowan, 'The medieval church in Argyll and the Isles', *Records of the Scottish Church History Society*, xx (1978), 15–29.
12. See lists in Watt, *Fasti*, 58–74, 266–88, 214–46, with biographies of many of these leaders in Watt, *Dictionary*.
13. Cf. the recent study of the implications of the parallel Latin literacy in England in M.T. Clanchy, *From Memory to Written Record: England 1066–1307* (London, 1977).
14. As noted in Durkan, 'Education', 72.
15. N. Orme, *English Schools in the Middle Ages* (London, 1973), 12–14, 60–63; or more briefly in N. Orme, *Education in the West of England 1066–1548* (Exeter, 1976), 2; cf. Durkan, 'Education', 67–73 where in a discussion of these schools in 16th. cent. Scotland the term 'Little School' is introduced for them.
16. For Elgin c.1500 see *Registrum Episcopatus Moraviensis* (Bannatyne Club, 1837), 262–3; for Aberdeen 1256 see *Registrum Episcopatus Aberdonensis* (Spalding and Maitland Clubs, 1845), ii, 44; for Brechin 1429 see *Registrum Episcopatus Brechinensis* (Bannatyne Club, 1856), ii, 26; cf. Durkan, 'Education', 90.
17. I.B. Cowan and D.E. Easson, *Medieval Religious Houses Scotland*, 2nd edition (London, 1976), 227–8; J. Durkan, 'The sanctuary and college of Tain', *Innes Review*, xiii (1962), 150; cf. Durkan, 'Education', 86.
18. Cowan and Easson, *Religious Houses*, 223; cf. Durkan, 'Education', 70.
19. *Liber S. Marie de Calchou* (Bannatyne Club, 1846), i, 142.
20. Orme, *West of England*, 2; see also 22; for a fuller analysis see Orme, *English Schools*, 87–115.
21. *Aberdeen Registrum*, ii, 45; *Brechin Registrum*, ii, 26; cf. Durkan, 'Education', 76. See also K. Edwards, *The English Secular Cathedrals in the Middle Ages*, 2nd edition (Manchester, 1967), 194–7.
22. *Moray Registrum*, 270.
23. Ibid.; *The Records of Elgin* (New Spalding Club, 1903–8), i, 51, 105; A.L. Murray, 'The revenues of the bishopric of Moray in 1538', *Innes Review*, xix (1968), 48 (reference to a payment made in 1562).
24. *Elgin Recs.*, i, 89, 118.
25. *Records of Inverness* (New Spalding Club, 1911–24), i, 5, 53.
26. Durkan, 'Education', 90.
27. W. Fraser, *The Chiefs of Grant* (Edinburgh, 1883), iii, 258; see Watt, *Dictionary*, 187 for dating and for suggesting that this apparent Christian name may rather be a Latin form of the contemporary Gaelic word for "a teacher".
28. Ibid., 40, 298–9.
29. *Aberdeen Registrum*, ii, 45.
30. *Extracts from the Council Register of the Burgh of Aberdeen 1398-1570* (Spalding Club, 1844), 4–5. The council chose a new rector and presented him to the chancellor for official appointment.
31. *Calendar of Scottish Supplications to Rome* (Scottish History Society, 1934–70), i, 65; iii, 122, 133.
32. Cowan and Easson, *Religious Houses*, 118–19.
33. For an explanation of the Dominican educational structure as a whole in the English province of the order see W.A. Hinnebusch, *The Early English Friars Preachers* (Rome, 1951), 209–10, 332–42. From 1349 the Scottish houses had direct access to Dominican houses of study at the highest level elsewhere (*Book of the Old Edinburgh Club*, iii [1910], 85).
34. This mobility in Scotland is stressed by A. Ross, 'Some notes on the religious orders in Pre-Reformation Scotland', in *Essays on the Scottish Reformation 1513–1625*, ed. D. McRoberts (Glasgow, 1962), 195.
35. Hinnebusch, *Friars Preachers*, 337.
36. Ross, 'Some notes', 202; see also A. Ross, 'Incubi in the Isles in the thirteenth century', *Innes Review*, xiii (1962), 108–9 for sermon material based on experience of Dominicans on these tours.
37. E.M. Barron, 'An old Inverness school', *Transactions of the Inverness Scientific Society and Field Club*, ix (1918–25), 261–5.
38. *Inverness Recs.*, i, 239.
39. Cf. F. Wyness, *City by the Grey North Sea: Aberdeen* (Aberdeen, 1965), map opposite p.72.
40. Watt, *Dictionary*, ix.
41. Ibid., passim.
42. Ibid., 471, 66–67, 109 11.
43. D.E.R. Watt, 'Scottish student life abroad in the fourteenth century', *Scottish Historical Review*, lix (1980), 3–4.
44. Watt, *Dictionary*, 471, 285–6, 157–8, 15–16, 56–57, 64, 278–9, 558, 367.
45. See below, p.87.88.
46. Watt, *Dictionary*, 64, 278.
47. Ibid., 287–8 s.v. Johannis.
48. Ibid., 262 s.v. Nicholas de Hedon.
49. *St Andrews Acta*, 92, 97, 103, 150, 188; *Cal.Scot.Supp.*, ii, 195; *Glasgow Univ. Munimenta*, ii, 61, 68, 75, 84, 93, 175.
50. Watt, 'Student life', 15–16.
51. Watt, *Dictionary*, 208, 278–9.
52. Watt, 'Student life', 11–13.
53. See lists in Watt, *Fasti*, 214–15, 266–8, 58–60, with biographies of known graduates in Watt, *Dictionary*.
54. Watt, *Fasti*, 26–27; Watt, *Dictionary*, 180–1, 11–12, 181–2, 157, 287–8.
55. Watt, *Dictionary*, 409.
56. Ibid., 411–13, 450–1, 67–70, 503–6.
57. In 1411 the bishop of Argyll was authorised by the pope to treat senior university men on the same level as the sons of a king, duke, earl or sheriff when it came to accumulating ecclesiastical benefices to acquire a good income (*Calendar of Papal Letters to Scotland of Benedict XIII of Avignon 1394–1419*, ed. F. McGurk [Scottish History Society, 1976], 242).
58. Watt, *Dictionary*, 542–6.
59. Ibid., 502–6.
60. Ibid., 282–3.

THE MEDIEVAL CHURCH IN THE HIGHLANDS

IAN B. COWAN

The history of the medieval church in the Highlands is obscure; it is not only that records have failed to survive, but the paucity of religious houses also ensured that few formal collections of documents were ever amassed. The papal archives have remedied some of this deficiency, but the very remoteness of the Highland dioceses inevitably made contact with the papacy somewhat infrequent. In these circumstances, lack of information can be too readily equated with torpor, but from what little can be discerned it would be unwise to suggest that the unreformed church was any less mindful of its task in the Highlands than in any other part of Christendom.

This survey will concentrate on the mainland dioceses of Argyll, Caithness, Dunkeld, Moray and Ross, all of which lay either wholly or part in the Highland area. Only seven small monasteries — Ardchattan, Beauly, Kinloss, Pluscarden, Saddell and Urquhart lay within these bounds and of these Saddell was suppressed in 1507 while Urquhart and Pluscarden were united in 1454.[1] This union, which was occasioned because there were not more than six monks in the Valliscaulian priory at Pluscarden and not more than two in the Benedictine priory of Urquhart, certainly points to decay as do the frequent bitter disputes over the headship of both priories.[2] In c. 1507 James IV averred that Saddell had within living memory seen no monastic life and had fallen to the use of laymen.[3] Elsewhere the picture is no more encouraging and Hugh Fraser, Sheriff of Inverness, claimed on 18 January 1432 that the buildings of Beauly, which his ancestors had founded and endowed, were falling to the ground; a fate which was also said to have befallen Pluscarden in 1457.[4]

If this were so, and petitions should never be taken literally, the position soon improved. The newly united priory of Urquhart and Pluscarden settled under Benedictine rule at the latter site because the buildings there were more extensive and thereafter, if disputes over the headship did not cease, the strength of the community increased.[5] A prior and eight monks appear in 1508, a prior and twelve monks in 1524 and 1548 and at least nine monks were present at the Reformation when the house was still governed by a prior in religious orders.[6] Elsewhere in Moray, the abbey of Kinloss which had possessed a community of an abbot and twenty-four monks in 1229 still possessed at least nineteen monks in 1537 and only one less at the Reformation.[7] Here too, if Robert Reid, its abbot between 1529 and 1553, successively became commendator of Beauly and in 1541 bishop of Orkney, his nephew and successor Walter was nevertheless blessed as abbot and ruled as such at the Reformation.[8]

During this period, if we are to believe the Italian scholar Ferrerio, there had been a marked revival of religious life in the sixteenth century. The previous century had certainly been an era of mixed fortunes for the abbey with Abbot Adam of Terwas who died in 1401 castigated as a lewd liver; John Flutare degraded in 1440 and William Culross who died in 1504 given to fleshly pleasures and hunting. Nevertheless, even Culross, following the tradition of monastic copying at Kinloss, wrote various books of ritual and Flutare purchased a silver pastoral staff used thereafter by abbots at mass. The purchase of furnishings for the abbey church characterised most abbotships. John Ellon who died in 1467 bought an altarpiece and two silver candlesticks, but his preparations for building a bell tower had to be carried to fruition by his successor who also built a spire. In doing so, however, he clearly outstripped the resources of the abbey as he was not only forced to sell the organs, but also had to be restrained from selling a painting at the high altar before being forced from office in 1482.[9]

The succession of Thomas Crystall to the abbey in 1504 ushered in a new era in the abbey's history. In a series of lawsuits a number of endowments pertaining to the abbey were recovered from various expropriators including the earl of Huntly who had claimed the lands of Balloch in Strathisla. His contribution to the temporal welfare of the monastery was, however, secondary to his efforts to rescue the decayed and irreligious state into which Ferrerio claims it had fallen. This involved increasing the number of monks, which had fallen to fourteen, to more than twenty (a figure which squares with contemporary evidence), and also inculcating a greater vocational sense into the community.[10] To this end, Crystall sent two monks for instruction with the Blackfriars of Aberdeen and on their return one, Walter Hethon, became chanter and the other, James Pont, taught the younger brethren scholastic questions.[11] During the same period John Smyth, one of the monks, commenced his short chronicle and education was further promoted by the contribution of books, including the Old and New Testaments in six volumes, to the library for the use of the monks.[12] Physical repairs to the monastery's fabric also characterised his abbotship; the chapel of St Jerome was repaired and two clocks placed on the church, the smaller of which was used as an alarm in rousing the brethren to say lauds.[13] Spiritual services were certainly not neglected and the monks possessed a well-thumbed copy of Cistercian usages.[14]

Crystall's resignation on 4 July 1528 in favour of Robert Reid, sub-dean of Moray, who only professed as a monk on 11 July 1529 — a fact prudently omitted by Ferrerio — might have proved disastrous for the monastery, but in fact Reid proved to be an exemplary abbot.[15] Although his presence at the abbey must have been infrequent, he maintained the tenor of Crystall's reforms. He promoted the building of a fireproof library in 1538 and in the same year invited the celebrated painter, Andrew Bairhum to paint altar pieces for three of the chapels. Whether his example would have been followed by his nephew, Walter, who succeeded him in 1553 is imponderable, but the monastery was clearly in good shape, both spiritually and physically at the period of the Reformation.[16]

This is equally true of the priory of Beauly to which Robert Reid was provided as commendator on 1 November 1531, this following a struggle for possession with a canon regular, although it seems likely that Reid actually obtained possession in 1530 as Ferrerio avers.[17] At Beauly, which had been repaired in the fifteenth century, a decay of monastic discipline had apparently preceded this appointment and the monastery cannot have been unaffected by unsettled political conditions in the north in the latter part of that century.[18] A bull of excommunication issued on 4 July 1506 against plunderers who had stolen and concealed the possessions of the abbey was not promulgated until 1514, and difficulties at this time may have influenced the decision to extinguish the order of the Vallis Caulium and institute the Cistercian order; a transformation which was finally effected by a papal bull of 10 May 1510.[19] Thereafter the monastery appears to have recovered some of its lost vitality. The recovery of land and fishing rights were among the tasks which faced Reid, but his chief benefaction lay in the re-building of the nave and the restoration of the bell tower which had been destroyed by lightning. Four years later in 1544, he erected a new prior's house to replace the existing ruinous structure.[20] The monks themselves were not forgotten and five junior monks were reputedly seconded to Kinloss for three years for instruction under Ferrerio. The number of monks involved is questionable as the community always appears to have been small, but there were eight monks in 1560, each of whom received forty shillings per year, for their 'habit silver' and had for their 'flesh iijd in the day, for their fish ilk day ijd'.[21]

Little is known of the remaining monasteries within these bounds. The Premonstratensian abbey of Fearn situated near Tain was rebuilding throughout the fifteenth century, but in a letter of James V to Pope Paul III of 9 March 1541, the house is described as ruinous and neglected. If true this might be attributed to a series of commendators who, commencing with Andrew Stewart, bishop of Caithness, held the abbey from 1508. Nevertheless, the convent appears to have consisted of five or more canons at the Reformation.[22] Ardchattan was similarly placed with six monks recorded in 1538 and at least three or four at the Reformation. The priory which was held *in commendam* by John Campbell, bishop of the Isles from 27 February 1545, is sometimes described as Cistercian, but in 1506 in a commission for its visitation by the prior of Beauly, it is said to be immediately subject to Val des Choux and there is no evidence that it became Cistercian.[23]

If monastic houses were sparse, those of friars were even more so. The Dominicans possessed friaries at Elgin and Inverness and the Franciscans and Carmelites were represented by one house each at Elgin and Kingussie respectively. If the Dominican friary at Elgin appears to have fallen under the control of the local family of Dunbar by 1526, a small community remained at the Reformation, and bedesmen were still being maintained in the Maison Dieu which had been granted to the priory in 1520/1.[24] If the state of this priory is, however, uncertain, each of the others exemplifies the theme of a late medieval revival in the fortunes of the church in the Highlands. The friary at Inverness was described as 'almost ruinous in its structure and buildings' on 18 March 1436, yet it was still an active force in the burgh when the community of a prior and four others placed their 'geir' in the custody of the magistrates on 20 June 1559. Its buildings remained undemolished, 13 February 1562, and this at least indicates that the house was not a target for the rascal multitude.[25]

Much more significance in terms of popular support may, however, be attached to the late foundations at Elgin and Kingussie. At the former which had seen a temporary settlement of Greyfriars in the thirteenth century, a new foundation evidently occurred in consequence of a papal bull of 19 March 1481/2 which sanctioned the erection of 'two or three' friaries of reformed Observants, although the actual foundation did not take place until the reign of James IV.[26] The foundation of the Carmelite house of Kingussie by George, earl of Huntly, who died in 1501, falls into the same period and again highlights the revival of interest in the orders of friars who were increasingly in demand as preachers.[27] At Dunkeld, Bishop Brown arranged that Friars Minor and Friars Preachers well acquainted with the Irish tongue should preach at least once a year in the upper parts of the diocese and hear confessions.[28]

In terms of devotion this was, however, the era of the collegiate church. If once again the Highlands were remarkably devoid of such institutions, the church of St Duthac at Tain made ample amends in terms of its importance as a place of pilgrimage. Although it was not formally erected as a collegiate church with a provost, five prebendaries, two deacons, a sacrist and assistant clerk until 12 September 1487 its clerics lived a collegiate existence from at least its reparation after a disastrous fire in 1427.[29] Favoured by kings, including James II who founded a chaplaincy there, but in particular by James IV who made frequent pilgrimages and offerings at the 'stok at Sanct Duthois' and founded an additional chaplaincy there, its drawing power in consequence was considerable.[30] Kilmun in Argyll could not match its importance in this respect, but the erection of the parish church of St. Mund on 5 August 1441 at the petition of Sir Duncan Campbell of Lochawe into a collegiate church for five chaplains, one of whom was to be the provost, and a parochial chaplain who was to take part in divine services with the other chaplains, ensured its position as one of the more important ecclesiastical centres in the West Highlands.[31]

Cathedrals could be of equal importance as pilgrimage centres and in this respect all five dioceses were not only well served, but continued to expand in the course of the fifteenth and early sixteenth centuries. Such expansion was not without its difficulties, however, for at Dornoch the original cathedral constitution utilised as prebends all existing parish churches whose revenues were not required as mensal or common capitular churches. This had initially resulted in a chapter consisting of the bishop, four dignitaries, an archdeacon and four canons, including the abbot of Scone in respect of his appropriated church of Kildonan. When an additional parish of Assynt was created in the mid-thirteenth century, it too became a prebendal church. However, further expansion did take place at some point before the Reformation as the hospital of Helmsdale (x 1558) and the chaplaincy of Kinnald (x 1560) were utilised to endow two further prebends, making a final establishment of thirteen prebends in all.[32]

Expansion on a similarly modest scale also took place at Elgin in which the erection of twenty-three prebends before 1242 left little further scope for the erection of further canonries. Prebends *ad vitam* were created from time to time and one of these, based on the revenues of the parish church of Kincardine, achieved permanence from 1537. A further sixteenth-century development saw the addition of the prebend of Unthank which raised the number of prebends to a final total of twenty-five.[33] Development at Lismore, on the other hand, seems to havd been limited to the creation of life prebends. Initially this chapter consisted of dean, chanter, chancellor and treasurer, the last three having been added to the existing deanship, archdeaconship and four simple prebends, making nine canonries in all to which Bishop Martin added Kilcolmkill as a specified tenth prebend. At about the same time the precentorship, initially held by the priors of Ardchattan, became a secular benefice c. 1371, and this may have marked the finalisation of the earlier constitution. Further prebends were subsequently erected, but it is significant that evidence relating to their prebendal status, and that of Kilcolmkill, are restricted to the period of their foundation. Prebends for life were certainly not unknown, as for example in 1506 when the church of Knoydart was erected by the pope '*in canonicatum et prebendam ad vitam*'. This practice may reflect a situation parallel to that in the Irish diocese of Cloyne, 'in which there was no fixed number of canons'. The likelihood that this was the case, and that no permanent prebends were added to those established by the original constitution, is strengthened by the fact that evidence for the existence of prebends at the Reformation is restricted to the four dignitaries, archdeacon and the four original prebends.[34]

Such modest developments were overshadowed by the changes which took place at Dunkeld and Fortrose in the century before the Reformation. At the former, the state of the chapter in the century or so after 1274 appears to have remained static at four dignitaries, archdeacon, sub-dean, sub-chanter and fifteen canons. Seven more prebends were to be added before the Reformation. Of these seven, three, Aberlady, Alyth and Muckersie, were erected between 1452 and 1469, and another, Ferdischaw, which had apparently previously been a prebend was reconstituted between 1484 and 1506. The remaining three prebends, Fearn, Forgandenny and

Lundeiff, appear as such for the first time in the fifteenth century and appear to have been instituted during that period.[35]

Similar changes characterised developments at Rosemarkie, although insufficiency of evidence makes the exact extent of the fifteenth century changes difficult to determine. By 1255/6, four dignitaries, an archdeacon, sub-dean, sub-chanter and several undesignated prebends had been established in the cathedral situated at modern Fortrose. The abbot of Kinloss was a canon of Ross in respect of his appropriated church of Avoch before 5 January 1324/5 and in the same century four other prebends, Contin, Cullicudden, Logie-Easter and Newnakle with Roskeen have been noted. Seven more prebends — Alness, Dingwall, Kilmuir-Easter, Kiltearn, Kincardine, Kirkmichael and Lumlair — appear in the following century and yet another, Kilchrist only materialises in 1560. Several of these prebends would appear to be fifteenth-century creations. All in all, twenty-one prebends involving the revenues of thirty-one churches were involved, and these, with six churches pertaining to the chapter in common, account for every church in the diocese.[36]

The administrative expansion within cathedral churches in the later middle ages is paralleled by diocesan development of a similar scale. Deans, whose prime function was to represent the clergy of the diocese at episcopal elections, and of whom there is no initial trace in either Caithness or Ross, had apparently ceased to function in Argyll and Dunkeld as chapters developed there.[37] In Moray, on the other hand, if deans continued to exist in an administrative capacity, they were, with the exception of a recognisable continuity of deans in the deanery of Inverness, extremely elusive after the erection of the chapter.[38] Intermittent references to later deans, and a dean of Angus within Dunkeld diocese by 1479 may simply point towards spasmodic attempts to parallel the administrative framework achieved in larger lowland dioceses.[39] The sixteenth century saw further efforts in this respect and although the situation in Moray does not appear to have improved and Caithness remained devoid of deaneries, a dean of Dingwall materialises in the diocese of Ross in 1530.[40] In Argyll likewise although it seems likely that Bishop Martin as part of his reorganisation of the chapter and diocese may have reconstituted the early deaneries as administrative units of Cowal, Lochaw and Kintyre, for a brief appearance is made by a dean of Cowal in 1364 and a deanery of Lochaw in 1434; this attempt appears to have failed.[41] A further reconstitution appears to have taken place in the sixteenth century with again three deaneries; Kintyre which re-appears in 1520 and Lochaw and Morvern which appear for the first time in 1541 and 1545 respectively.[42] This thesis is complicated, but not necessarily invalidated, by the naming of the three deaneries of the diocese in 1539 x 41, Argyll, Lorn and Bute.[43] The evidence is more specific at Dunkeld for there Bishop Brown's biographer Alexander Myln relates that 'as the population grew, the bishop by his official's advice divided the whole diocese into four deaneries'.[44] These deaneries, excluding that south of Forth, were known as Atholl and Drumalban, Angus and Fife, Fothriff and Strathearn, and their first deans were apparently appointed on 22 April 1505.[45]

Similar developments had also taken place in the judicial sphere, and with the exception of Argyll, jurisdiction exercised by the bishop's official in the ecclesiastical courts in these dioceses was supplemented by the appointment of commissaries. In Dunkeld this occurred before 1467 when a commissary with general authority appears and thereafter commissaries with limited authority for Tullilum and South of Forth were established in the early sixteenth century.[46] A parallel development occurred in Moray diocese with the appearance of a commissary general in 1464 and a commissary with limited authority for Inverness in 1522.[47] In Ross, too, commissaries appeared after 1451 and although in Caithness the first commissary does not appear until 1522, this exhibits not only an expansion of judicial services in the Highland area but also demonstrates a new vitality in the ecclesiastical organisation of the dioceses concerned.[48]

The records of the commissary courts within these dioceses are not extant but some insight into their activities is recorded in a description of the activities of David Abercrombie, commissary general of Dunkeld at the end of the fifteenth century, who it was said was 'the first man who effectively punished the excesses and crimes of the Highland folk'.[49] This task was made no easier in so far 'as he came of a noble Highland house and persons guilty of incest, adultery and fornication summoned for correction presumed to call themselves kinsmen in expectation of indulgent dealing'. However, the commissary's approach it is said, was to aver that for this reason and for the good of their souls, correction would be even more severe.[50] Yet another canon, Thomas Greig, prebendary of Alyth and dean of Atholl who 'kept open house in Highland fashion' punished judiciously all public offenders, whether they were clergy or country folk, and had succeeded, it was claimed 'in routing out abominable sins in Atholl and Drumalban.'[51]

Such administrative development was not, however, paralleled in all branches of the church's activities. Less concern was certainly evident in terms of justice, and the provision of schools and hospitals presents a much more uneven picture. In terms of education there is little information, but the cathedrals, with the possible exception of Lismore, must have maintained both grammar and song schools. The foundation of a perpetual chaplaincy in St George's hospital at Dunkeld in 1506 for the grammar schoolmaster was not likely to be an entirely new departure, and a song school also existed there.[52] At Elgin, too, although the town council in 1552 attempted to make one of the chaplains, Thomas Rag, desist from teaching on a free-lance basis, he was alternatively encouraged to join the grammar master in the common school.[53]

Institutional provision for the poor was much less satisfactory. The dioceses of Argyll and Ross apparently possessed no hospitals, and decline is evident in the diocese of Caithness in which the hospital of St John at Helmsdale which was apparently a going concern with a master in 1471 is subsequently described in 1509 and 1514 as a chaplaincy united to Dornoch cathedral.[54] On the other hand, the hospital of St Magnus which first appears on rcord in 1358 and is described as St Magnus de Skymer on 23 September 1440 and St Magnus Martyr on 1 June 1448, but as the poors hospital of St Mary, Caithness diocese on 3 February 1474/5, evidently continued in being until at least the Reformation, being leased with its revenues by the master on 5 and 24 March 1580/1.[55] In the diocese of Moray, hospitals such as St Nicholas beside the bridge of Spey are equally shadowy; the master is mentioned in a charter, 10 June 1471, and the building is said to have survived the Reformation, but nothing further can be substantiated.[56] So too with the undoubtedly pre-Reformation '*domus leprosorum*' mentioned at Forres in 1565, but of the 'houses of the lepers of Elgin' mentioned in 1291, there is no further trace.[57] A similar fate threatened the Maison Dieu at Elgin which in 1445 was reported to have been long void and wont to be assigned to clerks as a secular benefice, though originally founded for the maintenance of poor brothers and sisters. In consequence it may have been to safeguard the hospital, rather than to encompass its demise, that James, bishop of Moray granted it to the Blackfriars of Elgin on 17 November 1520 and certainly although its revenues appear as pertaining to the friars in 1561–72, there is also about this time a record of payment to three bedesmen.[58] Hospitals, through inadequate endowment, were always subject to decay and although Bishop Brown of Dunkeld (1484–1514/5) revived and augmented an earlier foundation, the hospital of St George, for a master and only seven poor folk highlights the inadequacy of institutional provision for the poor within the highland area.[59] The bonds of kinship may have provided an adequate substitute, and individual churchmen were certainly not unmindful of their obligations in this direction as exemplified by George Hepburn, dean of Dunkeld (1497–1527) who not only provided a weekly boll of meal 'for certain decrepit poor folk in the city' but also ordered porridge to be supplied every day when there was a dearth in the country.[60]

If the social benefits conveyed by the Church are questionable, spiritual services were no less so. Parochial revenues were seen as a means of endowing other religious institutions. In this respect by far the largest number of churches and their associated teinds were appropriated in the highland dioceses to the upkeep of the bishop and the cathedral chapter. In Caithness and Ross every church within the diocese had its revenue directed towards this purpose, the tally in the former being seven mensal, twelve prebendal and three churches held in common while in the latter, two mensal, thirty-one prebendal and six common churches constituted the full complement.[61] The almost total absence of religious houses contributed to this situation. In Caithness the church of Kildonan doubled as a prebendal church appropriated to Scone, as did Avoch, appropriated to Kinloss in Ross.[62] Otherwise religious houses were only represented in Ross by a transitory annexation of the parish church of Dingwall, first to Urquhart and then to Pluscarden, the appropriation of the vicarage of Tarbat to the abbey of Fearn and the union of the vicarage of Tain to the collegiate church there.[63]

The presence of several religious houses in Moray provided the basis for a somewhat different pattern of appropriation in that diocese. Beauly possessed the revenues of the parishes of Abertarff and Conveth with its associated chapel of Comar; Urquhart had possessed the revenues of Bellie, Dalcross with its chapel of Kilravock, and Urquhart; the revenues of all three passing to the united priory of Pluscarden in 1453/4, thereby joining those of Dores and Pluscarden which had previously pertained to that priory.[64] Kinloss on the other hand, as a Cistercian foundation, had originally rejected the idea of appropriating parochial revenues, and although Avoch had been annexed by 1274/5, the only other church pertaining to the abbey was that of Ellon in the diocese of Aberdeen which was granted to it by Robert I in 1310 and eventually confirmed to the monks in 1328 by Bishop Henry Cheyne on condition that twenty-four merks were assigned from the fruits for the erection of a prebend in Aberdeen cathedral.[65] Otherwise, of the remaining churches within the diocese, thirteen were assigned as mensal, no fewer than thirty-five as prebendal, five as common to the chapter and three assigned for the upkeep of the chaplains of the cathedral.[66] Other than this only eleven other churches within the diocese were appropriated; two to Beauly, five to Pluscarden and four to institutions outwith the diocese.[67] Two of these churches — Aberchirder and Inverness — pertained to the abbey of Arbroath, the parish church of Kiltarlity to the hospital of Rathven which also supported a prebend in Aberdeen cathedral and the church of Rothes appropriated to the hospital of St Nicholas beside the bridge of Spey.[68] This hospital, however, appears to have been secularised before the Reformation, and the parsonage was again treated as an independent parsonage; it thus joined the churches of Boleskine, Bona, Dunlichity, Essie and Glass as the only free parsonages in the diocese of Moray.[69]

In Dunkeld likewise the majority of the diocesan churches, although by no means all from the Highland area, were similarly utilised, seventeen being attached to the *mensa* of the bishop and twenty-three acting as prebendal churches.[70] The church of Abernyte supported four vicars choral and four other churches were possessed by the chapter in common.[71] Unlike Moray, however, in which few churches were appropriated to other institutions, Dunkeld, which contained the abbey of Inchcolm in one of its many detached portions, but only the tiny priory of Strathfillan in the main part of the diocese, was flanked on its eastern and southern borders by a number of religious houses, all of which took their share of parochial revenues. Thus, Cambuskenneth, Coupar, Dunfermline, Inchaffray and Scone possessed two churches apiece, while Arbroath, Culross and the priory of St Andrews each had one appropriation.[72] Inchcolm, on the other hand, possessed five churches, all of which lay in the diocesan enclave bordering on the Firth of Forth.[73] Only seven churches—Ardeonaig, Blair in Atholl, Kilmaveonaig, Lude, Rannoch, Struan and Weem remained unappropriated and these significantly all lay in the deanery of Atholl and Drumalban which, with the exception of Strathfillan, was devoid of religious houses either within its bounds or on its boundaries.[74]

A similar pattern emerges in the diocese of Argyll in which, of the seventeen unappropriated churches, ten lay in Morvern in which no religious house was to be found and in which not a single church was appropriated.[75] Throughout the rest of the diocese, a very different picture emerges and only seven churches out of thirty-eight in Lorn, Glassary and Kintyre escaped appropriation.[76] The bishop of Argyll held six mensal churches and four were annexed as prebends.[77] The collegiate church of Kilmun also held six churches and the priory of Ardchattan accounted for another five.[78] As the abbey of Saddell apparently possessed no churches, all other appropriated churches were held by institutions outside the diocese. Of these Paisley and Iona possessed three churches each, Inchaffray two and Kilwinning and Fail one apiece.[79]

Appropriations inevitably contributed to the poverty of parochial incumbents in all five dioceses. Nevertheless, it should not be thought that free parsonages were any better in this respect; vicars or chaplains were found in both appropriated and unappropriated churches and failing a proper vicarage settlement might in the former be denied both security of tenure and stipend. Those problems were not confined to these dioceses, but further problems peculiar to the highland area might arise. The plea made in the diocese of Argyll, that no-one should have a benefice unless he speaks the idiom which the greater part of the people spoke, would be equally appropriate in any Highland diocese in which the size of parishes also militated against effective parochial service.[80] The poverty of the vicars also contributed to rapacity on their part and the pillorying of such clergy by contemporary lowland satirists has its Highland counterpart in Makgregouris Testament in which the following legacics are left to both curate and vicar:

> 'To my curate, negligence I resign
> Therewith his parishoners for to teach.
> Another gift I leave him as condign,
> Sloth with ignorance, seldom for to preach,
> The souls he commits for to bleach
> In purgatory till they be washen clean
> Pure religion thereby for to sustain
>
> * * * * *
>
> To the vicar I leave diligence and cure
> To take the upmost cloth and kirk cow
> More to put the corpse in sepulture
> Have poor widow six grice and a sow,
> He will have one to fill his belly fou,
> His thought is more upon the pasch fines
> Than the souls in purgatory that pines.'[81]

From this it may be inferred that the administrative development of the late mediaeval church in the Highlands was not matched by its concern for the spiritual welfare of its parishioners. Yet the picture is not entirely black. In Dunkeld diocese in particular serious attempts at reform were made during the episcopate of Bishop Brown. As several parishes were considered too large he set about sub-dividing some of them. To this end the parish of Little Dunkeld which was large, scattered and sixteen miles in length was reformed by retaining the original parish church and establishing a new one at Caputh in which the windows were glazed, a reredos painted and the choir built at the bishop's expense. Later on, as the bishop thought that the population had further increased and that in the upper parts of the parish of Caputh Irish was spoken, he built and endowed in honour of St Anne, a parish church on his lands of Dowally. Reforms did not stop there, as he also restored the parish church of St Servanus, the principal church of the parish of Tibbermore, and appointed a vicar perpetual there.[82]

Bishop Brown may have been exceptional in his efforts, which also extended to the laying of the foundations of a bridge over the River Tay, but bishops elsewhere, such as Gavin Douglas at Dunkeld, Andrew Forman, bishop of Moray and David Paniter, bishop of Ross, were all men of distinction who may not have been unmindful of their diocesan duties.[83] Other agencies also endeavoured to maintain ecclesiastical standards. Town councils in particular took their duties seriously. An appointment to an altar in Elgin made by the town council in 1546, not only provided honest board in the houses of eight and, at the most fourteen, neighbours, but stipulated that the chaplain was to 'say mas and sing devyn service within the said paroche kirke at all dais, houris and tymes he beis disposit thairto'.[84] At Inverness on 29 April 1557, the council, with no thought of impending religious change, 'for uphald of dale service into thair kyrk for the glore of God and honor thair kyrk', augmented 'Schir Andrew Brebner Chepland to Sant Pettyr with fowyr merkis yerle to be payit of the common gud of Innernes, with the oblation and anwell of Sant Duthace altar'.[85] Elsewhere churches were being maintained and repaired, but against this may be set the case of the parishioners of Inverchaolin who in 1549 'wad nocht ansuer Schir Robert Maxvall vyker of the fruttis, or to the tyme at he mendit his part of the kyrk'.[86] The evidence is disparate but the evidence in favour of both physical and spiritual regeneration is as strong as that for decay and decline. The dilemma as to which of these forces was the more influential is at present unresolved, but the strength of Catholicism in many parts of the Highlands after the Reformation may suggest that the medieval church in that area was still an active force in the mid-sixteenth century.

FOOTNOTES

1. Cowan and Easson, *Religious Houses*, 61, 77–8, 84–5.
2. *CPL*, x, 253–4; *Cal. Scot. Supp*., i, 147; ii, 194; iii, 107–8, 122, 124, 133, 174.
3. *James IV Letters*, no. 149
4. *Cal. Scot. Supp*., iii, 72; *CPL*, xi, 330.
5. Peter F. Anson, *A Monastery in Moray* (London 1959), 91–104.
6. Cowan and Easson, *Religious Houses*, 61.
7. Ibid., 76
8. Ibid., 76
9. Ferrerius, *Historia*, 28–35
10. Ibid., 35–8, 57–84, Cowan and Easson, *Religious Houses*, 76.
11. Ferrerius, *Historia*, 80
12. Kinloss *Recs*., 12; Ferrerius, *Historia*, 77.
13. Ibid., 71
14. A. Ross, 'Notes on the Religious Orders' in *Essays on the Scottish Reformation*, ed. D. McRoberts (Glasgow, 1962), 214.
15. Reg. Supp. (Vatican Archives), 1955, fos 92v–93v; *Kinloss Recs*., 11; cf. 49–50; Ferrerius, *Historia*, 46–53.
16. Ibid., 47–8.
17. Ibid., 40; Cowan and Easson, *Religious Houses*, 80.

18. *Beauly Chrs.*, 105 and n.
19. Ibid., 177–181; *LP Henry VIII*, 1^2, 1522.
20. Ferrerius, *Historia*, 47–8.
21. Ibid., 49; *Beauly Chrs.*, 236–7, 256, 268.
22. Cowan and Easson, *Religious Houses*, 101–2.
23. Ibid., 83–4.
24. Ibid., 118.
25. Ibid., 119.
26. Ibid., 131.
27. Ibid., 137.
28. Myln, *Vitae*, 30.
29. Cowan and Easson, *Religious Houses*, 227–8.
30. *Fraser Papers*, no. 229; *TA*, i, 266; *RSS*, iii, nos. 182, 195.
31. Cowan and Easson, *Religious Houses*, 223.
32. Ibid., 203–4
33. Ibid., 206–7.
34. Ibid., 210–11.
35. Ibid., 205–6..
36. Ibid., 207
37. D.E.R. Watt, *Fasti Ecclesiae Scoticanae Medii Aevi* (Scottish Record Society 1969), 36–7, 122–3.
38. Ibid., 242–3.
39. Ibid., 123, 243.
40. Ibid., 242–3, 287.
41. Ibid., 37
42. Ibid., 36–7.
43. Ibid., 37.
44. Myln, *Vitae*, 29–30.
45. Watt, *Fasti.*, 122–4.
46. Ibid., 125–6.
47. Ibid., 245–6.
48. Ibid., 73–4, 288.
49. Myln, *Vitae*, 60–1.
50. Ibid., 61.
51. Ibid., 66–7.
52. Ibid., 41–2, 59.
53. *Elgin Recs.*, i, 118.
54. Cowan and Easson, *Religious Houses*, 181.
55. Ibid., 191.
56. Ibid., 191.
57. Ibid., 178–9.
58. Ibid., 179.
59. Ibid., 175.
60. Myln, *Vitae*, 55.
61. Ian B. Cowan, *The Parishes of Medieval Scotland* (Scottish Record Society 1967), 216, 218.
62. Ibid., 11, 99.
63. Ibid., 46, 194–5.
64. Ibid., 4, 16, 34–5, 43, 47, 109, 165, 205.
65. Ibid., 11, 61–2.
66. Ibid., 217–8.
67. Ibid., 214, 223.
68. Ibid., 1, 89–90, 109, 173.
69. Cowan and Easson, *Religious Houses*, 191; Cowan, *Parishes*, 19–20, 53, 62, 74, 173.
70. Ibid., 217.
71. Ibid., 4, 217.
72. Ibid., 6, 16, 36, 39–40, 49–50, 70, 78, 102, 138, 142, 152, 170, 176, 190–1.
73. Ibid., 2, 10–11, 43, 46–7, 130, 173.
74. Ibid., 8, 18, 105, 140, 168, 193, 207.
75. Ibid., 7–8, 60–1, 75, 98, 102, 104, 125–6.
76. Ibid., 37, 95, 97–8, 103, 106.
77. Ibid., 222; Kilmore and Kilcolmkill have since been adjudged independent parsonages (see above).
78. Ibid., 214, 220.
79. Ibid., 86, 88, 97, 100–2, 106, 148.
80. Reg. Supp., 592, fo. 127.
81. Breadalbane Papers cited Cosmo Innes, *Sketches of Early Scotch History* (Edinburgh, 1861), 362–3.
82. Myln, *Vitae*, 42–4.
83. Ibid., 46; Dowden, *Bishops*, 82–86, 165–7, 226–8.
84. *Elgin Recs.*, i, 87.
85. *Inverness Recs.*, i, 7.
86. Prot. Bk of Sir John Crawford (SRO), fo. 41a.

THE CLÀRSACH

J. MACKENZIE

The clàrsach is by far Scotland's oldest musical instrument and we have stone carvings dating from c.800 depicting this small harp. It is the Highland version of the Celtic Harp, a triangular-frame harp similar to those played in Mesopotamia almost five thousand years ago.

The word 'clàrsach' comes from Gaelic, meaning a smooth, flat board, also wedge-shaped and hollowed-out. The early clàrsaich were, in fact, made from hollowed-out bog willow, strung with horse-hair, gut or wire. All Celtic harps are derived from the small, eight-stringed 'cruit'; the Breton 'talen' and the Cornish 'telain' being smaller than the Clàrsach, the Welsh 'telyn' larger and the Irish 'clairseach' almost identical — the distinguishing feature being the graceful harmonic curve of the Clàrsach (known as the Highland Hump.)

The Clàrsach was developed in Scotland by the Irish missionary monks who followed St. Columba and who had often been trained at the Papal Music School. For seven centuries Ireland was famed for her supremacy in harp music but, by the 12th century, Scotland seems to have taken the lead in the skill and technique of her harpers. The historian, Giraldus, speaking at Oxford University in 1187, said 'Scotland has not only attained to the excellence of Ireland but has in musical science and ability even far surpassed it.'

The golden era of Scottish harp music was from the 12th to the 17th centuries when professional harpers were employed at Court, by the Church and by most Clan Chiefs — both for entertainment and for encouragement in battle. There were also itinerant harpers who were welcomed as entertainers, chroniclers and news-bearers. Harps are notoriously difficult instruments to play and tune, so the Clàrsach was never a true folk instrument. It was played by professionals and gifted amateurs, like King James I who 'touched the harp like another Orpheus.' After a strenuous, seven-year training a harper could expect a house, land and a respected social position near the head of the Chief's retinue. Among Scotland's most celebrated harpers were Ruaridh Dall Morison (blind Rory), harper to the MacLeods at Dunvegan from 1681, and John MacLean, Laird of Coll who was a gifted player and composer.

Clàrsaich were beautifully carved, inlaid with gold and silver and often decorated with precious stones or crystal. If strung with gut they were held on the right shoulder and played with the finger-tips — if strung with silver and brass wire they were held on the left shoulder and played with long finger-nails. A harper who displeased would be silenced by having his nails cut short!

In the 16th century two things caused the rapid decline of the Clàrsach — the fanatical zeal of the Reformers and the arrival of the new keyboard instruments which were easier to play. Harps were burnt by the Reformers as 'instruments of Satan' and, although harp melodies were taken over by pipes and fiddles, the harmonies and playing techniques were lost.

Fortunately two ancient harps survived — the Queen Mary and the Lude harp — so that when, in 1891, Lord Archibald Campbell led a Clàrsach revival by ordering nine new instruments to be made, these old harps were available as models. The revival has continued steadily until now there are enough harpers in Scotland to support five Clàrsach competitions at the annual National Mòd and several clàrsach-makers.

The modern Clàrsach, made from a variety of hardwoods with spruce soundboard and brass modulation blades (invented in the 16th century), is the ideal accompaniment to Gaelic songs as well as being a beautiful solo instrument.

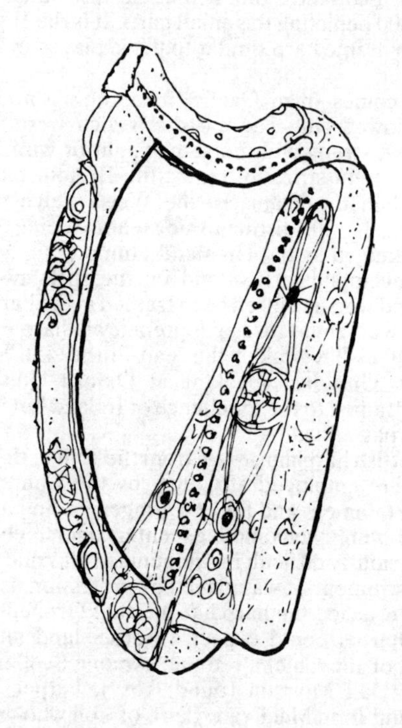

The "Queen Mary" Clàrsach

X'81

HIGHLAND FAMILY ORIGINS — PEDIGREE MAKING AND PEDIGREE FAKING

DAVID SELLAR

There is a well known story told in the *History of the MacDonàlds* attributed to Hugh MacDonald of a great feast given by the Lord of the Isles at his castle of Aros in Mull in the fifteenth century: 'One John Macdonald, tutor to Roderick his nephew, Laird of Mudort, and MacLean and some other gentlemen conversing, MacLean kept silent for a time; at which John Macdonald asked the reason of his silence? He replied, he had no occasion to speak. The tutor said, he knew very well MacLean's office was to set the Macdonalds in order to-morrow at dinner, and that he should see all the principal men there placed according to their rank and station; but if MacLean would give him a black hound he had, he would supply his place the next day. MacLean consented to this, and gave the hound. At dinner time next day, John stood at the end of Macdonald's table, and desired the Laird of Ardnamurchan to sit down. This family, indeed, might claim to be lords since King David Bruce's time; but the old Scots were careless of their prerogatives. Then he desired MacFinnon and MacQuire to sit [MacKinnon and MacQuarry], for MacQuire was an ancient Thane. Then desired Beatton, the principal physician, then MacMurrich, the poet, to take their seats. Now, saith he, I am the oldest and best of your surnames here present, and will sit down; as for these fellows who have raised up their heads of late, and are upstarts, whose pedigree we know not, nor even they themselves, let them sit as they please. MacLean, MacLeod of Harris, and MacNeill of Barra went out in a rage, and very much discontented . . . determined, as soon as an opportunity offered, to be fully revenged of John Macdonald for the affront, as they thought, he had given.'[1] The affront given was a serious one. Gaelic society in both Scotland and Ireland until the end of the old order was intensely aristocratic and lineage conscious. To suggest that a man 'knew not his ancestors' was one of the worst insults which could be offered. The quality of a family's pedigree — and very often that meant its length — reflected, supported and sometimes even explained its position in society. The keeping of the family pedigree was a function of a member of the learned professional classes, the *seanchaidh*, whose 'work was to hand down to posterity the valorous actions, conquests, battles, skirmishes, marriages and relations of the predecessors by repeating and singing the same at births, baptisms, marriages, feasts and funerals, so that no people since the Curse of the Almighty dissipated the Jews took such care to keep their Tribes, Cadets and branches, so well and so distinctly separate.'[2] In Gaelic society, a pedigree was a political statement, and not infrequently an exercise in political propaganda. Because antiquity was at a premium, forgery and manipulation, some of it very skilful, became a commonplace.[3]

The pedigree of the *Dal Cais*, the Munster family to which Brian Boru (d. 1014) belonged, and from which the later O'Briens descend, is a classic and well researched example of a manipulation of a genealogy to reflect enhanced political status and aspirations. The *Dal Cais* did not belong to the ruling kindred of Munster, the *Eoganachta*, who had ruled at Cashel since the fifth century. Indeed, they probably belonged to a group of subject peoples, the *Déisi*, who originally had no place in the elaborate scheme of genealogies of the Gael. However, as the *Dal Cais* rose in importance in the ninth and tenth centuries, eventually reaching the throne of Munster, their obscure pedigree was manipulated to reflect their new political standing and legitimise their position, and was grafted on to the stem from which the *Eoganachta* had sprung.[4]

In Scotland one pedigree which should also, true or false, be regarded as a political statement, is that of Macbeth. It has perhaps not always been realised how close the earliest surviving record of his pedigree is to Macbeth's own time. Macbeth died in 1057, his relative and eventual successor as Mormaor of Moray, Maolsnechtai, in 1085. Their pedigree appears already in the Irish manuscript *Rawlinson B 502*, compiled about 1130, the very year in which the last Mormaor of their kin, Angus, the nephew of Maolsnechtai, was killed at Stracathro in Angus, fighting the forces of David I.[5] Given these dates, it seems reasonable to assume that the genealogy of Macbeth preserved in *Rawlinson B 502*, and repeated in various later manuscripts, is the official pedigree which Macbeth himself put about and wished to be believed — a political document which can be safely backdated to his reign. According to later chroniclers such as Fordun, Macbeth's mother was the daughter of his predecessor but one as King of Scots, Malcolm mac Kenneth (d. 1034). Macbeth's pedigree, however, gives no hint of this, but traces his descent back patrilineally to two Dark Age kings of Dalriada of the tribe of Loarn, Ainfcellach (d. 719), and his father, Ferchar Fota (d. 697). Whether or not this claim has a sound genealogical basis — and the possibility should not be ruled out — the fact that the claim was made at all is evidence that the house of Loarn and its kings had not been forgotten in eleventh century Scotland, and that there was political advantage to be gained in claiming descent from them.

The most important single source for the origins of the later highland clans is the collection of pedigrees preserved in the manuscript now generally known, from its supposed date of composition, as *MS 1467*.[6] *MS 1467* gives the earliest and in many cases the only surviving account, within a purely Gaelic cultural context, of the descent of many families. Unfortunately, it is a difficult and suspect guide, rendered the more so by the form in which it has been twice edited. The manuscript itself bears every sign, where some measure of comparison with other sources is possible, of having been copied carelessly and in haste. In addition, nineteenth century scholars, finding parts of it difficult to read, stained the manuscript with chemical, which may have assisted them, but has certainly not helped later generations. *MS 1467* was edited by W.F. Skene in 1839 in *Collectanea de Rebus Albanicis*.[7] The transcriptions given there are unreliable and sometimes ludicrous; yet these are the transcriptions relied on by Skene in his *Highlanders of Scotland*,[8] and some of them are repeated still. To confuse matters further, the MS is referred to in *Collectanea* not as '*MS 1467*' but as '*MS 1450*'. This has led not a few subsequent clan historians to believe that two manuscripts exist, sometimes in conflict. *MS 1467* was edited again in part (and under that name) by Skene in his later and more reliable work *Celtic Scotland* in Appendix VIII to Volume III.[9] The transcriptions given there are more accurate than, and frequently differ greatly from, those in *Collectanea*. Unfortunately Skene, as was his wont, did not go out of his way to draw attention to his errors; he preferred to correct his earlier work *sub silentio*.[10] Unfortunately, too, the pedigrees in Appendix VIII are not a straightforward edition of *MS 1467*: they are a conflation made by Skene from various manuscript sources, including *MS 1467*, with little indication of the variants among the originals. For example, the MacDougall pedigree is noted 'From Book of Ballymote and ms. 1467. It also occurs in the Book of Lecan under the name of "Clan Somairli";' and the MacLean pedigree is noted

'From ms. 1647 [sic], MacFirbis and MacVurich.'[11] *MS 1467*, then, vital as it is, is a very uncertain guide, and a modern critical edition of it an urgent need.

It is easy, as Professor Barrow has reminded us, in criticising Skene, to undervalue his achievement. After one hundred years Skene's great pioneering work on *Celtic Scotland* has still not been superseded, and his chapter on 'The Clans and their Genealogies' remains the essential introduction to that subject, whatever one's reservations on matters of detail.[12] In that chapter, and in Appendix VIII, already referred to, on the 'Legendary Descent of the Highland Clans, according to Irish MSS.', Skene divides the traditional pedigrees of the clans into five distinct groups: 'I. CLANS supposed to be descended from FERGUS LEITH DERG, Son of Nemedh, who led the Nemedian colony to Ireland; II. CLANS supposed to be descended from COLLA UAIS, son of Eochaidh Doimlein, King of Ireland; III. CLANS supposed to be descended from the HY NEILL or race of Niall Naoi Giallach, King of Ireland, through Niall Glundubh, head of the northern Hy Neill and King of Ireland, slain 917; IV. CLANS supposed to be descended from CORC, son of Lughaidh, king of Munster, of the line of Heber; and V. CLANS supposed to be descended from the Kings of Dalriada in Scotland.' I have tried elsewhere to assess the genealogical traditions of some at least of the families in each of Skene's first three groups.[13] Skene's fifth group, for which *MS 1467* is the main authority, consists of pedigrees in which descent is claimed, however sketchily, from the Dalriadic house of Loarn; within this group ten families claim this descent through an ancestor, unknown to contemporary record, named Cormac son of Airbertach. See table A p.107.

The ten families are the '*Clan Ainnrias*' or Gillanders (identified by Skene, misleadingly, as will be argued, with the Rosses), the MacKenzies, the Mathesons, the MacDuffies or MacPhees, the MacNabs, and MacGregors, the MacQuarries, the MacKinnons, the MacMillans and the Clan Gille-Adamnain (identified by Skene with the MacLennans). The study of the pedigrees of these families provides an object lesson in the art of pedigree making and pedigree faking.[14] The descents claimed from Cormac are set out in Table A, as are the ascents from Cormac himself back to Feradach Finn of the tribe of Loarn, the father of the historical Ferchar Fota (d. 697). The table shows the number of generations claimed in each case between Cormac and Feradach Finn. Also shown are the number of generations between Cormac and the eponyms of the later families which claimed descent from him, and between Cormac and his latest descendants to be named in *MS 1467*.

It will be appreciated at a glance that the pedigrees show wide variations and are in every case too short. The number of generations given between Cormac and his supposed ancestor Feradach Finn are wildly inconsistent, as are the generations between Cormac and the latest descendant in each family. It has long been recognised that some at least of the pedigrees must be spurious. Skene, however, noticed that four of the pedigrees — MacQuarry, MacKinnon, MacMillan and Clan Gille-Adamnain — appeared to be different in kind from the others, and to be consistent with one another; the number of generations back to Cormac is fewer in these pedigrees and in each case the eponym of the later family appears as a son of Cormac. Skene suggested that these four pedigrees at least might be genuine as far back as Cormac, and that Cormac himself might be a historical character. Skene also noted as a pointer to the historicity of Cormac and his father a gloss on the MacMillan pedigree in MacFirbis' *Book of Genealogies*, 'This Airbertach inherited twelve *treba* among the Norse, viz. Greagruighe of the warriors called Mull and Tiree and Cruibhinis or Craobhinis.'[15]

Skene's surmise as to the historicity of Cormac and the genuine basis of these four pedigrees was unexpectedly vindicated recently by an inscription discovered by Dr Kenneth Steer and Dr John Bannerman in a survey for their work on *Late Medieval Monumental Sculpture in the West Highlands*.[16] One of the most striking stones in the whole West Highland sequence, and one of the earliest, is the gravestone of Gille-Brigde (or Bricius) MacKinnon at Iona. Steer and Bannerman date this stone to about 1350 AD, although if the stone were indeed commissioned by Gille-Brigde himself, as they argue, a date of up to fifty years earlier would appear more probable on genealogical grounds.[17] The stone bears two inscriptions. One, long known, states that the stone marks the burial place of Gille-Brigde and two of his sons. The other, which was previously undetected, reads + HIC IACET. FINGONE. MAC. CARMAIC. ET FIN/LAID MAC. FINGONE. ET EOGAN.' 'Here lies Finguine the son of Cormac and Finlay the son of Finguine and Eogan.'[18] The names given tally exactly with those given in *MS 1467* and other genealogical sources as the immediate ancestors of Gille-Brigde: his father Eogan, his grandfather Finlay, his great-grandfather Finguine (the MacKinnon eponym), and his great-great-grandfather, the mysterious Cormac. The stone, however, is a far better authority than *MS 1467*, both in terms of date and known provenance.

Dr Bannerman's note on the stone points out the implications of the discovery of this inscription for the study of West Highland genealogy. The historicity of Cormac is apparently confirmed, as also the belief that four kindreds took their names from his sons. 'That Finguine and his three brothers should give their names to four kindreds has many parallels in both Scotland and Ireland,' writes Bannerman, 'none more significant from our point of view than the emergence of the three distinct but related kindreds named after the immediate descendants of Somerled (d. 1164). Similar conditions of comparatively sudden territorial expansion, apparently so characteristic of the process of kindred-fragmentation, seem to have been experienced by Cormac's kindred at a time when his father Airbertach was their leader.' Bannerman then suggests that territorial expansion may have been made at the expense of the Norse, and postulates that Airbertach may have been a contemporary and ally of Somerled. 'It is difficult to see how the conditions of expansion implied in the fragmentation of the original kindred could have occurred, otherwise than by supporting the rising star of Somerled and his descendants.'[19] The hypothesis is attractive and plausibly argued. It is interesting to note in passing that the account of the feast at Aros, already mentioned, singles out two of the four kindreds in question as being of unassailable antiquity: 'Then he desired MacFinnon and MacQuire to sit, for MacQuire was an ancient Thane.'[20]

If Cormac, son of Airbertach, is to be regarded as a historical figure, what then of his own ancestry? The MacQuarry genealogy in *MS 1467* includes the names of Macbeth, Finlay and Ferchar Fota in Cormac's descent from Feradach Finn. There can be no doubt, as Bannerman points out, that the historical Macbeth, son of Finlay, who claimed descent, as already noted, from Ferchar Fota, is intended. It is true, also, that the number of generations given between Cormac and Macbeth is chronologically feasible. However, it is more difficult to follow Bannerman in believing this descent to be genuine and holding that Cormac and the four kindreds named from his sons did indeed descend from the historical Macbeth. If Macbeth had left direct descendants in the male line, it is almost inconceivable that no contemporary reference to them should survive, and that we should have to rely on a fifteenth century genealogical manuscript for knowledge of their existence. We know from Macbeth's pedigree, however, that descent from the tribe of Loarn was still prized in eleventh century Scotland. I would suggest that Cormac and his father Airbertach, who lived a century or so after Macbeth, were Gaelic aristocrats who belonged to or

Table A

Families descended from Cormac son of Airbertach, and through him from Feradach Finn of the tribe of Loarn, according to *MS 1467*.

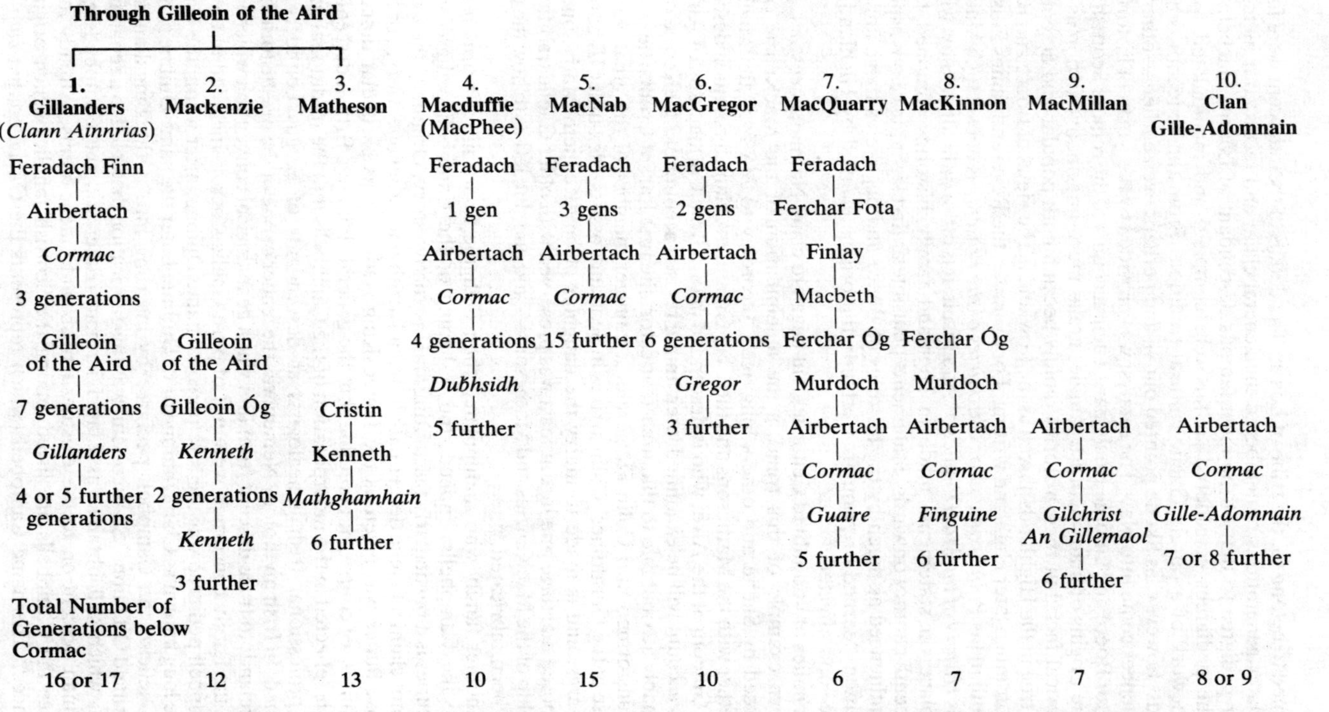

Through Gilleoin of the Aird: 1. **Gillanders** (*Clann Ainnrias*)	2. **Mackenzie**	3. **Matheson**	4. **Macduffie** (MacPhee)	5. **MacNab**	6. **MacGregor**	7. **MacQuarry**	8. **MacKinnon**	9. **MacMillan**	10. **Clan Gille-Adomnain**
Feradach Finn			Feradach	Feradach	Feradach	Feradach			
Airbertach			1 gen	3 gens	2 gens	Ferchar Fota			
Cormac			Airbertach	Airbertach	Airbertach	Finlay			
3 generations			*Cormac*	*Cormac*	*Cormac*	Macbeth			
Gilleoin of the Aird	Gilleoin of the Aird		4 generations	15 further	6 generations	Ferchar Óg	Ferchar Óg		
			Dubhsidh		*Gregor*	Murdoch	Murdoch		
7 generations	Gilleoin Óg	Cristin	5 further		3 further	Airbertach	Airbertach	Airbertach	Airbertach
Gillanders	*Kenneth*	Kenneth				*Cormac*	*Cormac*	*Cormac*	*Cormac*
4 or 5 further generations	2 generations	*Mathghamhain*				*Guaire*	*Finguine*	*Gilchrist An Gillemaol*	*Gille-Adomnain*
	Kenneth	6 further				5 further	6 further	6 further	7 or 8 further
	3 further								
Total Number of Generations below Cormac									
16 or 17	12	13	10	15	10	6	7	7	8 or 9

Note: The earliest name specifically given in each pedigree is indicated (eg. in the case of the MacKenzies, Gilleoin of the Aird). The eponymous ancestor of each family is italicised, as is Cormac. See also Table B for the descents from Gilleoin of the Aird.

claimed to belong to, the tribe of Loarn. The details of their descent were forgotten, but later generations remembered the general claim and recorded it by tacking on their pedigree to that of the most famous descendant of Loarn, Macbeth.

The pedigrees considered so far were compiled and manipulated within the framework of a purely Gaelic cultural tradition. From the sixteenth century onwards, however, as Skene pointed out — and perhaps even earlier — other cultural influences come into play. The catalyst was provided by the works of historians such Hector Boece and George Buchanan. Their accounts of the remote Scottish past and of the origins of many Scottish families are as much imaginative fiction as they are historical fact, but their histories rapidly became both popular and accepted. This was true in the Highlands as well as the Lowlands. The views of Boece and Buchanan colour much later Highland writing. For example, the Reverend James Fraser refers to both in his *Polichronicon* or *Chronicles of the Frasers*, as does 'Hugh MacDonald' in his *History of the MacDonalds*.[21] As a result, it is often difficult to know what value to place on statements made in Highland family histories compiled from the sixteenth century onwards. Statements plausible at first sight prove on inspection to be influenced as much by the histories of Boece and his like as by genuine Gaelic tradition, learned or popular. Certainly the origins claimed by Highland families were soon affected.

Families of undoubted Celtic descent began to claim Norman ancestors. The best known example of this trend is the manipulation of the MacKenzie pedigree, exposed by Skene and others long ago. According to *MS 1467* the MacKenzies, together with the Mathesons and the Clan Gillanders, claim a common descent from one Gilleoin of the Aird, who is descended in turn from Cormac, son of Airbertach. This account will be examined later. In the revised account of MacKenzie origins — probably attributable to that arch-fabricator, the first Earl of Cromartie — Gilleoin is transformed into Colin Fitzgerald, a younger member of the great Anglo-Irish house of the Geraldines. Colin arrives in Scotland, assists Alexander III at the battle of Largs, and is made to marry the daughter of one Kenneth Matheson. By this supposed marriage one link at least was preserved with older Gaelic tradition — the kinship of the MacKenzies and Mathesons — and one clue left as to how the pedigree had been fabricated.[22]

Another family who manipulated their pedigree to acquire a Norman ancestor were the Campbells. Indeed, the reshaping of the Campbell pedigree over the centuries is a particularly fascinating and instructive story. Originally the Campbells did not claim a Gaelic descent at all, but a British one, from one Mervie or Smervie, whose father was given as the famed King Arthur. This particular descent from Arthur is, of course, not credible, but the general claim to a British descent is clear, and is reflected in the incorporation of the Campbells into the traditional scheme of the professional Irish genealogists as descendants of Fergus Leithderg, son of Nemed. In Irish mythology Nemed was the leader of one of the pre-historic invasions of Ireland; to trace descent from him was a genealogical convention which indicated that the family concerned were not of pure Gaelic stock.[23] Included in the earliest Campbell pedigree was the rare personal name Duibne, after whom the Campbells were long known as Clan Dhuibne or O'Duibne. Later the name Duibne was utilised to Gaelicise the Campbell pedigree by inserting into it the Fingalian folk-hero Diarmaid O'Duibne. So successful was this fabrication that it led to a renaming of the clan, which still obtains, as Clan Diarmaid. Later still the Campbells grafted a Norman descent on to the existing British and Gaelic stems. Already in Hector Boece the Campbells are listed among the Scottish families which originated in France.[24] The name Campbell (which represents the Gaelic epithet *cam beul*, or 'twisted mouth', and was originally spelt *Cambel*) was equated with *De Campo Bello*, and kinship was claimed with the family of Beauchamp, or *De Bello Campo*. Happily, enough traces of the original claim to British ancestry survived in later composite seventeenth century accounts to yield the surprising information that Mervie, or Smervie, who appears as the son of Arthur in the earliest Campbell pedigrees, is none other than the Myrddin or Merlin of Welsh tradition, in his northern guise as the bard Laloecen, who went mad after the battle of Arderydd in 574, and met a three-fold death at Drummelzier on the Tweed.[25]

Not all the newly fabricated pedigrees claimed a Norman ancestor. Some looked to the early kings of Dalriada who figured in Boece's history. Instructive here is the case of the MacGregors. *MS 1467* deduces their descent from Cormac, son of Airbertach. Hector Boece, however, in his history had transformed the obscure king Girig, who reigned with Eocha, grandson of Kenneth MacAlpin, from 878–889, and whose origins are still unclear, into the victorious monarch Gregor or Gregory the Great, conqueror of Danes and Irish alike. Here was an ancestor worthy of Clan Gregor! By the end of the sixteenth century the MacGregors claimed descent from a brother or son of Kenneth MacAlpin, unknown to history, named Gregor, who is clearly modelled on the Gregory of Boece. Strangely, in Boece, Gregory is not descended from Alpin.

The MacGregor claim to descend from Alpin seems to stem in its developed form from a sixteenth century treatise referred to in *Douglas' Baronage* entitled *A Latin History of the Alpinian Family*. It is doubtful whether this work still exists, but it is possible to form an idea of its contents from *Douglas* and from later accounts of the MacGregor and MacKinnon families.[26] It was clearly a work of fiction beside which Boece and Buchanan seem positively veracious. A detailed, but entirely spurious pedigree was concocted linking the first MacGregor on historical record in the late fourteenth century step by step back to king Alpin. Each link in the chain was duly provided with a wife: for example, Dongallus, who died c. 900 (or so we are told) marries Spontana, sister of Duncan, king in Ireland, and his son Constantine marries Malvina, daughter of 'king Donald VI'! Other families, too, were drawn into the same scheme of descent through younger sons: the MacQuarries from Gorbredus, brother of Dongallus, the MacKinnons from Findanus, son of Dongallus, and the MacNabs, MacKays, Grants and Griersons at later points in the pedigree. The inclusion of MacKinnons, MacQuarries and MacNabs with the MacGregors presumably reflects the common kinship claimed for these families as descendants of Cormac in fifteenth century Gaelic tradition as exemplified in *MS 1467*. Such a tradition is further illustrated by the well-known bonds of friendship entered into by MacKinnons and MacNabs in 1601, and MacKinnons and MacGregors in 1671.[27] As already seen, the MacKinnons and the MacQuarries probably did indeed descend from Cormac, his sons Finguine and Guaire being their true eponyms; the MacGregors and the MacNabs almost certainly did not. There seems to be no reason to believe that MacKays, Grants, Griersons and MacGregors were originally related.

The later Skene was well aware of the spurious nature of these connections, but the earlier Skene had given them credence by his use of the appellation 'Siol Alpine' in *The Highlanders of Scotland*, and they have found their way into many modern accounts of family origins.[28] *The History of the Clan Gregor* by A.G.M. MacGregor, is only too typical in its lack of a critical approach. 'The renowned ancestor to whom we look as the Founder of our Race,' we read, 'was King Gregory, who reigned from 878 to 890. No documentary evidence can be adduced to prove descent from a source so remote; and allusion to it is not made here as to an established historical fact, but because the tradition has been constantly handed down that Gregory, of the race of

Scotland's early kings, was the ancestor of the Clan which bears his name.' A footnote observes that Skene, 'while deducing the race from another source, . . . remarks that the Clan Gregor, having recognised Gregory "as their eponymous ancestor, their descent from him is now implicitly believed in by all the MacGregors". . . After this record we may surely preserve our belief, which is thus itself established as a matter of history.'![29] The MacKinnons, too, have swallowed the story hook, line and sinker, and repeated it in many clan histories, rejecting their genuine and interesting descent from Cormac, son of Airbertach.[30]

How did this preposterous fiction first gain credence? The clue may lie in a genealogy and a praise-poem written by Duncan MacGregor to John MacGregor of Glenstrae early in the sixteenth century and recorded in the *Book of the Dean of Lismore*. Although later than *MS 1467*, these probably preserve the original and most authentic MacGregor tradition of ancestry, as both Skene and W.R. Kermack in *The Clan MacGregor* recognise.[31] The ancestry of the eponymous Gregor — who must have lived in the fourteenth century, and not the ninth — is taken back, not to Cormac, but to Gille-Faolain, 'the servant of St Fillan', the son of Aodh Urchaidh (Hugh of Orchy). As Kermack points out, the name Gille-Faolain links the MacGregors with the monastery of St Fillan in Glendochart, and suggests a kinship, or at least an association, with the MacNabs, whose name indicates descent from the Abbots of Glendochart. As already noted, MacGregors and McNabs are frequently bracketed together in genealogical tradition, genuine and spurious.

The praise poem gives the name of the father of Aodh Urchaidh as 'Conan' — *Konane* in the original: 'Conán of venturous troops was father of Aodh of Orchy, son of Ailpín the brilliant, stern of temper, high king of mighty blows puissant'. In the next stanza Alpin is called 'heir of Dugall'. The genealogy also names the grandfather of Aodh Urchaidh as Alpin, but renders the intermediate name *Kennane*, suggesting 'Cianan' rather than 'Conan'; *Kennane* is described as *ard ri* or high king of Alban.[32]

It seems likely that the original MacGregor pedigree claimed descent through Gille-Faolain and Aodh Urchaidh from Cianan (or Conan), son of an otherwise unknown Alpin, and descendant of an equally unknown Dugall. Later an attempt was made to latch on the descents from Cormac son of Airbertach and these names were omitted. The original tradition survived, however, and by the sixteenth century the Alpin of the pedigree was identified with the ninth century king of that name (who had no known ancestor named Dugall), and Cianan (or Conan) was identified with the famous Kenneth MacAlpin his son, King of Alban. Later still the conveniently named Gregory the Great was inserted into the pedigree — at the expense of Kenneth himself in some accounts — but descent from Alpin was still maintained.[33]

Three further families who deduce their descent from Cormac son of Airbertach in *MS 1467* are the MacKenzies, the Mathesons and the Clan Gillanders (Skene's 'Clan Andres or 'Clan Anrias'). The descent from Cormac, as already seen, is probably a fabrication. However, a common intermediate ancestor, 'Gilleoin', termed *na hAird* or 'of the Aird', is claimed by all three families, and in the case of the MacKenzies and the Mathesons, at least, this claim is probably correct. The pedigrees in *MS 1467* are set out in Table B. In the original they are not as clear as might be wished: some names are garbled or difficult to read, and it is not entirely clear where the Matheson line joins the MacKenzies. I have followed Skene in using the pedigrees in the so-called *Black Book of Clanranald* to help resolve difficulties: although late and untrustworthy, they appear to preserve intact segments of genuine material, which can be collated with the pedigrees in *MS 1467*. In the event I have arrived independently at the same conclusion as Skene[34] — although not without some hesitation, for my reconstruction varies from that suggested by Mr William Matheson in his *Traditions of the MacKenzies.*[35] Only two names in the pedigrees can be identified with certainty in the contemporary historical record: Kenneth, the son of the Matheson eponym (Coinneach mac Mathghamhna), in 1262 and 1263; and Paul Mactire in the mid-fourteenth century.[36]

Who was Gilleoin of the Aird? Skene identified the Aird as the Aird of Ross or Ardross in central Ross-shire, but there can be no doubt, as Matheson has shown, that the Aird in question is the territory south of the Beauly Firth and west of Inverness, still known in Gaelic as *Aird MhicShimi.*[37] Early in the thirteenth century the Aird formed the centre of the lordship of the Anglo-Norman incomer, John Bisset.[38]

Skene identified the Clan Gillanders with the Rosses, and suggested that all three families belonged to the same stock as the Celtic Earls of Ross of the O'Beolan line.[39] Although he has been widely followed in this, the suggestion seems to be quite without foundation. Matheson has argued persuasively that Clan Gillanders original tradition of descent was a Scandinavian one, and that they are to be associated with the MacLeods rather than the Mathesons and MacKenzies.[40] The Gillanders pedigree in *MS 1467* may be accurate as far back as the third Paul, but beyond that the likelihood is that is has been simply tacked on, perhaps inadvertently, to that of the true descendants of Gilleoin of the Aird. Quite apart from this, Skene's suggestion that the Clan Gillanders belonged to the stock of the Celtic Earls, and that the Rosses of Balnagown did not, appears to proceed on a misreading of Sir Robert Gordon, 'From this second sone of the Earle of Ross, the lairds of Balnagown ar descended; . . . wher yow may observe, that the laird of Balnagown his surname should not be Rosse, seing there was never any Earle of Rosse of that surname; bot the Earles of Rosse wer first of the surname of Builton [i.e. O'Beolan], then they were Leslies, and last of all that earldom fell by inheritance to the Lords of the Yles, who resigned the sam into King James the Third his hands, the yeir of God 1477: So I doe think that the lairds of Balnagowne, perceaveing the Earles of Ross decayed, and that earldom fallen into the Lord of the Yles his hands, they called themselves Rosses, therby to testifie ther descent from the Earles of Rosse. Besyds, all the Rosses in the province ar unto this day called in the Irish language, Clan-Leamdreis [i.e. Clan Gillanders]', which race, by ther owne tradition, is sprung from another stock.'[41] Read carefully, Sir Robert is saying that the Rosses of Balnagown descend from the O'Beolan earls, and that the Clan Gillanders do not, although they too took the surname of Ross. There seems no good reason to doubt this.[42]

It has also been suggested from time to time that the MacKenzies and the Mathesons may share a common ancestry with the MacLeans. Despite the arguments in favour of this proposition put forward by Matheson in the *Traditions of the MacKenzies*, I think the case has still to be made out.[43] In *MS 1467*, as already noted, the MacKenzies and the Mathesons are descended from Gilleoin of the Aird. The MacLeans, on the other hand, are descended from their eponym, Gilleoin Mor. It is clear that in *MS 1467* Gilleoin of the Aird and Gilleoin Mor, supposing they both existed, are different persons. They are given a different ancestry — although both are brought back ultimately to the tribe of Loarn — and Gilleoin Mor would appear to have lived at a slightly later date than Gilleoin of the Aird. Nevertheless, the two Gilleoins were assimilated in later Gaelic tradition, and a common ancestry claimed for MacKenzies and MacLeans, albeit rather hesitantly. Thus, in the *Black Book of Clanranald*, written about 1700, the MacLeans are traced back to Gilleoin Mor '7 dir cuid occ *gur* on Ghioll eoin mhóir so a tañig c*lann* choiñdigh' ('and some of them say that it is from this Gilleoin Mor that the MacKenzies have come'), and the Mathesons from Gilleoin of the Aird, 'ciogh be é soin do tigearñ cl*oinne* Ghiollaeoin' ('whatever may be his relationship to the chief of the MacLeans').[44] The identification is reflected also in the fabricated accounts of Norman descent: the MacKenzie forebear Colin Fitzgerald, who represents the Gilleoin of the Aird of the Gaelic pedigrees, was given a younger brother 'Galen' who is made the ancestor of the MacLeans![45] Matheson does not accept the identification of the two Gilleoins, but believes that the fact that the identification was made may reflect an underlying tradition of kinship. I think it more probable that the false identification came first, and tradition of kinship followed.

The clue to the true associations of Gilleoin of the Aird, and therefore of the MacKenzies and the Mathesons, may lie in contemporary references to the family of de Ard, or del Ard. Sir Cristin del Ard appears several times on record between 1296 and 1329. In 1296 he was taken prisoner by the English, along with the Earl of Ross, at the battle of Dunbar. In 1297, the beleaguered English governor of Urquhart Castle, Sir William Fitz Warin, petitioned Edward I for his release, saying that his father John of the Aird, described as 'a certain noble man,' had great influence in the area and was well disposed towards the English.[46] Later Cristin was granted one third of the barony of Deskford, and also the lands of Invercabok and Lichtoun, by Robert I, and the lands of Bught, near Inverness, by the Abbey of Arbroath.[47] This last grant was subject to the requirement that the lands must not be alienated without the Abbey's approval. In 1328 Cristin witnessed a charter to the Priory of Beauly, by William de Fenton, one of the Bisset co-heirs to the barony of the Aird.[48] Cristin's father John is probably to be identified with the *Johanne filio Cristini* and the *Johanne filio Christini MacGillo* who witnesses charters to Beauly by David de Innerlunan, c. 1275, and Andrew de Bosco and his wife Elizabeth Bisset, another Bisset co-heir, in 1278.[49] Two further Beauly charters granted in the early fourteenth century by Bisset co-heirs, Cecilia Bisset and Patrick de Graham, are witnessed respectively by *Haraldo filio Dofnaldi del Ard*, and by *Johanne filio Cristini del Ard* (presumably the son of Cristin) together with *Haraldo filio Dofnaldi*.[50] Clearly the Aird in the territorial designation *del Ard* is be be identified with the Aird of John Bisset's lordship, and it seems probable that there is some connection, as yet unascertained, between the family of del Ard and the Bisset co-heirs.

A prominent bearer of the surname del Ard later in the fourteenth century was Weland del Ard who married Matilda, daughter of Malise, Earl of Strathearn, Orkney and Caithness. Their son, Alexander del Ard, who was at one time a claimant to the Orkney earldom, appears to have died without issue.[51] His sister and heir, Margaret del Ard, married Alexander Chisholm. In 1368 Alexander was apparently co-portioner of the Bisset inheritance, along with William de Fenton and Hugh Fraser of Lovat. From Margaret and Alexander descend the family of Chisholm of Comar by a junior line; the elder line terminated in the fifteenth century with the heiress Catherine Chisholm who married Walter Haliburton.[52]

Little or nothing has been written about the patrilineal ancestry of Weland del Ard, but that he was a descendant, perhaps a grandson, of Cristin del Ard seems certain. The surname del Ard and the Bisset connection alone point strongly towards such a relationship. More conclusively, however, lands granted to Cristin appear later in the hands of Weland's descendants. Cristin had been granted the lands of Invercabok, they were resigned to Robert II by Weland's son, Alexander del Ard.[53] Cristin had been granted the lands of Bught on condition that they should not be alienated without approval; in 1464 the Abbey of Arbroath complained that John Haliburton of Kinrossie, the son of Walter Haliburton and Catherine Chisholm, and heir of Weland, had alienated these lands.[54] A skeleton reconstruction of the del Ard pedigree is set out in Table C (p.114).

The family of del Ard were clearly of first importance in the North in the fourteenth century. Although connected with the Bisset co-heirs, and perhaps sharing in their inheritance, they were apparently of Gaelic descent, their earliest recorded member being John *filius Christini MacGillo*. The name 'Gillo' in Cristin's patronymic is a garbled or abbreviated form of a Gaelic personal name beginning *Gille-*, 'servant of', and may indeed represent *Gilleoin*. Whether the bearer of this name was Cristin's father or some more remote ancestor is impossible to determine.[55]

When the MacKenzie and Matheson pedigrees in *MS 1467* are compared with what can be gleaned of the family of del Ard, the similarities are immediately apparent. The common ancestor of the MacKenzies and the Mathesons, Gilleoin, is given the designation 'of the Aird', from that same Aird which gave its name to the del Ard family. In addition, the name Cristin, a favoured name of the del Ard family, occurs in both MacKenzie and Matheson pedigrees.[56] These parallels are unlikely to be mere coincidence. I would suggest that the MacKenzies and the Mathesons may have been junior branches of the family of del Ard, whose senior line terminated with an heiress in the fourteenth century, and that their descent back to Gilleoin 'of the Aird' is in substance correct and preserves a memory of this connection.

Beyond that, no trustworthy information has survived. Skene's suggestion of a genealogical connection with the Celtic Earls of Ross by way of the Clan Gillanders cannot be sustained. The identification of Gilleoin with the ancestor of the MacLeans is late and unconvincing, while the descent claimed in *MS 1467* from Cormac son of Airbertach, like the similar descent claimed for the MacNabs and the MacGregors, is equally an exercise in the gentle art of pedigree faking.

Table B

Descents from Gilleoin of the Aird, according to *MS 1467* and the 'Black Book of Clanranald.'

Gilleoin of the Aird

- Gilleoin Óg
  - Kenneth[1]
  - Cristin
  - Angus
  - Kenneth
  - John
  - Kenneth
  - Murdoch
  - (MacKenzie)
- Cristin
  - Kenneth
    - Mathghamhain (Mathan)[2]
      - Kenneth fl. 1263
      - Murdoch
      - Duncan
      - Murdoch
      - Duncan
      - Murdoch
      - (Matheson)
    - Ewen
      - Cristin
      - Kenneth
      - Paul
      - Martin
      - Gillanders
      - Paul
      - Murdoch
      - Ewen
      - Tire
      - Paul (?'MacTire') fl. mid-14th century
      - (Gillanders)

1. This name appears as 'Agad' in *MS 1467*.
2. The Matheson pedigree in *MS 1467* is clear as far back as Mathan's father Kenneth. It ends with the name of Kenneth's father which, although indistinct, should probably be read as 'Cristin.' The Clanranald pedigree suggests that 'Cristin' is correct, and that he was the son of Gilleoin of the Aird.
3. See note 36.

Table C

The Del Ard Family

Cristin 'MacGillo'
- John 1275, 1278, 1297.
- Cristin del Ard fl. 1296–1329
- John 1315/25

Weland del Ard (perhaps grandson of Cristin) = Matilda of Strathearn, Orkney and Caithness

- Alexander del Ard d.s.p.
- Margaret del Ard = Alexander Chisholm
  - Thomas Chisholm
    - Alexander of Kinrossie
      - Catherine Chisholm = Walter Haliburton of Pitcur
      - John Haliburton of Kinrossie ↓
    - Weland (Wiland)
      - ↓ Chisholm of Comar

FOOTNOTES

1. '*History of the Macdonalds*', *Highland Papers I*, ed. J.R.N. Macphail (Scottish History Society, 1914), 45.
2. 'The Manuscript History of Craignish', *Miscellany IV*, ed. Herbert Campbell (Scottish History Society, 1926), 190.
3. This is true, not only of Gaelic pedigrees, but more generally in early Mediaeval Europe: the evidence is surveyed in David N. Dumville, 'Kingship, Genealogies and Regnal Lists', in *Early Medieval Kingship*, ed. P.H. Sawyer and I.N. Wood (University of Leeds, 1977).
4. F.J. Byrne, *Irish Kings and High Kings* (London, 1973), 11.
5. Rawl. B. 502, 162e 1 and 162e 21; see *Corpus Genealogiarum Hiberniae*, ed. M.A. O'Brien (Dublin, 1962), 329, 330; there is a facsimile edition by K. Meyer (Oxford, 1909).
6. National Library of Scotland, Adv. MS 72.1.1.; D. MacKinnon, *Catalogue of Gaelic Manuscripts in Scotland* (Edinburgh, 1912), 72, 106–8. See also J.W.M. Bannerman, Appendix II in K.A. Steer and J.W.M. Bannerman, *Late Mediaeval Monumental Sculpture in the West Highlands* (HMSO, 1977), 205.
7. *Collectanea de Rebus Albanicis* (Iona Club, 1839 and 1847), 357–62.
8. W.F. Skene, *The Highlanders of Scotland* (London, 1836), 2nd edn. with notes ed. Alexander Macbain (Stirling, 1902).
9. W.F. Skene, *Celtic Scotland*, 2nd edn. 3 vols (Edinburgh 1886–90).
10. As Macbain pointed out in 'Mr Skene *versus* Dr Skene', *Trans. Gaelic Society of Inverness* (T G S I), XXI (1896–7), 191.
11. *Celtic Scotland, III*, 470, 480.
12. *Celtic Scotland, III*, Chapter IX.
13. 'The Origins and Ancestry of Somerled', *Scottish Historical Review*, xlv (1966), 123–42; 'Family Origins in Cowal and Knapdale', *Scottish Studies*, 15 (1971), 21–37; 'The Earliest Campbells — Norman, Briton or Gael?', *Scottish Studies*, 17 (1973), 109–25.
14. The pedigree of the MacDuffies is not examined in this paper. According to 'A Fragment of an Irish MS. History of the Macdonalds of Antrim', *T G S I* XXXVII (1934–6), 277, 'it was more natural for a McDonald to be fostered by a McFee than by any other for the first that was called McDonald was fostered by Dushi MacMurphy . . .' Here we have an independent reference to the MacDuffie eponym which would place him in the mid-13th century.
15. *Celtic Scotland, III*, 345. Skene identifies *Craobhinis* with Iona. Bannerman discusses the gloss, which appears also on the MacKinnon pedigree, in *Monumental Sculpture*, 104–5: he points out that the exact meaning of *treba* (which Skene translates as 'tribes' or 'septs') has still to be elucidated.
16. Above, note 6.
17. A simple calculation based on the known dates of later members of the Mackinnon family, as disclosed in *inter alia, Monumental Sculpture*, leads to this conclusion.
18. *Monumental Sculpture*, 103.
19. *Monumental Sculpture*, 104–5.
20. Above, p. 103.
21. *Chronicles of the Frasers*, ed. Wm. Mackay (Scottish History Society, 1905), 14, 15, 17, 38, 50; 'History of the Macdonalds,' 10, 11, 30.
22. *Celtic Scotland, III*, 351–4. The exposure of this fiction has not prevented its repetition in many subsequent clan histories.
23. Thus the MacLeods, whose Scandinavian origin has never been doubted, were also brought down from Nemed. Skene's first group in *Celtic Scotland* are descendants of the Nemed, above p.105.
24. Book Twelve, chapter ten.
25. D. Sellar, 'The Earliest Campbells', above, note 13; W. Gillies, 'Some Aspects of Campbell History', *T G S I*, L, (1976–8), 256–95; A.O.H. Jarman, *The Legend of Merlin* (University of Wales, 1970).
26. Sir Robert Douglas of Glenbervie, *The Baronage of Scotland* (Edinburgh 1798), 'Macalpine', 'Macgregor', 'Macguarie'. Some MacGregor and MacKinnon accounts are noted below, notes 29 and 30.
27. *Celtic Scotland, III*, 363; W.R. Kermack, *The Clan MacGregor*, 2nd edn. (Edinburgh and London, 1963), 10.
28. *Highlanders*, 331.
29. A.G.M. MacGregor, *History of the Clan Gregor* (Edinburgh, 1898), I 5. It should be added, in fairness, that this is a useful and well documented history of the clan.
30. For example, D.D. MacKinnon, *Memoirs of Clan Fingon* (Tunbridge Wells, 1884); A.M. Downie and A.D. Mackinnon, *Genealogical Account of the Family of MacKinnon*, 2nd edn. (London, 1883); and C.R. MacKinnon, *The Clan MacKinnon* (Coupar Angus, 1958).
31. *Celtic Scotland, III*, 362–3; W.R. Kermack, *The Clan MacGregor*, 2nd edn. (Edinburgh and London, 1963), 5–10.
32. *Scottish Verse from the Book of the Dean of Lismore*, ed. W.J. Watson (Scottish Gaelic Texts Society, 1937) XXVII, 204–17; *The Dean of Lismore's Book*, ed. Thomas M'Lauchlan (Edinburgh, 1862), 101, 106*, 107*. I am most grateful to Mr Donald Meek of Edinburgh University for checking the original manuscript. Mr Meek comments that the variation between *Koñane/Conan* and *Kennane/Cianan* suggests that the poet or the scribe was uncertain as to the original form of the name and he confirms that there is no linguistic evidence to support the jump from *Cianan* or *Conan* to *Kenneth*: I owe the readings *Koñane* and *Kennane* to him.
33. Douglas, *Baronage*, 'Macgregor'.
34. *MS 1467*, 1r.d22, d25, d35; 'Black Book' in A. Cameron, *Reliquiae Celticae*, ed. A. MacBain and J. Kennedy (Inverness, 1894), 300, and original MS (National Museum of Antiquities M.C.R. 40), 176. I am most grateful to Dr John Bannerman and Mr Ronald Black of Edinburgh University for discussing these readings with me.
35. W. Matheson, 'Traditions of the Mackenzies, *TGSI*, XXXIX-XL (1942–50), 193–228.
36. Skene's *Highlanders*, 322, 331 and Macbain at 417; *Celtic Scotland, III*, 486; 'Traditions of the Mackenzies', 208;

W. Matheson, 'The Pape Riot and its Sequel in Lewis', *TGSI*, XLVIII (1972–74), 426. It is not clear whether 'Mactire' is patronymic or a by-name.
37. 'Traditions of the Mackenzies', 214–16.
38. A.A.M. Duncan, *Scotland — The Making of the Kingdom* (Edinburgh, 1975), 198; see also E.C. Batten, *The Charters of the Priory of Beauly* (Grampian Club, 1877).
39. *Highlanders*, 322–5 and Macbain at 417.
40. 'Traditions of the Mackenzies', 196; 'The Pape Riot', 424–7.
41. Sir Robert Gordon, *Genealogical History of the Earldom of Sutherland* (Edinburgh, 1813), 36.
42. See Macbain's comment in *Highlanders*, 417, and F.N. Reid, *The Earls of Ross* (Edinburgh, 1894).
43. 'Traditions of the Mackenzies', 217–24.
44. 'Black Book' and original MS, as above, note 34.
45. *Celtic Scotland, III*, 351–2; 'A Brief Genealogical Account of the Family of MacLean', *Macfarlane's Genealogical Collections, I*, ed. J.T. Clark (SHS, 1900), 119 is sceptical. For a recent survey of 'Maclean Family Manuscripts' see N. Maclean-Bristol in *Notes and Queries* of the Society of West Highland and Island Historical Research, X (Dec. 1979), XI (March 1980).
46. For Cristin's career see *Beauly Charters*, 84–6, and *The Scots Peerage* ed. J. Balfour Paul (Edinburgh, 1904–14), IV, 44–5. Both these accounts are vitiated by the suggestion that Cristin del Ard was also known as Cristin de Forbes, see below, note 55. See also W. Mackay *Urquhart and Glenmoriston* 2nd edn. (Inverness, 1914), 19–23.
47. *Reg. Mag. Sig.*, I, App. II, 387, 388, 502; *Arbroath Liber* (Bannatyne Club, 1848–56), I, 305–7.
48. *Beauly Charters*, 84.
49. *Beauly Charters*, 61, 64.
50. *Beauly Charters*, 74, 79.
51. G.E.C., *The Complete Peerage*, X, App. A, 31; *Inchaffray Charters* (SHS, 1908), lxx, lxxi; *Beauly Charters*, 89, 90, 98, 99; A. Mackenzie, *History of the Chisholms* (Inverness, 1891).
52. *Registrum Episcopatus Moraviensis* (Bannatyne Club, 1837), 369; Mackenzie, *History of the Chisholms*.
53. *Reg. Mag. Sig.*, I, 600. The teutonic name Weland may have come to the north with Weland of Stiklaw in the late 13th century; see Barbara E. Crawford 'Weland of Stiklaw: a Scottish royal servant at the Norwegian Court, *Historisk Tidskrift* 4 (1973), 329.
54. *Arbroath Liber*, II, 138–40.
55. It has often been conjectured, for example in Balfour Paul's *Scots Peerage*, IV, 44, that Cristin del Ard was also known as Cristin de Forbes and is the ancestor of the later family of Forbes. The identification stems from the misreading of a charter, now in the Scottish Record Office, Forbes muniments no. 390 Professor A.A.M. Duncan has kindly communicated to me by letter his reading of the name in question as *Cristino d[e]l [Ar]d* (as opposed to *de Forbes*). Professor Duncan's view confirms that of earlier record scholars.
56. See Table B.

Beauly Priory Church
West Front

THE CLAN SYSTEM — FACT OR FICTION?

R.W. MUNRO

The beginning of the distinction made between the Highlands and Lowlands can be fairly well pinned down to the time of the historian John of Fordun, and well-documented events following on it in the late 14th century such as the foray which ended bloodily somewhere in Stormont, and the affair on the North Inch of Perth. But it is not so easy to determine the date when people began talking about the 'clan system', and it is worth beginning with a reminder that there are those who do not believe such a thing ever existed.

I make no claim that the existence of *clans* was unique to the Highlands (or even to Scotland for that matter), and it would be absurd to do so. But as the theme of this conference is the Middle Ages in the Highlands, most if not all of my evidence will be taken from the north and west of Scotland. And if any one should ask whether the phrase 'clan system' has any or more validity, say, in the Border country, that might be a subject for another time — and another exponent.

When I went to the great dictionaries to see how long the words 'clan system' had been in literary use, it seemed to be for less than a century. There was a quotation from the *Athenaeum* in 1887 which states that the Duke of Argyll had attributed 'all the evils of the Highlands' to the clan system and to Celtic feudalism — a reference plainly to the 8th Duke's two solid volumes entitled *Scotland as it Was and as it Is*, where the phrase is repeated more than once.[1]

Long before that, too, the father of the dictionary method had written — after reviewing the former state of the clans before the legislation which followed 1745 — of 'the *system* of insular subordination,' a system which, he commented, led to a feeling of content, but which he also stigmatised in a graphic Johnsonian phrase as 'a muddy mixture of pride and ignorance'[2] — a phrase with which I am fortunately not dealing here. General David Stewart of Garth, too, in his *Sketches of the Highlanders* (1822), wrote at some length on 'the system of clanship', and so did W.F. Skene in his early *Highlanders of Scotland* (1836).[3]

Perhaps the habit of talking about the 'clan system' really came into its own at the outset of the present century. Frank Adam, in a little book called *What is My Tartan?* (1906) gave ten pages to a chapter on the 'Rise and Decadence of the Highland Clan System', and it formed an even larger part of the bulky volume which the late Lord Lyon (Sir Thomas Innes of Learney) built on Frank Adam's later *Clans, Septs and Regiments of the Scottish Highlands* (1908 &c.)[4] In her *Social and Economic Development of Scotland before 1603* (1930), Dr I.F. Grant (to whom I gladly acknowledge my indebtedness) devoted a substantial portion to the Highlands, and 50 pages or so to 'the development of the clan system' and its economic aspects.

And so, whether in quotation marks or without them, the phrase has come to stay. 'The popular conception of a clan today', it was stated 25 years ago,[5] 'is that it comprised a chief and his followers, who all bore his name, and were related to him by ties of blood, near or remote'. A book published this year[6] is even more forthright: 'The modern popular image of the clan is of a body of people related by blood, descended from a common ancestor, inhabiting a clan territory, ruled by a chief who is head of the kin, wearing a clan tartan and all having the same surname'.

This picture is perhaps the outcome of a 'muddy mixture' of 18th century reality and 20th century romanticism. As one form of corrective I think it is worth putting forward some of the evidence, rather than trying to offer a dissertation, an analysis, or even a series of generalisations on what a clan really was — and a warning is necessary that what happened in one clan did not necessarily happen in the same way or at all in the others. The period covered will be from after the Wars of Independence to the time of James VI — and if my Middle Ages seem rather more 'senile' than those of other contributors it would be well to think of the later — and more abundant — material mainly as throwing light on what had gone before; and a good many dates will be necessary if any hints of development in the 'system' — or non-system — are to be noted.

In seeking a framework to indicate the many-sided life-style of the clans in this period, one might consider them as military, social, even cultural units. But if we are to seek a *system* we have I think to concentrate rather on *structure*. For this purpose I have chosen four main headings, which will inevitably be arbitrary and overlapping — Chiefship, Kinship, Territory, and Alliances. Unfortunately there is no authentic 'source-book of Scottish clanship' in existence, although there is more material for one than is generally realised. What I plan to do is to look at some examples of contemporary *written* sources, most of which can be found in print, taking them from as many different names and districts as possible. I am well aware that this will be only part of the story, and it has the disadvantage that in a region with a language of its own, where many agreements (for example) were by word of mouth rather than the pen, and oral traditions were late in being written down, direct evidence in written form is uneven and sometimes entirely lacking. Possible sources include documents, letters, statements incorporated in the public records, and (where they are dateable) family chronicles and poems. If clans can be seen to speak for themselves, and hold up a mirror to their own life, so much the better, but it would I think be a mistake to ignore outside (even if sometimes hostile) sources, so long as we keep their origin and possible purpose in mind.

In what follows, I shall quote as a peg on which to hang my extracts one or two of the current dubious, contradictory, or even plainly absurd notions, and then go on to cite some of what I consider to be relevant written evidence.

Chiefship

An obvious starting-point in any discussion of clanship is the position of the chief, but whether he is to be regarded simply as the patriarchal head (or root) of the family tree or the apex of the feudal pyramid is not so easy to decide. This is where we come to the contradictions. A whole book has been writen — Audrey Cunningham's *Loyal Clans* (1932) — on the basis of the total incompatibility of 'patriarchy' and 'feudalism', and a belief that this was the cause of most of the troubles of the Highlands. On the other hand, an authority on Celtic law[7] has said: 'I think the Celtic system was one which very readily adapted itself to the feudal system because it was a system which in many of its aspects was of a feudal nature'. Innes of Learney[8] declared roundly that 'the clan system *was* feudal', and wrote of the 'colourful and happy regime of feudo-clanship' and the 'mischievous doctrine' of a conflict between the two 'designed by English politicians for the destruction of the Scottish social system'. More calmly, it has been said[9] that 'although the theories of landholding that underlay the two systems were so different, in practice Gaelic clanship and feudalism were very much alike'.

My first quotation is on a chief's duty to his followers. In a Lamont indenture (in

Scots, 1433) between Robert Lawmanson of Inveryne in Cowal and Finlay Ewenson of Ardlamont, the former promises Finlay and his heirs to be 'leal and good as his lord and chief of kin ought to be to their near cousin and man', while Finlay was to become man to Robert and his heirs against all mortals, the King and Steward of Scotland only excepted.[10] What a chief passed on to his heir is shown by a document of 1488: John Ross of Balnagown, seeing in his old age the turbulence and destruction suffered by himself and his kin and friends (he had seen the earldom of Ross forfeited, and his own son with 17 local landed gentlemen and many common soldiers killed), and looking for a quiet life and for the good rule of his heirs and kin, 'freely and irrevocably' made over to his grandson and heir apparent David (and to Sir Gilbert Keith of Inverugie, probably his son-in-law) 'the haill rule of his person, his house and place of Balnagown, kin, men and friends', with the writs and manrents (bonds of personal service) of all his lordship of Balnagown with its pertinents, with all his goods.[11]

A powerful chief could keep law and order, and look after his tenants. Bishop Leslie, writing of William Mackintosh of Dunachton (c. 1540/50), said he defended his clan against the invasions of their enemies, their neighbours, and caused minister justice to them in the manner of the country, so that none should be suffered to make spoil or go in sorning, as they call it, or as vagabonds in the country.[12] In 1570 Colin Campbell of Glenorchy promised some of his followers and their men who had been robbed by the MacGregors that they would be protected, supplied and maintained at his expense — 'Spare neither my gear nor your own,' he told them, 'for God leaving us our healths we will get gear enough'.[13]

For the bardic view of the chief's role, I must reluctantly rely on translation. MacGregor verse tells of a chief whose bravery and skill ever brings victory, the 'falcon of the three glens, bountiful friend of church and bards, of handsome form'; the figure used on the death of a McNeill chief is that 'the topmost nut of the bunch is plucked'; and a later Maclean poem sees the chief as taking the helm to steer his ship.[14]

Although many feuds and controversies can be traced to the Highlander's flexible attitude to succession, unlike the more rigid feudal system, the difference did not always lead to serious divisions. This can be illustrated by chronicle reference to a peaceable 'abdication', and oral tradition of a chief 'deposed'. On Lachlan Mackintosh's death in 1407 at a 'good age' he was succeeded by his only son Farquhar, whom the Kinrara MS calls 'tall of stature, but slender of body, of a brown complexion and sullen disposition'. Farquhar lived for another ten years, and had three sons and several daughters; but 'his friends of the name of Clanchattan were altogether dissatisfied with his way of managing affairs. Therefore he willingly renounced his inheritance and birthright in favour of his uncle Malcolm and betook himself to a private life, reserving only two estates which he and his posterity enjoyed for 200 years or thereby.' Malcolm is said to have 'entered the estate with the general approbation and applause of his friends' in 1409, and had a chief command at Harlaw.[15] Nearly a century later, a chief of the MacDonalds of Keppoch, Iain Aluinn (John the handsome or splendid), who had handed over a noted cattle lifter when ordered to do so by Mackintosh as Steward of Lochaber (by whom he was hanged), was deposed by the 'elders' or 'head men' of the clan as unfit to lead them, and was replaced by an uncle while his own descendants were long recognised as 'the race of the elder brother'.[16]

In several clans from 1400 onwards when the chief's son was under age at his father's death he was not passed over but a 'tutor' appointed (as will be mentioned later). During the minority of a Mackintosh chief, his cousin Donald was served 'nearest agnate' at Inverness on 2 April 1561 by a jury said to be composed of burgesses of the town and members of the clan.[17] Sir Humphrey Colquhoun of Luss was killed in a feud with MacFarlanes and MacGregors leaving daughters only, and his brother Alexander had himself retoured as tutor in 1592 — the first and only Highlander to appear in the tutorship retours before 1600, although later a Mackinnon chief (remembered in clan tradition as 'John the Dumby') was found '*incompos mentis, fatuus et naturaliter ideota*' and a brother was authorised to act for him.[18]

In the Highlands, even more than the Borders, 'the land was hilly and the King remote',[19] and many chiefs enjoyed their own hereditary powers of jurisdiction. The barons of Argyll and the Isles who figure in the St Andrews Parliament of 1309 were no doubt the more important tenants of a man who regarded himself as a sovereign prince, but only the King could create 'free baronies', with power over life and limb, &c., and their own feudal courts.[20] By the earliest Campbell charter of Lochow (1315), King Robert granted to Colin son of Sir Neil Campbell and his heirs in the conventional feudal formula the whole land of Lochawe and Ardscotnish to be held in one free barony, in wood and plain, meadows and pastures, muirs and marshes, waters and mills, patronage of churches, huntings and hawkings, and all other liberties, privileges and just pertinents, as well not named as named.[21] In the earldom of Strathearn the barony of Tullibardine was granted to Sir David Murray in 1444, and in Atholl the barony of Strowan went to Robert Duncanson in 1451 as reward for his diligence in hunting down Robert Graham and other regicides.[22]

A good many records of baron courts have survived from the 17th century (Glenorchy begins in 1621, Menzies in 1622), but they are extremely fragmentary for earlier centuries. The general keeping of law and order were their main purpose, but they could also regulate the baron's right to services and labour, and other social and economic powers such as that of 'thirling' his tenants to his mill, brewery and smithy.[23] Through them he could exercise a paternal authority over the people of the barony, and they were therefore a convenient means by which to administer the affairs of a clan.[24] Sir Thomas Innes's picture of them as centres of popular local self-government may be overdrawn (and too much based on Cromwellian regulations) though it might have more validity for post-1600 baron courts.[25]

In the absence of earlier records, we must have recourse to chronicles. Fraser of Lovat, strangely enough, was a lord of parliament long before his various lands and baronies were united and erected into one free and entire barony of Lovat.[26] The Wardlaw MS mentions that the Tutor of Lovat held courts and sat as his nephew's bailie in 1559 in Stratherrick and Abertarff; and we hear of his successor doing the same 30 years later in the same areas and also in Glenelg, Glenstrathfarrar and other Lovat properties.[27] It was a Lovat maxim that the first duty of leading men of the clan to their chief was to watch and guard his territory, 'to live upon the marches, skirts and extremities thereof, to keep off thieves and sorners'; these courts gave every gentleman his own particular post, and also tacks and leases were settled, preference being given to 'long time tenants' who were confirmed in their holdings.[28]

Kinship

Dr Johnson wrote of Highland chiefs that their power was strengthened by the kindness of consanguinity, and the reverence of patriarchal authority, adding: — 'The Laird was the father of the clan, and his tenants commonly bore his name'.[29] The phrase 'kin-based society' or 'kingroup' is now gaining ground in serious historical writing,[30] yet Gordon Donaldson has said that, from documentary evidence after the 16th century, neither kinship nor a common surname was an important element in a clan beyond the inner circle of the chief's family and the cadet branches of his house[31] — and how wide a circle that usually was should be remembered. On the question of whether kinship was a more important element in Highland society than in Lowland, which Professor Donaldson also raises, I would draw attention to Professor Smout's comment that 'Highland society was based on kinship modified by feudalism, Lowland society on feudalism tempered by kinship.'[32]

It was Donald Gregory's belief that the bulk of the population of the Highlands came of families which had been on the same lands from remote times, probably 'under a succession of different, and quite unrelated, chiefs'.[33] He was surely right, but even where the chief family was not itself of native stock, the spread of junior branches and intermarriages within a compact community would soon strengthen the ties of kinship and common descent.

It was of course the duty of all able bodied clansmen to serve and follow their chief in all his affairs and business, in peace and in war. This was obvious either from kinship custom or feudal law, and would not normally fall to be recorded. Documents which state this among near kin are unusual (the only one I know of is in my own clan, which was not I think a particularly unruly one),[34] and later I shall be referring to bonds by those not of the chief's kindred.

What can be said of so-called 'clan councils'? In the time of the MacDonald lords, we are told, 'there was great peace and wealth in the Isles through the ministration of justice'.[35] At Finlaggan in Islay, according to Donald Monro's account written only about 50 years after the fall of the Lordship, fourteen councillors 'sat down in the Council Isle, and decernit, decreitit and gave suits furth upon all debaitable matters according to the laws of Ranald McSomharkle callit in his time King of the Occident Isles, and albeit their Lord were at his hunting or at ony other games, yet they sate every ane at their council ministering justice'.[35] In a bard's appeal for justice to the Lord of the Isles, we find him asking to have replenished his stock of horses, cattle and gear taken from him by 'thiggers' or beggars.[36]

There is a telling instance among the Rosses of how the cadets tried to restrain their chief in 1577. Fearing that the folly of Alexander Ross of Balnagown would bring about the ruin of his house and loss of his lands, and replacement by a stranger would be to his and their 'utter wreck', fourteen principal gentry of the clan signed a petition exhorting him to serve God, obey the Regent (Morton), and seek remedy for the troubles which threatened; they asked Balnagown to confer with them, lest he 'perish his house, kin and friends, and *tyne the riggs that his fathers wan*'.[37] By way of contrast, there was an ailing Grant chief who sought reassurance from his clan. In 1584 the Laird of Grant, having lost his son and heir and found himself 'mishandled' by his neighbours, sent his surviving son and grandson with a letter asking 'his most special friends and kinsmen' if they had any fault to find with him so that it might be amended. The day his message was received the gentlemen of the clan met in the Kirk of Cromdale and sent a reassuring answer, which unanimously declared that they found no fault with their 'chief and master' and would support him against all invaders not only with their goods but with their lives.[38]

If a minor succeeded to chiefship the leading men of the clan would have a hand in tutor-making. When Hugh Lord Lovat died in 1577, leaving a son only seven years old, there was some doubt whether the office should go to the child's uncle, or to a great-uncle who had been tutor to the young chief's father 20 years earlier. A great meeting of the leading Frasers, not less than 300 with their followers, assembled near the 'Stockford of Ross' on the River Beauly to settle matters; both men argued their own cases, 'a great heat of unbecoming altercations ensued', and it was feared that the two factions might 'fall in blood'; but the older man withdrew, and Fraser of

Strichen became Tutor of Lovat 'by the unanimous consent of all present'.[39] In a Craignish charter of 1447, Duncan Campbell of Lochawe laid it down that the office of Steward of the lands of Craignish should, if the heir were a minor, be ruled by a tutor with the advice of the heir's kindred (*parentelae*) namely 'the Clandowill Craiginche'.[40]

On the downfall of the Lordship of the Isles in 1493, there is an example of how a clan were associated with the fate of their chief. The bard (almost certainly a MacVurich) lamented the fall of the House of the Isles in terms which suggest that the whole clan felt the blow to their pride and position — 'tyrants suffered a strong blast from the wise, strong tribe, though now they are unhonoured (or reproached) — there is no joy without Clan Donald'.[41] This great clan, of course, continued in its branches, for younger sons had been established on lands held of the head of the house as feudal superior; the connecting link was kinship with 'the royal blude of Clan Donald lineally descendit', and when the Lord of the Isles granted lands it was to individuals, whose heirs continued in possession throughout the Middle Ages.[42] The Macleans, however, fell into four or five main branches, independent of each other. A bitter dispute divided Duart and Lochbuie under James IV; Coll had charters to show that he held of the Crown direct, but Duart insisted that he should follow and serve him, and had Coll's lands and tenants despoiled.[43] In contrast to this may be cited two 'bonds of association' made by some of the leading Murrays, in which the leading place was taken by Sir John (later 1st Earl of Tullibardine), whose friendship with James VI may suggest (along with the terms of the bonds themselves) that the wording at least was not a native growth in Strathearn.[44]

On the contentious matter of surnames, I would first quote from a Highland writer who should have known better: 'Whether blood relations or not,' wrote the late W.C. Mackenzie,[45] 'all the clansmen bore a common name, by birthright or by adoption, and that name was derived from a common ancestor whose historicity was not always unassailable. The name was the binding link between the members of the clan.' — 'This is nonsense', countered Sir Thomas Innes;[46] 'until the mid 18th century the ordinary clansman had no "name" in that sense — it was the characteristic of the so-called "Lowland" names'.

First I would point out that 'the clan and surname of Macnelis' (McNeills of Gigha) is a perfectly good legal phrase which appears in the Privy Seal Register in 1531.[47] Yet just across the narrow sound which separates Gigha from Kintyre, in the earliest surviving Highland rental (1505) drawn up for Crown lands and printed in the *Exchequer Rolls*, among a bewildering multiplicity of surnames the name of the leading family (MacDonald) does not appear at all.[48] The reason is of course that until surnames were in common use and stabilised a man — or a woman — was known in a closely-knit community by his or her parentage and immediate relationship, perhaps with some personal characteristic tacked on. Chiefs as well as clansmen were called by these patronyms, so in 1472 we find the head of the Camerons as Allan MacDonald Dubh (the latinised form '*Alan Donaldi Duff, capitaneo de Clan Camroun*' being the first mention of this clan in the national records).[49] Even after surnames were introduced some remained unfixed, such as the surname associated with the Clan Donnachaidh. In 1451 'Robert Duncansoun de Strowane' was the style used in his barony charter, and the surname Robertson is believed to have been first taken by his son William; but up to 1600 at least the name 'Clandonachie' still persisted and was itself recorded as a surname.[50]

It is not really wise to be too dogmatic about dating the assumption of surnames in the Highlands, as it varied for different purposes. There is a much-quoted example in the Clan Grant — how in 1537 a parish clerk of Duthil on Speyside was to be elected and the proceedings preserved a list of parishioners none of them bearing the name Grant; while only 32 years later (1569) over 40 tenants in Strathspey are mentioned in a Crown remission — and all of them are called Grant.[51] The reasons have been much discussed, and explanations offered why surnames should be so suddenly adopted (in one generation); but surely the difference must be due to the first document having been drawn up locally and for local use, and the second being a public record framed in Edinburgh.[52] In other words, a man known among his friends and neighbours by his antecedents took (or was given) a surname when he found himself among strangers.

Before leaving the subject of surnames I would suggest that to think they meant nothing in the Highlands would be a great mistake. If they were not significant, why should the name of the 'Place of Weem' be changed to Castle Menzies, as testified by a Crown charter of 1510?[53] After succeeding to his mother's Gordon inheritance and being created Earl of Huntly, why did Sir Alexander Seton change his name to Gordon?[54] And I would urge those who do not know the exact words of the Act of 1603 proscribing and abolishing the name MacGregor to look it up in the Privy Council Register, and read there how it was done because 'the bare and simple name of McGregoure maid that haill clan to presume of their power, force and strength, and did encourage them, without reverence of the law or fear of punishment, to go forward in their iniquities'.[55]

Territories

What is claimed to be the first 'properly authenticated map, showing the position of the Highland clans' appeared in 1872 (previous maps had attempted no actual demarcation of territories). It used public and private records and histories to 'divide the land with the strictest impartiality', and drew the comment from a contemporary reviewer that 'every Highland gentleman should at once provide himself with a copy of this graceful volume, so well-fitted to add adornment to a drawing-room'.[56] In our own day the scholarly and artistic map entitled *Scotland of Old* is the work of Sir Iain Moncreiffe of that Ilk and Don Pottinger, where the lands for each name are coloured to indicate general spheres of influence, based on evidence from the period between 1560–1603, and an attempt is made to strike a balance between tenants, owners and feudal superiors.[57]

It needs to be emphasised that such 'clan maps' indicate areas where different names were mainly found — certainly not areas owned or peopled exclusively by the clans in question, but rather where a particular chief's authority was acknowledged, and so changing from time to time and merging at many points. For example, in Lochaber chiefs of Mackintosh received charters of lands occupied mainly by Camerons and MacDonalds who preferred to obey Lochiel and Keppoch, and Mackintosh's own country lay partly within Huntly's lordship of Badenoch.

Even more basic and controversial is the question — were there in fact any 'clan territories' or 'tribal lands'?[58] In the report of the Napier Commission (1884) this passage occurs: 'The opinion was often expressed before us that the small tenantry of the Highlands have an inherited inalienable title to security of tenure in their possessions while rent and service are duly rendered — an impression indigenous to the country though it has never been sanctioned by legal recognition'.[59] The Commissioners believed that this claim to permanent occupation was due to the clan system, but it is likely to have arisen from much earlier times than those we are discussing here.[60] It is a belief still firmly clung to, even when its precise historical origins are unknown, and has found expression in such unequivocal statements as this from a book by a former editor of Burke's *Peerage* and *Landed Gentry*: 'Under the clan system the land belonged to the whole clan, and it cannot be disposed of by the chief.'[61]

The Lord of the Isles bestowed lands on individuals and not on groups — as clearly in the 1408 Gaelic charter of lands in Islay as in the Latin ones couched in more formal feudal terms. There are many examples of chiefs granting lands to their followers. Dr I.F. Grant states definitely 'the chief owned lands as an individual and he allocated them as he chose',[62] and Dr John Cameron (the author of *Celtic Law*) accepted that 'the land had been the personal property of their ancestors (the Highland chiefs) long before the establishment of the feudal system'.[63]

Perhaps one should look for the origin of the notion in the status of 'kindly tenants', which the *Dictionary of the Older Scottish Tongue* defines as 'one who occupies land on favourable terms under a special lease which gives a sort of hereditary right'. Most of the examples usually cited are from the south and south-west of Scotland, and we find 'native and kindly tenants (of certain named lands) past memory of man' in the Borders.[64] Kindly tenants paid small rents but rendered certain services, including so many days' work at harvest.[65] The words 'kindly' and 'kindness' are obviously related to 'kin', and in fact the word 'kindness' was repeatedly used in documents to describe the kin relationship.[66]

Specific Highland evidence is harder to come by and indefinite: no general principle appears as to the length of time required to acquire this right, and the definiteness of such claims varied in different districts.[67] In Kintyre, where some 'native tenants' were believed to have a hereditary or prescriptive right to their holdings, it is said to have been acquired after a tenant had been in possession for three generations or 81 years.[68] In Islay the long dispute between MacDonalds and Macleans over the Rinns (1563–86) depended on the question as to whom these lands 'were most kindlie'.[69] From the Kinrara MS comes the example of a Macpherson tenant in Farr (Strathnairn) who 'falling short of his means and having no right to the roum (place) but a naked possession, sells his *dúchus* in kindness thereof' to a Mackintosh for 500 merks plus a lifetime payment of £20 Scots.[70] In a 1569 dispute between Donald Gormeson in Skye and the Mackenzies the Privy Council ordered that Donald was to be allowed to use his lands &c. in all times coming 'as his heritage and kindly rowmes conform to his rights and titles thereof'.[71] And when the MacGregors were being dispossessed during the 16th century they again and again vainly claimed a right of 'kindness', and Mary Queen of Scots asked the Menzies laird of Weem to allow those in Rannoch to occupy the lands they held before on reasonable terms.[72]

No talk on 'clan territories' would be complete without some reference to the practice of raiding. Hear Sir Walter Scott: 'The Gaels, great traditional historians, never forgot that the Lowlands had, at some remote period, been the property of their Celtic forefathers, which in their eyes gave them the right "to spoil the spoiler as we may, / and from the robber rend his prey".'[73] Clan feuds and raids are supposed to have been endemic in the 'system', but it is only fair to point out that the land available for cultivation was not evenly divided, and basic economic pressures were at the bottom of a large number of the troubles between Highland clans — the cause of feuds between MacDonalds and Macleans, Mackintoshes and Camerons, MacLeods and Mackenzies, and many more.[74] Nor should the clans in particular always be blamed, for it was Professor Hume Brown who pointed out that feuds in a state of feudal society were 'as natural as trade competition at the present day'.[75] When a whole clan or leading family became landless, the only source of livelihood was by raiding — such 'broken men' as had no chief or superior to obey were a constant source of concern to the King, Parliament and Privy Council.[76]

Distance was no object, and the mobility of the clans by the light of 'MacFarlane's lantern' was remarkable. Raids into Moray lands 'where all men takes their prey' were freely admitted by Cameron of Lochiel in the mid-17th century,[77] but there is plenty earlier evidence. A raid by the Munros as far as Strathardle in Atholl, when Mackintosh demanded 'road collop' on their way north and pursued them as far as Clachnaharry, has been dated three or even four centuries earlier.[78] For spoil on the grand scale the MacDonald raids on the Grant lands in Glenmoriston in 1513 and 1544 provide an example in detail.[79] Some of the tales of burning clans in churches can be discounted as propaganda, but the best (if not the only) case authenticated by public records was at Monzievaird near Crieff in 1490, when according to Pitscottie six score Murrays were burned by their Drummond foes who had Campbell of Dunstaffnage with them, and the chief offenders were tried and executed (although doubtless not all concerned bore those two surnames).[80]

Outsiders might rage at the 'wild wikked hielandmen', but it was James Fraser, minister of Kirkhill near Inverness, who described the men of Lewis as 'the stoutest and prettiest men, but a wicked bloody crew whom neither law nor reason could guide or model'.[81] (Here please remember that we are talking about the Middle Ages!)

Alliances

In introducing my final section, something may be said about the much-abused term 'sept'. The opening words of a 50-page chapter on 'The Septs of the Highland Clans' in *The Clans, Septs and Regiments of the Scottish Highlands* reads: 'This chapter must be regarded as a rather wonderful effort of imagination', and later in the book some 600 or 700 surnames are alphabetically apportioned to various clans.[82] One finds Miller for example as a sept of MacFarlane, and Smith of Clan Chattan, Black is distributed between the Lamonts, MacGregors and Macleans, but White or Whyte is given to MacGregor and Lamont while Bain (= fair) is allotted to the Mackays alone. These are, of course, simply occupational or descriptive names which might be adopted in any part of the country, and be used by the followers of many different chiefs. No wonder, when in 1956 the claiming of septs by different clan societies was causing some bitterness, the Lord Lyon (Innes of Learney himself) should write: 'I have for some time kept in view that "sept-snatching" seems to have superseded cattle-lifting in clan circles as an acquisitive operation.'[83] I cannot recollect the word 'sept' being used in connection with the Highlands earlier than the 17th century,[84] so I do not feel obliged to discuss it in speaking about the clans in the Middle Ages — except to remark that the 'subaltern tribes', of which Lord President Forbes of Culloden was later to write, existed even if the word did not, and to introduce some mention of alliances among the clans.

The word 'clan' has been used of relatively small family groups like the Mackays and the Brehons in Islay,[85] and also for huge confederacies like the Clan Donald and Clan Chattan, formed by alliances between great houses sprung from a common ancestor or between people of different origins, names and places of abode.

An example from Mackenzie history may be as appropriate as any to illustrate the extension of a family group by influential marriages. Colin Mackenzie of Kintail in 1572 married a daughter of Grant of Freuchie and had six chiefs as brothers-in-law, five of his six sisters having married (1) Glengarry and then Chisholm, (2) Mackintosh, (3) Ross of Balnagown, (4) Urquhart of Cromarty, (5) Munro of Foulis; three of Colin's daughters are stated to have been the wives of Fraser of Lovat, Maclean of Duart, and MacDonald of Sleat.[86] Some Mackenzie historian might find a study of the causes and effects of these marriages worth while — although perhaps they may not all have helped to make friends and influence people.

Something has already been said, both in this and other papers, of the Lordship of the Isles, and here I need only recall how their council included not only those of the 'royal blude' of Clan Donald, but also Macleans of Duart and of Lochbuie, MacLeods of Harris and of Lewis, four smaller lairds (Mackinnon, MacNeils of Gigha and of Barra, and perhaps MacQuarrie), with in addition four representatives of other landholding families of less degree.[87] Clan Chattan consisted of a number of clans and families, in which Mackintosh had the chief place. Membership remained remarkably constant from the earliest written evidence in the 16th century and probably long before that until the mid-18th century. The clan fell into two categories — those claiming to be of Mackintosh blood or descended from a common ancestor through an heiress; and a number of small clans which voluntarily placed themselves within the confederacy — for mutual protection was the keynote of their association.[88] One little-known document tells of a Clan Donald/Chattan alliance, whose operation (if indeed it was effective) has not I think been examined. Lachlan Mackintosh of Dunachton 'for himself and his haill kin of Clanchattan', and Donald Gorm of Sleat for himself and Angus of Kintyre 'with the remanent of their haill kin of Clan Donald', bound themselves to 'assist concur fortify maintain and defend' each other against everyone the King and Earl of Huntly excepted (and Mackintosh would use his good offices in any quarrel which Donald Gorm might have with the Lairds of Kintail or Harris).[89]

Bonds of manrent or personal service were usually contracts between a powerful magnate and men of less influence, the one promising protection in return for 'leal and true services' to be rendered.[90] The earliest such bond so far discovered is a Highland one (1442) in which Thomas Fraser of Lovat became 'lele man and trew' to Alexander Earl of Ross and Lord of the Isles under penalty of 1500 merks Scots, and it was presented for transumpt in Inverness by the Earl himself.[91] In 1501 Huntly was ordered as the King's Lieutenant in the North to buttress his authority by receiving such bonds from 'earls, lords, barons and head kynnismen' to compel their obedience and many are recorded;[92] but the Breadalbane papers include many bonds made with Campbell of Glenorchy by humble groups of followers — and while some may have been coerced into accepting his protection, one says specifically that he had been 'chosen of their own free motive to be their chief and protector', and promised at death to leave him 'ane cawylpe of kenkyngie . . . as is usit in the countries about'.[93] Such bonds, says the historian who has made a special study of them,[94] 'provide a wealth of evidence which exists precisely because they were expected to act as kinsmen, evidence which exists precisely because they were not kinsmen and therefore made written bonds setting out the obligations which were implicit and unwritten for the kin'.

It is a valid question whether the clan as a whole, or the principals only, had any say in these arrangements. When William Mackintosh, Dunachton's son and heir, gave Huntly his bond in 1543 for himself and his kin of Clanchattan, 21 of the leading men of that composite clan — Macqueens, Macphersons, Macphails and others — promised 'under pane of cursing' to renounce their dependence on their young chief if he broke his bond.[95] His son Lachlan 25 years later stipulated that 'albeit ony of my kyn and friends of Clanchattan or others my adherents allies or parttakers will not assist nor concur with me in service of the noble lords his heirs and successors that shall not be hurtful nor prejudicial to me and my heirs' &c.[96] When Argyll in 1559 proposed to transfer the 'manrent, homage and service' of 'the haill kyn and surname of the Clanlaurane and their posteritie' to his cousin of Glenorchy, he stipulated 'providing the said Colin obtain their consent thereunto'. The MacLarens had suffered two massacres within 17 years, and within four months 27 of them from about a dozen different households gave Glenorchy their bond of manrent, which was renewed a generation later, Glenorchy taking them under his protection on the narrative that the whole surname and clan had 'elected' (that is, chosen) him to be their chief.[97] In Lochiel's bond to Huntly in 1547 he promised 'by the advice of his kinsmen and friends *and clan*' to become the earl's man in return for Huntly's support and 'ane reasonable fee', and Huntly as Chancellor and Queen's Lieutenant in the North agreed to apply for a 19-year remission for past crimes committed by the Camerons — a remission issued less than a month later under the Privy Seal with a fascinating list of 200 clansmen named in the Register by their individual patronyms (although the clerk unfortunately stopped short of adding details of their domiciles).[98]

But now we are getting into the realms of Government policy, and it is time to call a halt. — I may have left you no clearer about whether or not there was anything in the Middle Ages which can properly be called a CLAN SYSTEM: but perhaps, however unsystematic my treatment of the subject, I have shown that, besides a good deal of fiction, there are plenty solid *facts* on which to base one's views of the clans of the Scottish Highlands in the Middle Ages.

FOOTNOTES

1. *Op. cit.* (2 vols 1887), i 29, 200ff, 224–5, 230, 232; *New. Eng. Dict.* ed. Murray, s.v. 'clan'.
2. *Johnson's Journey to the Western Islands & Boswell's Journal*, ed. Chapman (1934), 81.
3. Stewart, *Sketches*, i 2lff; Skene, *Highlanders*, ed. Macbain, 101.
4. Cited in this paper is the 8th edition, *The Clans, Septs and Regiments of the Scottish Highlands*, by Frank Adam, rev. by Sir Thomas Innes of Learney (1970). It is instructive to compare the definition of a clan put forward in the 18th cent. by Lord President Duncan Forbes of Culloden (*Culloden Papers*, 298), and accepted by Frank Adam (*What is my Tartan*, 27), with the legal and armorial definition given by the Lord Lyon at p 152 of the above edition (hereafter cited as Adam/Innes).
5. A. McKerral 'Clans and Clan Names', in *Common Errors in Scottish History* (1956), ed. G. Donaldson, 22–24.
6. D. Stevenson, *Alasdair MacColla and the Highland Problem in the 17th Century* (1980), 10.
7. Dr John Cameron, evidence in Maclean of Ardgour v. Maclean, 1938, quoted Adam/Innes 609.
8. Adam/Innes 62, 45, 102.
9. W.R. Kermack, *The Scottish Highlands: A Short History* (1957), 64.
10. *Inventory of the Lamont Papers* (SRS, 1914), no 24; H. McKechnie, *Lamont Clan* (1934), 63.
11. SRO Balnagown Papers, GD 297/164.
12. John Leslie, *Historie of Scotland*, trans. Dalrymple (STS 1895) ii 211n.
13. *Black Book of Taymouth* (Bannatyne Club, 1855), 387.
14. D. Thomson, *Introduction to Gaelic Poetry* (1974), 55, 132; *Dean of Lismore's Book*, ed. T. M'Lauchlan (1862), 128; W.J. Watson, *Bardachd Ghaidhlig* (1915), 205, and *Scottish Verse from the Book of the Dean of Lismore* (1937), 27, 60–61; A.A.W. Ramsay, *Arrow of Glenlyon* (1930), 23. From later poetry it is known that the bards could ridicule and condemn as well as praise the chiefs.
15. L. Mackintosh of Kinrara, 'Epitome of the Origin and Increase of the Mackintoshes', in W. Macfarlane, *Genealogical Collections* (SHS, 1900), i, 182–3, and MS English version fo. 13–14. Kinrara names the writers of three earlier accounts on which he drew.
16. D Gregory, *History of the Western Highlands and Isles* (1836), 108–9; N.H. MacDonald, *Clan Ranald of Lochaber* (1971), 6–7 (a Gaelic source might offer a clearer idea of the words 'elders' or 'head men'). For a warning against a too rigid system of 'numbering' chiefs see Socy. of West Highland and Island Historical Research, *Notes & Queries* (1977), iv 13–15.
17. A.M. Mackintosh, *Mackintoshes and Clan Chattan* (1903), 365; this record is not in *Mackintosh Muniments* (1903), ed. H. Paton. I have not seen the original.
18. *Inquisitionum ad Capellam Dom. Reg. Retornatarum* (1811), ed. T. Thomson, *Inq. de Tutela* nos. 1241–2 (17 Jan 1592), *& Abbrev. Inq.* no. 554 (4 Oct 1636); W. Fraser, *Chiefs of Colquhoun* (1869) i 165; D. Mackinnon, *Chiefs and Chiefship of Clan Mackinnon* (1931), 19.
19. T.C. Smout, *History of the Scottish People 1560–1830* (1969), 47.
20. W.C. Dickinson, *Carnwath Court Book* (SHS 1937), xxi, xvi–ii.
21. *Reg. Mag. Sig.* (1306–1424), app. i, no 106; facsimile in *Diplomata Scotiae* (1739), ed. J. Anderson, no. xlvii.
22. *Reg. Mag. Sig.*, 26 Jan 1443/4, 15 Aug 1451.
23. W.C. Dickinson, *Scotland from the Earliest Times to 1603* (1961), 91–2.
24. Dickinson, *Carnwath*, xxi; Kermack, *Scottish Highlands*, 65.
25. Adam/Innes 71–73, 124 & refs. cited. See, for example Grant court books SRO ref. GD 248/37/1; Ross of Balnagown in W. Macgill, *Old Ross-shire and Scotland* (1911), ii 34ff; Taymouth in *Black Book*, 352ff; Menzies in SRO ref. GD 50/136 & 137, and *Inverness Gaelic Socy. Trans.* (1963), xxxix/xl 103ff.

26. *Reg. Mag. Sig.*, 26 March 1539; *Scots Peerage*, ed. Sir J.B. Paul, v 523.
27. J. Fraser, *Chronicles of the Frasers* (SHS 1905), 146, 184–5.
28. Ibid., xxxii, 184–5, 250.
29. *Johnson's Journey*, 77.
30. *Scottish Society in the Fifteenth Century* (1977), ed. J.M. Brown, 235, 57–60; K.A. Steer & J.W.M. Bannerman, *Late Medieval Monumental Sculpture in the West Highlands* (RCAHMS, 1977), 88.
31. Donaldson, *Scotland — James V to James VII* (1965), 13.
32. Smout, *Scottish People*, 47.
33. Quoted by McKerral in *Common Errors*, 23.
34. *Calendar of Writs of Munro of Foulis* (SRS, 1940), no 160; *The Munro Tree, 1734*, ed. R.W. Munro (1978), M/71.
35. Donald Monro, *Description of the Western Isles, 1549* (1961 edn), 57. For a reference to the council of the Earl of Ross sitting in Dingwall see above page 31.
36. Watson, *Dean of Lismore*, 66–81; Thomson, *Gaelic Poetry*, 48–50.
37. Balnagown Castle MSS; Macgill, *Old Ross-shire*, ii 2–3, no 1006.
38. W. Fraser, *Chiefs of Grant* (1883), iii 157–8.
39. *Chron. Frasers*, 177.
40. Argyll writs, 20 Feb. 1446/7 in *SHS Miscellany* (1926), iv 293.
41. Thomson, *Gaelic Poetry*, 50; M'Lauchlan, *Dean of Lismore's Book.*, 95–7.
42. D. Monro, *Western Isles*, 102; I.F. Grant, *Social and Economic Development of Scotland to 1603* (1930), 186, 187.
43. *Reg. Mag. Sig.*, 1 Dec 1528; *Reg. Privy Council*, i 311–13, 322–3; Gregory, *Western Highlands and Isles*, 111, 190.
44. *Chronicles of the Atholl and Tullibardine Families* (1908), ed. John Duke of Atholl, i 19–21.
45. W.C. Mackenzie *The Highlands and Isles* (1949 edn), 820.
46. Adam/Innes, 104.
47. *Reg. Sec. Sig.*, 4 Jan 1530/1.
48. *Exch. Rolls*, xii 698–709; McKerral (*Common Errors*, 22, *Kintyre in the Seventeenth Century* 9, 12), pointed out that the MacDonells of Dunivaig were then under forfeiture, Largie family used name Macrannaldbane, and Sanda not yet founded.
49. *Reg. Mag. Sig.*, conf. 24 Oct 1495; J. Stewart of Ardvorlich, *The Camerons* (1974), 262–3.
50. *Reg. Mag. Sig.*, 15 Aug 1451; J.A. Robertson, *Earldom of Atholl* (1860), 40–42.
51. *Chiefs of Grant*, i 99 (1537 list not printed), iii 137–8.
52. Dr Ian Grant (Scottish Record Office), per G. Donaldson, *Scottish Genealogist* (1974), xxi 64.
53. *Reg. Mag. Sig.*, 2 Oct 1510.
54. J.M. Brown in *Scottish Society in the Fifteenth Century*, 60; *Scots Peerage*, iv 523.
55. *Reg. Privy Council*, vi 558n, xiv 400–2.
56. T.B. Johnston & J.A. Robertson, *Historical Geography of the Clans of Scotland* (2nd edn. 1873), 5, 7, 40.
57. Published by John Bartholomew & Sons Ltd., Edinburgh; *Scotland's Magazine*, Aug 1960.
58. Grant, *Social and Economic Development*, 487; Steer & Bannerman, *Monumental Sculpture*, 148.
59. *Report of HM Commissioners in Inquiry into the Condition of the Crofters and Cottars in the Highlands and Islands of Scotland* (1884), i 4, 8, 110.
60. I.F. Grant, *Highland Folk Ways* (1961), 7, 8n.
61. J. Hunter, *Making of the Crofting Community* (1976), 157, 265; L.G. Pine, *Highland Clans* (1972), 26, 33.
62. *Social and Economic Development*, 487, 523; and see Donaldson, *Scotland — James V to James VII*, 13.
63. 'Law in the Glens', *The Highlands and the Highlanders* (Glasgow Empire Exhibition, 1938), 68–9.
64. *Reg. Privy Council*, i 432; *DOST* iii 429.
65. Donaldson, *Scotland — James V to VII*, 239.
66. J.M. Brown in *Scottish Society*, 58.
67. Grant, *Folk Ways*, 7.
68. McKerral, *Kintyre*, 134.
69. *Reg. Privy Council*, per *Book of Islay*, ed. G.G. Smith, 70–72; MacFarlane's *Geog. Coll.*, ii 190.
70. MacFarlane's *Gen. Coll.*, i 353, and Kinrara English MS, 111–12; A.M. Mackintosh, *Ms. and Clan Chattan*, 376; A.G. Macpherson, 'An Old Highland Genealogy and the Evolution of a Scottish Clan' *Scottish Studies* (1966), x 33. *SND* iii 171 defines 'duchas' or 'duchus' as (1) paternal seat, dwelling of a person's ancestors, and (2) possession of land by whatever right . . . if one's ancestors have lived in the same place.
71. *Reg. Privy Council*, ii 10.
72. Grant, *Folk Ways*, 8; Cunningham, *Loyal Clans*, 131–2; Ramsay, *Arrow of Glenlyon*, 38–9; *Reg. Privy Council*, i, 289–90; Hist. MSS Comm., vi, 692.
73. Scott, *Lady of the Lake* (1810), canto v, 7 and note.
74. Grant, *Social and Economic Development*, 525.
75. *Scottish Historical Review* (1906), iii 161.
76. Grant, 525; *APS* iii 461ff, iv 71ff; *RPC* esp. iv xlii-ix, 781ff.
77. *Chiefs of Grant*, ii 76 (18 Oct 1645).
78. A.M. Mackintosh, *Ms. and Clan Chattan*, 80; A. Mackenzie, *History of the Munros* (1898), 23–7; *Munro Tree*, L/ln; C.I. Fraser of Reelig, *Clan Munro* (1954), 19; W. Matheson, 'Traditions of the Mackenzies', *Inverness Gaelic Soc. Trans*, (1963), xxxix/xl 204–5.
79. *Reg. Mag. Sig.*, 4 May 1548; W. Mackay, *Urquhart and Glenmoriston* (1914), 471–8.
80. R. Lindsay of Pitscottie, *Historie and Chronicles of Scotland* (STS 1899), i 237; *Treasurer Accts.*, i 170; *Exch. Rolls*, xii pp l–lii; *Reg. Sec. Sig.*, i 613; *Acts of Council 1478–95*, 167–8; G. Donaldson, *Scotland — The Shaping of a Nation* (1974), 236.

81. *Chron. Frasers*, 41. The MacLeods of Lewis of course suffered considerable provocation from the 'Fife Adventurers' (*ibid*. 239–40), who were supported by the king and privy council.
82. Adam/Innes, 295, 554ff.
83. Report in *North Star* (Dingwall), 29 Dec 1956.
84. For 1618 example see Sir T. Innes, *Tartans of the Clans and Families of Scotland* (1964 edn.), 9n; for MacDonalds of Glencoe as 'sept' or 'sect' see *Papers illustrative of the Political Condition of the Highlands of Scotland* (Maitland Club, 1845), 62, 65, and *Culloden Papers* (1815), ed. H.R. Duff. 19.
85. *Book of Islay*, 364.
86. D. Warrand, *Some Mackenzie Pedigrees* (1965), 10–13; *Scots Peerage*, vii 500–3.
87. D. Monro, *Western Isles*, 102–3; A Matheson in *SHR* (1963) xlii 50n.
88. J. Dunlop, *Clan Mackintosh* (1960), 15–18, 21.
89. SRO Register of Deeds, recorded 24 March 1817; *Collectanea de Rebus Albanicis* (Iona Club, 1839), 97–9.
90. J.M. Brown, *Scottish Society*, 56–58.
91. *Ibid*. 56n, and 'Bonds of Manrent in Scotland before 1603' (unpub. Glasgow Ph.D. thesis, 1974), ii 496; *Munro Writs*, no. 18.
92. *Reg. Sec. Sig*. i 722; *Spalding Miscellany* (1849), iv 179ff. For Taymouth bonds see *Black Book*, 175ff.
93. *Black Book of Taymouth*, 185–6. For *calp* and *ceann cinnidh* see A.A.M. Duncan, *Scotland — The Making of the Kingdom* (1975), 108, and Adam/Innes 488, 610.
94. J.M. Brown, *Scottish Society*, 58. On lack of class consciousness in Scotland see G. Donaldson, *Scotland — James V to VII*, 14–15.
95. *Spalding Misc.*, iv 260.
96. *Ibid*. 225.
97. *Black Book*, 201–3, 257; but see M. MacLaren of MacLaren, *The MacLarens* (1960), 57.
98. *Spalding Misc.*, iv 217–19; *Reg. Sec. Sig.*, iii 2204; J. Stewart, *Camerons*, 33.

Earliest known Coat of Arms of Inverness from a Painted Panel, dating from Charles Ist's reign, in Town House.

THE CRUSADES AND THE SCOTTISH *GAIDHEALTACHD* IN FACT AND LEGEND

ALAN MACQUARRIE

Did the Scottish *Gaidhealtachd* play any part in the great European Crusades, or indeed in the Crusading movement in general? At first sight it might appear unlikely, and certainly historians in the past have not looked at the question very seriously. Perhaps vague later traditions, in which the Highlands so abound, might be regarded as a more fruitful source of material than ascertainable fact. In many cases, after all, that which cannot be proved is just as interesting as what is known to have happened.

The area we are considering has thrown up many traditions about the Crusades. We shall turn our attention first to those which relate to the Crusades only in a vague or general way, and which cannot be connected with specific incidents. The most famous such tradition concerns the *bratach shithe* or fairy banner of Dunvegan. 'The legend of its origin is that a MacLeod who had gone on a Crusade to the Holy Land when returning home in the garb of a pilgrim was benighted on the borders of Palestine in a wild and dangerous mountain pass, where by chance he met a hermit who gave him food and shelter. The hermit told him that an evil spirit guarded the pass and never failed to destroy the true believer; but by the aid of a piece of the true cross and certain other directions given by the hermit, this MacLeod vanquished and slew the "she-devil" . . . around whose loins this banner had been tied; and in reward for conveying certain secrets which she wished some earthly friends to know, she revealed to her conqueror the future destinies of his clan, in whose family this knowledge was supposed to be deposited until its final extinction, and desired that her girdle be converted into this banner, which was to be attached to her spear, which became the staff which is now lost.'[1] It would be wasted labour to try to recover the facts behind this supposed crusader's relic. The same is probably true of another tradition relating to a mysterious object in the possession of the Macphersons of Cluny. In 1883 James Mitchell was shown round the hall of Cluny Castle by the chief: 'In the hall are various relics of the olden time . . . There is . . . a very curious belt of thick red morocco leather, with clasps and devices in silver of a religious and oriental character. This had been in the family since the time of the Crusades, one of the Cluny race having gone to Palestine to fight against the Turks. The country people believe there is a charm in the belt, particularly for the safe delivery of women in childbirth.'[2] There are similarities between both these curious objects: neither of them has an origin which can be definitely ascertained, both are believed to have magical or supernatural properties, and both have been traditionally associated with the Crusades — mysterious happenings in far-off lands, participation in which would convey prestige on any status-conscious family.

There are plenty of examples of talismans and charm-stones which have subsequently been connected with the Crusades. The best-known example is the 'Lee Penny,' which was used for magical purposes long before Sir Walter Scott wrote a romance around it.[3] The Stewarts of Ardvorlich (on the south shore of Loch Earn) possess the *clach dearg* of Ardvorlich, and were accordingly reckoned the chiefs of the Stewarts of Balquhidder; it had properties to cure sick cattle when they drank water in which it had been dipped. The family tradition is that it was brought back from a crusade.[4] In 1890 the National Museum of Antiquities received 'a charm-stone used in Argyll, a polished slice of silicious fossil wood, set in silver, and said to have been brought from the Holy Land.'[5] Sir Colin Campbell of Glenorchy (who died in 1480) had an amulet which he 'woir when he fought in battell at the Rhodes agaynst the Turks,' and which was still at Taymouth Castle long after his time. The austere modern editor of the *Black Book of Taymouth* comments only that it 'would seem to have been used for more homely purposes afterwards.'[6] Further south, on the bank of the Kirtle Water, there is a stone built into Bonshaw Tower known as the Crusader Stone: 'The tradition of the Irvings is that an Irving on the First Crusade brought a stone back from the walls of the Old Temple at Jerusalem, had it blessed by the pope at Rome, and fixed it where it now rests in the tower at Bonshaw.'[7] A more sober modern judgment is that the stone is of local origin, that the carving on it is of the same sixteenth-century date as the rest of the tower, and that 'of course it has nothing whatever to do with the Crusades.'[8] But we may perhaps regard this contemptuous dismissal as being a little unfair to a family who were only trying to add a little lustre to their pedigree. Others had done it before. John Barbour had written a genealogy of the Stewarts, in an attempt to show that their origins were rather more grand than was in fact the case, in the course of which he sent Alan son of Walter Stewart off to the siege of Antioch with Godfrey de Bouillon. Walter Bower pointed out that Antioch fell to the Christians in 1098, while Alan son of Walter died more than a hundred years later.[9] It is worth noting, however, that a Breton ancestor of the Stewarts, Alan son of Flaald, *had* been on the First Crusade[10] — perhaps showing how legends can be derived from facts. Clearly numbering a crusader among one's ancestors was something which conveyed prestige, and this was no less true of Celtic Scotland than of any other part of the country.

Unlike the case of this Stewart ancestor, we cannot now hope to recover the truth behind all these hazy traditions, or to ascertain which ones are more respectable than others. But there is also a surprising amount of genuine historical fact worth examining as well, and it could be suggested that, in the light of factual evidence, all these later traditions are not to be dismissed out of hand as nonsense, but some of them at least may have a basis in truth.

It is often thought that the call of Clermont in 1095 came at a time when Scotland, and particularly the Highlands and Islands, were so remote from the central gravitational forces of Christendom that Pope Urban's appeal for the rescue of the Holy Land cannot have penetrated so far. A.O. Anderson was aware that several contemporary writers mention *Scotti* in connection with the First Crusade, but he thought that these were probably Irish.[11]. The Irish historian Michael Dolley, on the other hand, has written:

> On 15 July 1099, to shouts of "God wills it," a random and ragged but reasonably representative array of the chivalry of Western Europe stormed Jerusalem . . . We should not be surprised that there were no Irishmen among these knights . . . Where Europe was concerned Ireland was a land apart, and Irish society was something quite unique.[12]

The last point is of equal validity for Celtic Scotland, whose social structure was very similar to that of Ireland, but the statement as a whole is impossible to accept. There are a number of references to Scots and Irish taking part in the First Crusade in contemporary chronicles which cannot be explained away. The problem is to determine how the message of Clermont reached Scotland, and then to determine what part the Scots themselves played in the crusade.

Contact between Celtic Scotland and the papacy was certainly sporadic in the late eleventh century. When Gregory VII sought to stop certain irregular practices in Man and the Isles, he wrote to Lanfranc Archbishop of Canterbury asking him to intervene, which suggests that he was aware of what was going on, but able to intervene only indirectly.[13] At Clermont itself there were no bishops from the British Isles present, though Lanfranc's successor Anselm sent a representative.[14] Most of the participants at the council were French, as were most of those who responded to the call. But the message spread rapidly beyond the bounds of France. William of Malmesbury describes how

> The Welshman abandoned his poaching, the Scot his life among fleas, the Dane his continuous drinking, and the Norwegian gorging himself on fish.[15]

William was writing a generation after the events he describes, and his assertion that there was no-one left to cultivate the fields cannot perhaps be take too seriously. But there can be no doubt that the army was large and drawn from a wide range of nationalities. The contemporary historian Ekkehard of Aura thus describes the multinational character of the army of the First Crusade:

> About one hundred thousand men joined the army of the Lord, from Aquitaine, Normandy, England, Scotland and Ireland, Brittany, Galicia, Gascony, Wales, Flanders, Lorraine, and other Christian peoples whose names are not known or heard of now. Moreover, and more wonderful, [the news], flying across the ocean with accustomed speed, made the people of the islands of the sea enlarge the army of the heavenly King . . . There were those who took nothing but bread and water for food, while others used silver rather than iron for all their utensils.[16]

Otto of Freising, whose mid-twelfth-century account is largely based on Ekkehard's, adds that the crusaders were drawn

> not only from the land, but from the islands of the sea and inhabitants of the furthest ocean.[17]

Another twelfth-century chronicler, Sigebert of Gembloux, describes the army as being drawn together from rich and poor

> from Spain, Provence, Aquitaine, Brittany, Scotland, England, Normandy, France, Lorraine, Burgundy, Germany, Lombardy, Apulia, and other kingdoms.[18]

We cannot hope to know the names of any of the humble men whose presence in the army is so often stressed by chroniclers — what we might term the 'bread and water' crusaders. But one important Hebridean chief did take the cross. Lagmann, King of Man and the Sudreys, was struck with remorse after blinding and mutilating his rebellious brother. The *Chronicle of Man* states that

> he freely laid down the government, and, signed with the cross of the Lord, set out on the journey to Jerusalem, in which also he died.[19]

The chronology of this chronicle (which was not being kept contemporaneously) is severely at fault during the late eleventh century, but references to such contemporary figures as Malcolm III of Scotland (died 1093) and 'Murecardus Obrien rex Ybernie' (i.e., Muirchertach Ua Briain King of Munster, who died in 1119)[20] make it clear that the passage must refer to the 1090s. Lagmann is said to have taken the cross, an action which was an innovation of the Council of Clermont; and the *Anglo-Saxon Chronicle* records that the preaching of Pope Urban caused 'a very great stir' in England at Easter 1096, when 'a countless number of people with their wives and families set out, wishing to fight against the heathen.'[21] Lagmann and those who went with him probably crossed the English Channel in the summer of 1096, and joined the assembling forces of Robert Duke of Normandy:

> Then in the month of September Robert Count of Normandy, brother of King William, set out on that adorable journey, having as companions Robert Count of Flanders and Stephen Count of Blois . . . With them went the English and Normans and Eastern Franks, the Flemings and groups (*cunei*) of all the peoples scattered between the British Ocean and the Mediterranean Alps.[22]

Cuneus meant originally a wedge or phalanx of soldiers, but in Medieval Latin came to mean a less disciplined group. Among these *cunei* was a particularly interesting one which caught the notice of the Picard writer Guibert de Nogent, who gave a vivid description of what he saw:

> You should have seen the groups (*cuneus*) of Scots, ferocious among themselves but unwarlike elsewhere, coming forth from their marshy lands with bare legs, shaggy cloaks, a purse hanging from their shoulders; their abundant arms seemed ridiculous to us, but they offered us the help of their faith and devotion. God be my witness, I have heard men from I know not what barbarous nation coming into our seaports, whose language is so uncouth that they seem to have no voice; but crossing their fingers one over the other in the sign of the cross, they thus indicated (because they could not speak) that they journeyed in the cause of the faith.[23]

This suggests an attitude to the Scots, and perhaps in particular to highlanders, which we shall meet again; they were admired for their steadfastness, but their clothes were outlandish and their language barbarous.

Such men might have been expected to succumb early to the hardships of the journey and the unfamiliar Mediterranean climate; but they were still with the army when it left Constantinople and pressed on towards Antioch in the summer of 1097:

> Whoever heard such a number of languages in a single army, when it contained Franks, Flemings, Frisians, Gauls, Allobrogians, Lotharingians, Germans, Bavarians, Normans, Englishmen, Scots, Aquitanians, Italians, Danes (*Daci*), Apulians, Iberians, Bretons, Greeks, Armenians? If a Breton or German had wished to speak to me, I would have been able to answer neither.[24]

Fulcher of Chartres, who wrote these words, was travelling in the company of Stephen Count of Blois, and would have been well able to describe the composition of the northern army. He would have been rubbing shoulders with Bretons and Germans, and probably with Scots as well; presumably he would not have been able to answer their questions either.

This is the last glimpse we catch from contemporary writers of the Scots actively engaged upon the First Crusade; we can only speculate on whether they reached Jerusalem. Despite A.O. Anderson's doubts, we can accept that these *Scotti* were in fact Scots; Professor Duncan has shown that Guibert de Nogent elsewhere uses the word *Scotti* to mean Scots,[25] and Ekkehard of Aura, writing c. 1115, does in fact distinguish 'Scotia et Hibernia.' Lagmann King of Man and the Sudreys was a Hebridean *Gall-ghàidhil* who can perhaps best be described as Hiberno-Scottish.

There was a strong connection between the kings of Man and the kings of Munster during this period. When Lagmann's death became known in the Isles, the *proceres Insularum* sent to Muirchertach Ua Briain of Munster asking him to send a regent until the boy-king Olaf son of Godred should be fully grown; the man sent by him was 'Dompnaldus filius Tadc', possibly a grandson of Brian Bóromha and a leading member of the O'Brien kin-group.[26] The O'Briens also seem to have been on friendly terms with the kings of Scotland at the same time. The *Annals of Innisfallen* contain the following odd entry under the year 1105:

> In the above year a camel (*in camall*), which is an animal of remarkable size, was brought from the king of Alba to Muirchertach Ua Briain.[27]

It is worth asking where could this *animal mirae magnitudinis* have come from, and how could King Edgar (if he is the *ríg Alban* referred to) have acquired it. It is very possible that its appearance in Scotland is connected with the return of the crusaders from Jerusalem; otherwise its presence in Scotland is very difficult to explain.

Another Scot, from the eastern fringe of the area we are considering, may have brought back from the First Crusade a rather less ambitious souvenir. 'In 1823 the interesting discovery was made in the churchyard [of Monymusk] of a Moorish gold coin . . . It was identified as belonging to the Murabetîn dynasty of Morocco and bears the Arabic date 491 (A.D. 1097). It . . . is in beautiful condition, having clearly been in brief circulation before the moment of burial.'[28] Alternative explanations might be found to explain how an Arab coin found its way into the Garioch, but the date it bears points clearly in the direction of the First Crusade.

The twelfth century is on the whole a disappointing time for the avid hunter after Scottish crusaders. Some Scots responded to the mission of Hugh de Paiens, founder and first master of the Knights Templar, who came to Scotland in 1128 seeking recruits to go to Jerusalem.[29] Ailred of Rievaulx asserts that David I longed to join the Second Crusade (1147), but was dissuaded by 'the council of priests and abbots, the tears of the poor, the sighs of widows, the desolation of the people, and the clamour and outcry of the whole kingdom.'[30] Those Scots who were less susceptible to such pressures set out with an Anglo-Flemish fleet in the spring of 1147.[31] At the end of June, the fleet, having sailed from Dartmouth, arrived before Lisbon and joined the king of Portugal in besieging the city. As the siege dragged on over the summer months, many of the English began to regret that they had not headed straight for Jerusalem, and spoke of lifting the siege. But one of the English captains, Hervey de Glanville, made a stirring speech to remind them of their loyalty; and the climax of his argument was this ringing taunt:

> Who would deny that the Scots are barbarians? Nonetheless, while in our company they have never trespassed against the laws of duty and companionship.[32]

It would be interesting to imagine the feelings of any of these steadfast Scots had they chanced to overhear the captain's speech. Their barbarity, and the difference of language which that seems to imply, makes it likely that these were Scots from the *Gaidhealtachd*.

It may have been on their way to join the Second Crusade that a group of Highland Scots was noticed by a Premonstratensian monk near Cambrai, who commented on a curious feature of their dress:

> In our own times in western Scotland the people do not all wear drawers (*feminalia*), but all the knights and townsmen wear them; the rest make do with a general covering which covers them at the front and back, but underneath it is open at the sides. This was told me by certain clerics who had come from these parts . . . And some of these people, who were passing through our land on pilgrimage (*peregre*), were clearly seen not to be wearing drawers.[33]

This is perhaps the earliest scholarly commentary on what the Scotsman wears under his kilt. More seriously, it is of interest to note the difference drawn between 'knights and townsmen' and the rest of the population with their curious mode of dress. It is not certain when the writer could have seen the Scottish pilgrims he mentions, though it must have been around the middle of the twelfth century (he died in 1183). The word 'pilgrimage' was often applied to the Second Crusade (1147–8), and these Scottish pilgrims may well have been taking part in that event.

Professor A.A.M. Duncan has written of a 'marked lack of enthusiasm in Scotland for the recovery of Jerusalem after its fall in 1187.'[34] Such Scots as took part in the Third Crusade (1190–2) probably served under the leadership of Robert de Quincy, the only Scottish nobleman whose presence on the Crusade is certain. For the Highlands and Islands we have no evidence. The *Chronicle of Man* notes the fall of Jerusalem in 1187, the departure of kings Richard and Philip in 1190, and the imprisonment of Richard in Germany in 1193, but does not mention any local participation. The Irish annals ignore the events completely.[35]

There may have been an upsurge in interest in the crusades early in the following century. The Cardinal Legate John de Salerno, sent by Innocent III to Scotland in 1201–2, seems to have preached the cross while he was there, for in the following year David Rufus of Forfar set out for Jerusalem.[36] The *Book of Clanranald* thus describes the death of Ranald, son of Somerled:

> After having received a cross from Jerusalem, partaken of the body of Christ, and received unction, he died, and was buried at Reilig Oghran in Í [Iona] in the year of our Lord 1207.[37]

This phrase is ambiguous; it could mean that Ranald had received relics brought back from Jerusalem, but may be more likely to mean that he took the cross on his deathbed, commuting the crusader's vow for a money payment in return for the plenary indulgence granted to crusaders. The *Book of Clanranald* is a very much later compilation, and contains such chronological mistakes as associating Ranald with the defeat of the Norse in 1263. Unfortunately, there seems to be no other evidence relating to Ranald's association with the Crusades.

The Fourth Crusade (1204) resulted unhappily only in the destruction of the eastern Christian city of Constantinople, and a new crusade was soon required for the defence of the Holy Land. Our information here is much more rewarding. There were legates preaching the cross in Scotland in 1212, as a result of which, Bower tells us,

> A seemingly innumerable multitude throughout the whole of Scotland . . . took the cross; few of them, however, were among the rich and powerful of the kingdom. [38]

An exception was Saher de Quincy, son and heir of the Robert de Quincy who had joined the Third Crusade. In 1218 he set about the fulfilment of his vow by having a ship prepared in Galloway for his crusade, and then sailed to Bristol to have it fitted out.[39] The de Quincy family's connection with Galloway dates from some years later, when in 1233 Saher's son Roger married Helen, daughter of Alan of Galloway; but Alan of Galloway had himself been married to a lady of the family of de Lacy, constables of Chester, and Ranulf earl of Chester joined this crusade — this may provide a clue why Galloway should have been chosen as the starting point for Saher de Quincy's crusade.[39a] From the Celtic earldom of Lennox, further up the Firth of Clyde, came crusaders who have left behind them ample testimony of their sojourn on the Mediterranean. It is not certain that they took ship with Saher de Quincy, but other facts about their voyage are well known.

Two of these crusaders were the bards Muiredhach Albanach and Gilla Brigde Albanach. The designation *Albanach* does not invariably mean a Scotsman, but can mean one who resides or has resided in Scotland. In the case of Gilla Brigde, he 'seems to have been a native of Scotland, whose woods he loved by birthright.'[40] Muiredhach Albanach Ó Dálaigh, on the other hand, was active in Ireland before he was banished in c. 1213;[41] but in a later poem he writes:

> Let me go to my own land . . .
> to Scotland of the woods and the grass,
> of the feasts, the hills, and the isles.
> I will visit Ireland again.[41a]

After 1213 he came to Scotland and took service with Alwin (Ailin or Alun) earl of Lennox, who died c. 1217, and to whom Muiredhach addressed an elaborate praise-poem.[42] It is probably no coincidence that he left Lennox shortly after Alwin's death, for there would have been little employment for him during the minority of Alwin's son Amhlaimh. Some fifteen years after his exile, c. 1228, Muiredhach returned to Ireland, but seems to have settled finally in Scotland, where his descendants became the hereditary bardic family of MacMhuiredhaich or MacVurich.[43]

The two poets seem to have had two other companions on the voyage, both of whom died on the return journey.[44] One of these was probably Aed mac Conchobhair Maenmuige, whose *obit*, 'returning from the Jordan and from Jerusalem,' is given s.a. 1224.[45] To him was addressed Muiredhach Albanach's poem *A Mhuiredhaich, meil do sgin*, which must have been written shortly before their departure. It includes the lines:

> Protect us in the hot land,
> gentle Lady Mary.[46]

The fourth companion cannot have been Cathal Croibhdearg Ó Conchobhair, who also died in 1224, as he died in Ireland in the habit of a Franciscan.[47] He is traditionally thought to have been the companion mentioned in Muiredhach Albanach's poem *An foltsa dhuit, a Dhé athar*, which must have been written shortly before setting out. In it the poet describes how he has been newly tonsured along with a companion:

For four years until this night
has this fresh mass of hair been on me;
I will now reap its bending crop;
this will be the requital of my deceitful poems.[48]

Presumably the shearing was part of their initiation as pilgrims. Perhaps the poet had allowed his hair to grow since the time of his banishment, some four or five years before he set out on crusade.

Gille Brigde Albanach, in his poem *A ghilli gabhus an stiuir*, describes the anxiety of the crusaders as they sail from Acre towards Damietta, in the Nile Delta:

Lad who takest the helm,
you travel often to unknown lands;
you have almost deserved anger;
many havens have you visited.

Let us make a hard decision;
these clouds are from the north-east;
let us leave the bases of the rough mountains of Greece;
let us strive to make Damietta.

These clouds from the east are dark
as they drive us from Acre;
come, Mary Magdalen,
and wholly clear the air.

Distress of one night or of two
would cause me no grief;
the whole season in distress
is a long stretch, great Mary.

Lady of the undulating hair,
thou hast kept us all the autumn
on the bright-edged Mediterranean;
O modest one with the yellow locks.

Brigid of the bright bosom,
though we have been sailing for some time,
our sailings here have been enough for me,
maiden of Europe, beloved one.

Take care as you voyage,
to steer the helm aright;
if the ship carry us of,
on what beach, lad, will it land?
Lad who takest the helm.[49]

We may guess that the crusaders sailed to Acre in the summer or early autumn of

1219 (Saher de Quincy died at Damietta on 3 November 1219). When they reached Acre they would have learnt that the main body of crusaders had passed on to Egypt, and set out after them, possibly coasting Cyprus ('the bases of the rough mountains of Greece') on the way. How long they remained with the army at Damietta is impossible to say, though since the *obit* of Aed is not entered in the Irish annals until 1224 they may have remained right up until the evacuation of Damietta in September 1221, and thereafter have made their leisurely way back through the Mediterranean. Muiredhach Albanach's poem *Fada is chabhair a Cruachain* finds him on board ship off Monte Gargano on the Adriatic in homesick mood:

Help from Cruachan is far off
across the wave-bordered Mediterranean;
the journeying of spring separates us
from these green-branched glens.

I give God thanks . . .
up against Monte Gargano;
between Monte Gargano and the fair-ditched lands of Cruachan
the distance is not small.

It would be as the reward of heaven tonight
if we could touch off Scotland of the lofty manors;
that we might see the haven . . .
or whiff the air of Ireland.[50]

There is an unmistakeable note of relief in the quatrain attributed to Muiredhach Albanach, which he spoke 'at the head of Lochlong in Argyllshire when he sat down to rest himself when he returned thither from Rome':

As I sit on the hillock of tears,
without skin on either toe or sole;
O King! — Peter and Paul!
Far is Rome from Lochlong.[51]

A final glimpse of Muiredhach's achievement in 'going round the world' comes in a poem written shortly after his return to Ireland in c. 1228. In it he boasts:

I come . . .
from over the bright-surfaced Mediterranean;
I am going round the world.[52]

The next major crusading venture to have an impact in the Scottish Highlands was the Crusade of St Louis in 1248–50. Matthew Paris tells us that in 1248 Hugh de Châtillon, Count of St-Pol, had a great ship constructed in Scotland, 'ad Ylvernes, scilicet in Muref' (i.e., at Inverness in Moray), in which he could boldly cross the sea with men from Blois and Flanders and the Low Countries, to join the forces of King Louis IX of France when Damietta was again besieged by the crusaders.[53] Professor Duncan has pointed out that there was 'a substantial Flemish settlement in Inverness and the Moray Firth towns' by the mid thirteenth century;[54] Mr William Matheson has drawn attention to an interesting tradition relating to Coinneach mac Mathghamhna, who was alive in the mid-1260s: as a young man he was banished by his father for repeating unpleasant predictions learnt from the singing of birds (which he understood), joined a ship bound for France, and came to the favour of the French king. The king gave him a ship in which he travelled to distant lands, always being able to understand the language that was spoken wherever he went. Finally, having grown rich as a result of his unusual gift for languages, he returned to Kintail and was met by his father. The latter failed to recognise him and treated him with marks of great respect (which presumably no self-respecting Highland chief would ever have shown towards his own son), and waited on him at table — thus fulfilling the birds' original prediction. As Mr Matheson writes, 'To suppose that Coinneach mac Mathghamhna took part in the Crusade of St Louis is of course a flight of fancy, but it may serve to illustrate how a historical personage could become the hero of a type of tale in existence long before his time.'[55] There is no reason to doubt that Coinneach *did* visit far-off lands and acquire a gift for languages in the mid-thirteenth century; and we know of the Count of St-Pol's crusading ship sailing from Inverness in 1248. To connect the two is tempting, but must remain speculative.

The last of the great crusades took place in 1270. A number of Scots, including both Bruces and Balliols, took part in it, and Scotland seems to have been better represented at Acre in 1271 than ever before. The most interesting Scottish representatives from the point of view of the history of the *Gaidhealtachd* were the earls of Atholl and Carrick. David de Strathbogie Earl of Atholl was a descendant of the earls of Fife and held the earldom of Atholl at least from 1264, though by what right is uncertain. Adam de Kilconquhar Earl of Carrick seems also to have been a member of a cadet branch of the comital family of Fife, who married the daughter of the last Celtic earl of Carrick before departing on crusade.[56] Presumably both earls were accompanied by retinues drawn from within their earldoms. At any rate, both earls died in the Holy Land (of disease), and it was the younger Robert Bruce, son the of lord of Annandale, who brought back the news of Earl Adam's death to his young widow. Fordun tells us that when she heard the news, the countess caused violent hands to be laid upon Bruce and had him imprisoned until he consented to become her husband himself.[57] Perhaps this tale suggests something of the romantic aura which surrounded a returned crusader, that women were prepared to resort to violence to gain his affections.

By the Treaty of Perth (1266) the Western Isles passed from the nominal control of the Norwegian crown to that of the Scottish crown. This did nothing to bring the Isles closer to the cosmopolitan mainstream of Mediterranean Europe; if anything, the involvement of the Highlands and Islands in the large-scale wars in Scotland from 1296 onwards was a distraction from more distant adventures. These wars made it impossible for Scots to contemplate aiding in the recovery of the Holy Land after the fall of Acre in 1291. This point was made in a letter from the Scottish nobility to King Philip IV of France in 1309, apologising that they could not join his projected new crusade until peace had been restored; among the senders were the earls of Ross and Lennox, Alexander of Argyll, Donald of Islay, 'the barons also of the whole of Argyll and the Isles (*Ynchegallya*), and the inhabitants of the whole kingdom of Scotland.'[58] After the death of Bruce there was a modest Scottish crusade under Sir James Douglas which came to an untimely end with his death in Spain in 1330, but most of the participants in this appear to have been lowlanders.[59]

Throughout the later Middle Ages there were spasmodic attempts to revive the crusading ideal, and in these Scots played their part as they had done earlier. The brothers Norman and Walter Leslie were crusading in Prussia in 1356,[60] and in 1365 they were present at the storming of Alexandria by King Peter of Cyprus, in which at least one Scottish knight lost his life.[61] In the 1450s and '60s a number of Scots were fighting against the Turks in Asia Minor, including one group who 'had become so poor that they cannot return to their native parts without the alms of the faithful,' and required the intervention of the Pope to assist their repatriation.[62] In 1442 the Grand Master of the Knights of Rhodes granted a pension from the Knight's lands in Scotland to a certain layman called 'Dignetus (? = Donnchad?) le Scot' for his services performed at Rhodes and elsewhere; his name has undergone corruption, but may conceal a Gaelic christian name.[63] He was not himself a knight of Rhodes, unlike Sir Colin Campbell of Glenorchy, who died in 1480, and (according to the *Black Book of Taymouth*) 'Throch his valiant actis and manheid was maid knicht in the Isle of Rhodos, quhilk standeth in the Carpathiane Sea neir to Caria ane countrie of Asia the les, and was thrie sundrie tymes in Rome.' Mention has already been made of the amulet which Sir Colin is said to have worn 'when he fought in battell at the Rhodes agaynst the Turks;' and he is traditionally known as *Colin Dubh na Roimh*.[64] His activities in the Mediterranean are probably also to be placed in the period round the fall of Constantinople (1453), when other Scots were joining in the losing battle against advancing Ottoman power. Lastly should be mentioned a certain 'Johannes Grandus' (i.e. John Grant), a siege-engineer involved in counter-mining activities during the defence of Constantinople in 1453. He was a member of the company of the Genoese captain Giustiniani, and is described as a German in the Greek sources. But, as Sir Steven Runciman has pointed out, Grant is not a German name, and it is suggested that he may well have been a Scot from Speyside or Aberdeenshire who had served as a mercenary in Germany before enlisting with Giustiniani.[65]

It is clear that, considering both fact and legend, it would be difficult to sustain the view that the medieval Highlands and Islands were 'a land apart', especially since it is equally clear that their inhabitants did not want to be cut off or separate from the European mainstream. Perhaps there had been a tradition of interest in and pilgrimage to far-off lands even before the Christian era, which is reflected in the voyages of Brendan, Columbanus and Columcille, and in the interest which prompted Adamnán to write his *De Locis Sanctis*, which later came to comprehend the Crusade and the pilgrimage to Jerusalem. The length of the journey, the danger, the remoteness and sanctity of the places visited, all conveyed added prestige. There is certainly a note of pride in the words of Muiredhach Albanach, carried down by oral tradition from the thirteenth century to the eighteenth:

Far is Rome from Lochlong.

FOOTNOTES

1. F.T. MacLeod, 'Notes on the Relics preserved in Dunvegan Castle,' *Proceedings of the Society of Antiquaries of Scotland* (*PSAS*), xlvii (1913), 99–129, at p. 111
2. J. Mitchell, *Reminiscences of my Life in the Highlands* (1883: reprinted London, 1971), i. 192
3. Sir Walter Scott, *The Talisman* (various editions); cf. *PSAS*, iv, 222
4. I. Moncreiffe, *The Highland Clans* (London, 1967), 21
5. *PSAS*, xxiv, 411
6. *The Black Book of Taymouth*, ed. C. Innes (Bannatyne Club, 1855), p. ii
7. A.M.T. Maxwell-Irving, 'The Crusader Stone at Bonshaw,' *Transactions of the Dumfries and Galloway Natural History and Archeological Society* (*TDGNHAS*), xxxix (1960–61), 124–6
8. R.C. Reid, 'Bonshaw,' *TDGNHAS*, xx (1935–6), 147–56, at p. 149
9. R.L.G. Ritchie, *The Normans in Scotland* (Edinburgh, 1954), 280 and nn.
10. Orderic Vitalis, *Ecclesiastical History*, ed. M. Chibnall (Oxford, 1969–in progress), v, 58
11. A.O. Anderson, *Early Sources of Scottish History* (Edinburgh, 1922), ii, 98
12. M. Dolley, *Anglo-Norman Ireland* (Dublin, 1972), 1
13. *The Chronicle of Man and the Sudreys*, ed. P.A. Munch (Manx Society, 1874), ii, 265

14. R. Somerville, 'The Council of Clermont (1095) and Latin Christian Society,' *Archivum Historiae Pontificiae*, xii (1974), 55–90, at 71–2
15. William of Malmesbury, *Gesta Regum Anglorum*, ed. W. Stubbs (Rolls Series, 1887–9), ii, 399
16. Ekkehard of Aura, 'Hierosolimitana,' *Recueil des Historiens des Croisades: Historiens Occidentaux* (*RHC Occ.*), (Paris, 1844–99), v, 16
17. Otto of Freising, *Historia de Duabus Civitatibus*, ed. A. Hofmeister (Hanover, 1912), 311
18. Sigebert of Gembloux, 'Chronicon,' *Monumenta Germaniae Historica: Scriptores* (*MGH Scrip*), (Hanover, 1826–in progress), vi, 367
19. *Chronicle of Man*, i, 54
20. *Annals of Innisfallen*, ed. S. MacAirt (Dublin, 1951), 278
21. *Anglo-Saxon Chronicle*, ed. G.N. Garmonsway (London, 1953), 232
22. William of Malmesbury, *Gesta Regum*, ii, 402
23. Guibert de Nogent, 'Historia Hierosolimitana,' *RHC Occ.*, iv, 148
24. Fulcher of Chartres, 'Gesta Francorum Iherusalem Peregrinantium,' *RHC Occ.*, iii, 366
25. A.A.M. Duncan, 'The Dress of the Scots,' *Scottish Historical Review* (*SHR*), xxix (1950), 210–12
26. *Chronicle of Man*, i, 54
27. *Annals of Innisfallen*, 262
28. *PSAS*, lix (1925), 65
29. *Anglo-Saxon Chronicle*, 259
30. John of Fordun, *Chronica Gentis Scottorum*, ed. W.F. Skene (Edinburgh, 1871), 242
31. Their progress was described by an eyewitness in *De Expugnatione Lyxbonensi*, ed. C.W. David (New York, 1936), passim.
32. Ibid., 106
33. Philip de Harveng, 'De Institutione Clericorum,' *Patrologiæ Cursus Completus . . . Series Latina*, ed. J.P. Migne (1844–55), cciii, col. 730
34. A.A.M. Duncan, *Scotland: the Making of the Kingdom* (Edinburgh, 1975), 446
35. *Chronicle of Man*, i, 78–80. The entries for the years between 1181 and 1189 are now missing in *Annals of Innisfallen* (cf. p. 314). *Annals of . . . the Four Masters*, ed. J. O'Donovan (Dublin, 1856), ii, 88–9, records Richard's first coronation in 1190.
36. *Charters of the Abbey of Coupar Angus*, ed. D.E. Easson (Scottish History Society, 1947), i, 24–6, 130–2
37. Alexander Cameron, *Reliquiae Celticae*, ed. A. Macbain and J. Kennedy (Inverness, 1892–4), ii, 156–7
38. Walter Bower, *Scotichronicon Johannis de Fordun cum Supplementis et Continuatione*, ed. W. Goodall (Edinburgh, 1759), i, 534
39. *Calendar of Documents Relating to Scotland*, ed. J. Bain (Edinburgh, 1881–8), i, no. 703

39a. K.J. Stringer, 'A New Wife for Alan of Galloway,' *TDGNHAS*, 3d Series, xlix (1972), 49–56

40. G. Murphy, 'A Vision Concerning Rolf MacMahon,' *Éigse*, iv (1945), 79–111, at 94–95
41. *Annals of the Four Masters*,iii, 178–81

41a. O. Bergin, 'Unpublished Irish Poems: xxviii — a Palmer's Greeting,' *Studies*, xiii (1924), 567–74, at 574

42. W.F. Skene, *Celtic Scotland* (Edinburgh, 1880), iii, 117–9, 454–5
43. D. Thomson, 'The MacMhuirich Bardic Family,' *Transactions of the Gaelic Society of Inverness* (*TGSI*), xliii (1966), 276–304, at 279–80
44. G. Murphy, 'Two Irish Poems written from the Mediterranean in the Thirteenth Century,' *Éigse*, vii (1955), 71–77
45. *Annals of the Four Masters*, iii, 214–5
46. *Measgra Dánta*, ed. T.F. O'Rahilly (Dublin, 1927), no. 69, p. 179
47. *Annals of the Four Masters*, iii, 210–15
48. *Aithdioghluim Dána*, ed. L. McKenna (Dublin, Irish Text Society, 1939–40), i, 174–6
49. I have freely adapted Murphy's translations in *Éigse*, vii, loc. cit.
50. Ibid.
51. D. Mackintosh, *Collection of Irish Proverbs* (2nd edn, Edinburgh, 1819), 190–1
52. Bergin in *Studies*, xiii, loc. cit.
53. Matthew Paris, *Chronica Maiora*, ed. H.R. Luard (Rolls Series, 1872–83), v, 93
54. Duncan, *Making of the Kingdom*, 478
55. W. Matheson, 'Traditions of the McKenzies,' *TGSI*, xxxix–xl (1942–50), 193–228, at 221–3
56. Duncan, *Making of the Kingdom*, 585
57. Fordun, *Chronica*, 303–4
58. *Acts of the Parliaments of Scotland*, ed. T. Thomson and C. Innes (Edinburgh, 1814–75), i, 459
59. The most detailed account is in I.M. Davis, *The Black Douglas* (London, 1974), 155–65, though it contains some inaccuracies. Douglas died on 25 Aug. 1330 (Fordun, *Chronica*, 353).
60. T. Rymer, *Foedera, Literae, Conventiones*, etc. (Record Commission edn, London, 1816–69), III, pt i, p. 339
61. Bower, *Scotichronicon*, ii, 488n.: Guillaume de Machaut, *La Prise d'Alexandrie*, ed. L. de Mas Latrie (Geneva, Société de l'Orient Latin, 1877), 86, records the death of an unnamed Scottish knight: for the Leslies' activities in Italy in 1364, cf. G. Canestrini, *Documenti per Servire alla Storia della Milizia Italiana* (Florence, Archivo Storico Italiano, 1851), 57–60
62. *Calendar of the Papal Registers . . . Papal Letters*, ed. W.H. Bliss and others (London, 1893–in progress), xi, 158–9, 519, 590
63. *Registrum Cartarum Sancti Egidii*, ed. D. Laing (Bannatyne Club, 1859), 66–7
64. *Black Book of Taymouth*, pp. ii, 10, 13
65. S. Runciman, *The Fall of Constantinople*; v. Notes & Queries XV, of the Society of West Highland and Island Historical Research, 1981. (Cambridge, 1965), 84

GAELIC POETRY AND HISTORICAL TRADITION

JOHN MACINNES

Poetry is not perhaps the most obvious area of Gaelic literature in which to look for direct evidence of an historical kind. At first sight it might seem a more profitable undertaking to study the considerable body of historical tales that have been recorded from oral tradition over the last two centuries and the oldest of which go back to Somerled's campaign against the Norsemen. But important as these stories are, their primary value is as literature. They are in general short dramatic narratives whose laconic style is often reminiscent of the Icelandic sagas, with which perhaps they share some degree of common ancestry. In the Gaelic stories interest focuses on personal relationships and individual feats, and events are depicted on a local rather than a national scale. Yet it is important to emphasise that the Gaelic sense of identity is conditioned and sometimes actually shaped by information that emanates from these historical legends as well as from other, less formally organised categories of tradition. Poetry and legend combine in tradition to create a native view of history. Even in the diminished traditional lore of our own times we can still find a surprising unanimity of opinion as to what constitutes the salient features of Gaelic history and the history of Scotland, which we still call Alba.

In certain ways poetry stands in contrast to the prose narratives. Poets are the spokesmen of Gaelic society; in all ages and at a variety of social levels poetry is the traditional medium for the expression of society's customary expectations. It is not a different awareness so much as a difference in artistic convention that makes the Gaelic poet concern himself with the national dimensions of a given issue. But it is also a matter of artistic lineage. A contemporary bard in a crofting township is the distant heir of the poets who once enjoyed the patronage of the kings of Scotland and the great magnates of the kingdom, and will make songs, as of right, on issues of national and international import. In this paper I shall try to indicate some of the main perspectives which poets have adopted down to the eighteenth century. This involves some consideration of the fascinating, and neglected, theme of prophetic tradition. I shall also discuss some aspects of the hostility between Clan Donald and the Campbells if only for the reason that it occupies a central place in Gaelic historical lore. Finally, I shall give a brief outline of the rhetorical strategy which Gaelic poets employed (and in some of its reaches employed unconsciously) in order that at least a conceptual unity of the Gaelic nation in Scotland should be preserved.

I am conscious of the fact that it may seem anomalous, in a conference devoted to the Middle Ages, that much of the verse cited in this paper is drawn from the vernacular poetry of the seventeenth and eighteenth centuries, the bulk of which is oral, rather than from the written record of classical Gaelic, which stretches back much farther in time. But as some of the examples may show, Gaelic poetry retained a peculiarly medieval quality long after what we normally think of as the Middle Ages had passed. This is certainly true of the rhetoric. There are, too, extraordinary survivals such as the following statement implies: 'I would drink a drink in spite of my kinsfolk: not of the red wine of Spain but the blood of your body, to me a better drink.'[1] This reference, one of half a dozen or so of its kind, is from an eighteenth century lament by the daughter of the Laird of Scalpay to her lover. The image may be no more than an expression of distraught grief. There is, however, a tale of the death of Martin of Bealach in Skye in the same century which suggests that the actual practice survived until then though in a greatly attenuated form. It is also a motif of certain Irish keens. Readers of Spenser's 'A View of the Present State of Ireland' will remember: '. . . the Gauls used to drink their enemies' blood and to paint themselves therewith, so also they write that the old Irish were wont; and so have I seen some of the Irish do but not their enemies' but friends' blood, as namely at the execution of a notable traitor at Limerick called Murrogh O'Brien, I saw an old woman which was his foster mother took up his head whilst he was quartered and sucked up all the blood running there out, saying that the earth was not worthy to drink it, and therewith also steeped her face and breast, and tore her hair, crying and shrieking out most terribly.'[2]

In the Middle Ages such practices were already old. There are also ancient survivals of belief. For instance, Donald MacDonald of Eriskay, the victorious hero of the Battle of Carinish in North Uist, which was fought in 1601 against the MacLeods, is described as having routed the 'Seed of the Mare',[3] a totemistic allusion which is presumably to be linked with names like *Arcaibh* (Orkney), 'among the Pig-Folk', or *Cataibh*, 'Cat-Folk' — the south and south-east of Sutherland according to local usage; the County of Sutherland in general usage elsewhere. Watson argues that in *Inse Chat* we have the pre-Norse name of the Shetlands; the first element in Caithness is from the same source. We may compare *Clann Chatain* or *Mac Gille Chatain*. According to tradition to dream of a cat is designative of a MacPherson or a Macintosh, both members of *Clann Chatain*. Apparently we have traces here of a system of dream interpretation which can be linked with these ancient totemistic names. To dream of a horse or mare signifies that a MacLeod is involved, and so on for a number of other kindred-groups. We may have a survival of a different kind in another paean[4] to the same victorious MacDonald warrior in 1601. This triumphal song seems to be a late example of the same kind of welcome as was performed three hundred years earlier when seven women of Strathearn 'came out to meet the King [Edward I] . . . and sang before him, as they used to do according to the custom of the time of the Lord Alexander, late King of Scotland.'[5]

There are thus certain areas of Gaelic tradition in which elements of great antiquity co-exist with those that reflect the history of more recent times. This is seen even in the name of Alba. In the oldest Gaelic literature it denotes the whole of mainland Britain but it appears also to have been used, perhaps anachronistically, in the restricted sense of 'Gaelic Britain' as opposed to Pictland, before coming to denote the Gaelic kingdom of Scone. It is now in Gaelic simply the equivalent of Scotland, from Shetland to the Borders. Behind the modern Gaelic usage, however, there probably lie various developments and adjustments which we cannot now reconstruct in any detail. Iain Lom of Keppoch in the seventeenth century talks of 'Orkney to Tweed'[6] and in the previous century not all Hebridean poets thought of the Isles as part of Alba. And what, for instance, is the precise significance of the name Drumalban in Lanarkshire? It is surely very significant that the men of Galloway at the Battle of the Standard in 1138 'cried out the war-cry of their fathers — and the shouts rose, even to the skies — *Albani, Albani*.'[7] This indicates that at that date the same Alba had cultural and ethnic affiliations which transcended the merely geographical limits of Scotia — Scotland north of Forth. The plain inference would seem to be that wherever the Gaelic language had penetrated, that area was part of Alba. Yet the men of *Innse Gall*, the Hebrides, may have had a different perspective. The *Gall* are of course the Norsemen; the connotation is the same in our name for Caithness, *Gallaibh*. But although we still call a Caithness man *Gallach* the simplex *Gall* in all Gaelic dialects means Lowland Scot and *Galldachd* the Lowlands.

Writing about the Highlands in the lifetime of Robert the Bruce, Professor Barrow has this to say: 'Neither in the chronicle nor in the record of the twelfth and thirteenth centuries do we hear of anything equivalent to the 'Highland Line' of later time. Indeed, the very terms 'Highlands' and 'Lowlands' have no place in the considerable body of written evidence surviving from the period before 1300. 'Ye hielans and ye lawlans, oh whaur hae ye been?' The plain answer is that they do not seem to have been anywhere: in those terms, they had simply not entered the minds of men. We commonly think of this highland-lowland dichotomy as being rooted deep in the history of Scotland, as being, indeed, imposed upon that history by the mere facts of physical geography. Yet it seems to have left no trace in the reasonably plentiful record of two formative centuries . . . [In the thirteenth century] the Gaelic language must have been perfectly familiar up and down the east coast from the Ord of Caithness to Queensferry. It must, moreover, still have been the ordinary working language of Carrick and the rest of Galloway.' [But after the partial retreat of Gaelic] 'Thus one great historic divide between Highlands and Lowlands had established itself before the end of the middle ages. The Highlands and Islands were now synonymous, as they had not previously been, with the Gaidhealtachd, the Gaelic speakers and their culture, while the Lowlands . . . became the country of the Sasunnach, the people who (whatever their racial origins) spoke and wrote a variant of the English tongue. Lowlanders, for their part, recognised the same division, though they thought in significantly different terms. They were not Sasunnach either to themselves or to the English south of the Border. They were Scots . . .'[8]

To the Gael, too, they are Scots. A Lowlander is unequivocally an Albannach and it would be a contradiction in terms to speak of an Albannach Sasunnach. And although Gaels recognise more or less the same division of the country into Highland and Lowland, there are certain subtle differences in that division which we are perhaps prone to ignore. It is not the fact of a geographical divide that the Gaelic names emphasise. Gaidlhealtachd and Galldachd are abstract terms, not ordinary place-names, and the areas they designate are not drawn with precise boundaries. The perspective here is cultural. Some tradition-bearers indeed extend the Gaidlhealtachd vaguely beyond the Highland Line. This may suggest some faint reflection of the limits of Gaelic speech, as described by Professor Barrow, before c.1350.

The creation of what we may call the Gaidhealtachd proper does not imply that the mandarin class of poets and shennachies deserted their memories of former greatness. In a classical Gaelic poem addressed to the chief of Clan Gregor (1461–1519) the poet, brother of the Dean of Lismore, says: 'Here is a quatrain I have found . . . thy history aright, up to Fergus son of Erc the warlike. In thy line, not niggard to help, the number who assumed a crown hath been kings two score and three: in the high enumeration knowledge of them is meet. Three in the north, three in the south were there, after Malcolm Canmore; twice five crowns is the tale from Malcolm to Ailpín. From Malcolm upwards their number known is fourteen men to Fergus. To what number then doth thy lineage extend? Reckoning may be made up to Fergus.'[9]

This 'high enumeration' is essentially the same as we find in the *Duan Albanach*, 'The Scottish Poem', composed during, or immediately after, the reign of Malcolm Canmore.[10] From such sources also the shennachie who recited in Gaelic the lineage of Alexander III at his inauguration in 1249 drew his information. Given the nature of Gaelic society and the immense importance of oral tradition at so many social levels, it would be strange if that information was restricted entirely to one social or professional class. Over three centuries after the date of the poem to the chief of the MacGregors, and from the same area of Perthshire, we have an interesting testimony to the state and content of oral tradition. It comes from Duncan Campbell, who was born in 1828 at Kerrumore in Glenlyon. He depicts a society of small tenants, farmers, and minor gentry, who were all Gaelic speaking. He tells us, and demonstrates his claim, that 'Our Glenlyon men of age . . . were wise and deep in traditional lore.' In one vignette concerning the coronation of Queen Victoria, in 1838, he describes his own aged grandmother discussing that event and adds: 'She and others of her generation enjoyed the liberty this occasion gave them for going . . . to the history of Scottish kings as far as Kenneth Macalpin, *which had come down by oral tradition* [my italics]. Long afterwards when I read the 'Duan Albanach', I was much surprised to discover that the substance of it was retained to a remarkable extent in the oral and local traditions which our aged people recalled and told . . . As for the later kings from the time of Wallace and Bruce, as Glenlyon was visited by so many of them for hunting purposes until the Union of the English and Scottish Crowns, there was nothing very strange in the fact that the traditions were fairly strong and unbroken.'[11]

We need not take it at face value that there was an unbroken continuity of oral tradition in the transmission of these facts. Oral tradition was probably reinforced throughout the ages from other sources, clerical and lay, including the parish school. It may be remarked that in modern Gaelic oral tradition Bruce and Wallace are both represented as being Gaelic speakers; and although this is sometimes demonstrably based upon (or reinforced by) English language sources, tradition bearers will cite it as evidence of the predominance of Gaelic at one time in Scottish history and, by implication, of the reality of a Gaelic Scotland. Except at that 'dynastic' level, however, Gaelic poets are not in general concerned with the earlier distribution of Gaelic culture or speech beyond the Highland Line. Around 1730 Edmund Burt has this to say of the Gaels: '. . . they have an adherence to one another as Highlanders, in opposition to the People of the Low-Country, whom they despise as inferior to them in Courage, and believe they have a right to plunder them whenever it is in their Power. This last arises from a Tradition, that the Lowlands, in old Times were the Possession of their Ancestors . . . When I mentioned this Tradition, I had only in view the middling and ordinary Highlanders, who are very tenacious of old Customs and opinions; and [now] I would be understood that it is very probable such a Notion was formerly entertained by some, at least, amongst those of the Highest Rank.'[12]

As to the first part of this, much the same sentiments could be heard expressed in the twentieth century. They also find expression in poetry though not over conspicuously and on the whole confined to a popular level of song. But as regards Burt's conjecture about 'the highest Rank', the only qualification to be made is that there must have been men of high rank still alive at that time who subscribed to the same principle. On the evidence of the poetry of that age some of them were MacDonalds.

The importance of Clan Donald in the history of Gaelic poetry cannot be over-estimated. This stems directly from their status in the Lordship of the Isles and from their continuing influence on the Gaidhealtachd after the Lordship was forfeited. In the twelfth century the Lordship emerges as a new focus of Gaelic culture and loyalty in Scotland. In terms of political and military organisation no less than cultural patronage and diversity it is as if Gaelic Alba had been reaffirmed and re-created within narrower territorial limits. The cultural inheritance of Somerled's heirs was a rich complex which on the one hand drew on ancient traditions of the *Cenél nGabhráin*,[13] going back to the foundation of the Scoto-Pictish kingdom; on the other upon those of the Gallghaidheal and the Norse kingdom of the Isles. The role played by the *Gall* of the North in the formation of this 'Nova Scotia' is not neglected by the poets. In their claims to Norse ancestry the MacLeods are outstanding, as when Mary MacLeod celebrates these descendants of a 'line of kings who laid Man under tribute . . . stately race, seed of Olver and Ochraidh; from the city of Bergen did your first title spring.'[14] But there were lesser kindreds also who remembered their Norse origin and in the sixteenth century a MacDonald song, the famous 'Lullaby' to Domhnall Gorm of Sleat contains the phrase 'when my King's son goes to Scotland': *Nuair théid mac mo Righ-sa dh'Alba*.[15] There may well have been atavistic longings, of which we have now little trace, to be found among the Gaelicised Norsemen comparable with those that are still fostered by the Scotticised Shetlanders. But this is not the norm. Even Mary MacLeod, in her elegy for Sir Norman of Berneray, is careful to state that 'One half of your kinship was with the race of Coll . . . from the province of Connacht.'[16] In the eighteenth century John MacCodrum says of Clan Donald: '. . . They came from Egypt in the days of Gathelus and Scota . . . Alba, though it is much to say, they divided from sea to moor, many great nobles were there who received their right from the hand of Clan Donald.'[17]

MacCodrum was illiterate. So was Eachann Bacach, a warrior poet of the Macleans. Yet he too shows his knowledge of the learning that was primarily cultivated and transmitted by the Gaelic *literati*, among whom the great literary dynasty of the MacMhuirichs was outstanding. Eachann's elegy for Sir Lachlan Maclean opens with the words: 'Your origins went back to Pharaoh.'[18] In the context of vernacular poetry as a whole such allusions may be no more than stray items, or decorative asides, from the 'Milesian Legend' — one of the constructions of medieval Gaelic pseudo-history (it features also, of course, in the Declaration of Arbroath) in which Gaidheal Glas (Gathelus), son of Scota daughter of Pharaoh, is the eponymous ancestor of the Gaels. But the references serve to illustrate two things. One is the deep consciousness of Gaelic identity and continuity of history, particularly within the Lordship. At the beginning of the seventeeenth century Sir James MacDonald of Islay claims that 'My race hes bene tenne hundreth yeeris kyndlie Scottis men, under the Kinges of Scotland.'[19] Dr John Bannerman sums up the developments that sustained such a claim: 'Indeed, it could be argued that the ultimate origin of the Lordship of the Isles lay in the erstwhile political fact of the Kingdom of Dalriada itself.'[20] The other point to be made about learned allusions in oral poetry is that they show the connection between vernacular and classical Gaelic poets, of which more later.

Sir James MacDonald's phrase 'under the Kinges of Scotland' may seem to stand in contrast to the line in Domhnall Gorm's 'Lullaby': 'When my king's son goes to Scotland.' This king is of course MacDonald. The Lord of the Isles is in modern Gaelic often referred to as *Tighearna nan Eilean*, which appears to be a direct translation from English. Genuine tradition-bearers do not use it. To them he is known simply by the cognomen MacDonald; in literary sources his usual title is King. The *Clanranald History*, for example, has 'John, son of Angus Og who was called MacDonald and Mormaer of the Isles and King of Fionnghall.'[21] *Am Mormhaire* (The Mormaer) is the normal and still current style of MacDonald of Sleat; otherwise *Am Mormhaire Domhnallach* or less commonly *Am Mormhaire Sléiteach* (the Gaelic adjectival forms of 'MacDonald' and 'Sleat'). The Gaelic *literati*, then, continue to use the title reflected in *Rex Insularum*. Thus Raghnall son of Somerled is in the *Clanranald History* 'Raghnall King of the Isles of the Norsemen and the Coastland of the Gaels; foremost of all Gaels and Norsemen . . .'[22] But there is never, so far as I know, any suggestion in poetry or elsewhere that the Gaels do not owe allegiance to the true line of Malcolm III no matter how much their loyalty might become obscured in the turbulence of history or how much hostility the policies of an individual monarch and the attitudes of the central authorities might provoke. In poetry the rhetorical topic of *rìoghalachd* — loyalty to the king and participation in the kingly virtues — is constantly reiterated.

Much of the rhetorical structure of Gaelic verse took shape in the work of the poets who wrote in what we know as Classical Gaelic, a standard language evolved sometime toward the end of the twelfth century. It remained the standard for the whole Gaelic speaking area, up to the middle of the seventeenth century in Ireland, and nearly a hundred years later in Scotland, where it came to an end with the death of the last representative of the hereditary bardic family of the MacMhuirichs.[23] A considerable amount of what has survived, though by no means all, of the work of this Bardic Order is praise-poetry. One of the earliest, if not *the* earliest, examples of the genre is a poem to Raghnall King of Man and the Isles from 1188 to 1226.[24] It has been ascribed to Muireadhach Albanach, ancestor of this same MacMhuirich family who for well over five hundred years held literary office first, apparently, under the patronage of the Lordship of the Isles in Kintyre and for over two centuries under that of Clanranald in South Uist. The MacMhuirichs have a fair claim to be regarded as the most illustrious family of learned poets and historians in Gaelic Scotland but there were, of course, others. The great early sixteenth century manuscript known as *The Book of the Dean of Lismore* is in part a collection of bardic poetry. Dr Bannerman observes that 'It has been noted before that the poetry of Scottish provenance, in both authorship and content, belongs overwhelmingly to a limited area of Scotland. Except for the earldom of Ross, whose links with the Lordship seem to have been at best tenuous and not of long duration, it is now possible to equate that sphere with the sphere of influence of the Lords of the Isles . . . Indeed, considering that the compilers were natives of Fortingall, the distribution pattern of the Scottish poetry, beginning, as it does, at Fortingall and proceeding west from there along a narrow corridor as far as Loch Awe, and then opening out dramatically to include a poem addressed to MacLeod of Lewis at one end of the Lordship and another to MacNeill of Gigha at the other end, would be an extraordinary one seen in any light other than that of the Lordship of the Isles.'[25]

'The only Scottish poet . . . who was certainly not a native of the area dominated by the Lords of the Isles is the only one for whom the compilers saw fit to record his place of origin, namely, Donnchadh Mór from Lennox.'[26]

W.J. Watson was of the opinion that 'there must have been, all over the north and north-east from Sutherland southwards, and eastwards by Aberdeen, to say nothing of Galloway, a very large amount of early Gaelic poetry, by trained professional bards and others, of which we have no record.'[27] But this does not necessarily follow. Even if we allow that there must have been poetry and song of one kind or another everywhere throughout the Gaidhealtachd, our classical bardic poetry, a special development of the high Middle Ages, dependent equally on a rigorous scholastic training and the availability of patronage, might well have failed to penetrate or failed to flourish in the greater part of the Gaidhealtachd outside the sphere of the Lordship's influence. In fact, the later distribution of some other forms of poetry tends to support this view.[28]

Dr Bannerman's delimitation of the bounds of the Lordship is based among other evidence on the so-called *M.S. 1467*, whose 'form and content leave no doubt that its compiler's intention was to set down the pedigrees of the chiefs of important clans who, in his opinion, recognised the authority of the Lord of the Isles at that time.'[29] The time was c.1400, when the Campbells had not yet become conspicuous in the role in which later tradition has made them famous. *The Book of the Dean*, incidentally, contains a considerable number of poems of Campbell provenance. Poem I in W.J. Watson's edition contains the verse 'Write expertly, learnedly . . . bring unto Mac Cailéin no poem lacking artistry to be read.'[30] It is by the chief of Macnab and appears to project an anthology, which Watson takes to be the manuscript actually compiled by the Dean of Lismore.

Watson comments: 'The reference in the poem to *Mac Cailéin*, the Earl of Argyll, as a shrewd and competent critic of poetry is specially interesting; and incidentally suggests that hostile relations between the MacGregors and the Campbells did not preclude friendly intercourse between Dugall MacGregor and the Campbell chief.'[31]

The MacDonald-Campbell 'feud', with the Campbells cast in the role of villain, is part of Scottish folklore. It is also deeply rooted in genuine Gaelic oral tradition. That it should have these sources and this distribution is itself a token of the importance of MacDonald influence in forming popular views. There is nowadays a salutary tendency on the part of historians to de-mythologise such accounts but this should not tempt us to set aside the facts that traditional Gaelic society accepted: an important element in all history is what people believe to have happened. To convert these traditions, for the sake of brevity, into modern terminology, we find the hostility between Clan Donald and the Campbells presented as if it were a dialectical opposition of resistance to and collaboration with the central authorities. (In documentary sources the concept of resistance is summarily expressed in the often quoted statement made by the commissioners of the Lordship in 1545).[32] There is no traditional memory of a time when the Campbells were under the sway of the Lordship. Throughout the wide area which the Lords of the Isles dominated, the custodians of tradition emphasise one point. That is, that the Campbells, being as truly Gaelic as any other *fine* or kindred, nevertheless took the side of the *Gall* of Scotland. There is a cultural dimension to this: an awareness of the encroachment of the *Galldachd* on the *Gaidhealtachd*. In the last quarter of the fifteenth century when the Lordship was under heavy attack by the central authorities and about to be forfeited by the Crown, Giolla Coluim mac an Ollaimh wrote a sad elegant poem *It is no joy without Clan Donald*. 'Alas for those who have lost that company; alas for those who have parted from their society; for no race is as Clan Donald, a noble race, strong of courage. There was no counting of their bounty; there was no reckoning of their gifts; their nobles knew no bound, no beginning, no end of generosity. In the van of Clan Donald learning was commanded, and in their rear were service of honour and self-respect. For sorrow and for sadness I have forsaken wisdom and learning: on their account I have forsaken all things: it is no joy without Clan Donald.'[33]

The apprehension expressed here must have been greatly increased in 1609 when the statutes of Icolmkill threatened among other things to suppress the bardic order itself. In the eighteenth century Alexander MacDonald was to coin or use a phrase that sums up the reaction to these ethnocidal policies: *Mìorun mór nan Gall* — the great ill-will and hostility of the Gall. The traditions of the Campbell lands do indeed reflect the separate identities of Gaidheal and Gall but explicit statements of that nature are not to be found.

The Campbell and MacDonald poet-spokesmen each make a unique and identical claim on behalf of their respective clans: to each of them belongs *Ceannas nan Gàidheal*, the 'headship', leadership and supremacy, of the Gaels. This formal attempt to wrest from Clan Donald their proud, ancient title raises the struggle above the level of any other vendetta in Gaelic history. The MacDonald claim in fact goes back beyond the eponymous Donald: 'The headship of the Gaels to the Seed of Coll'; the genealogy of John of Islay is then traced by this poet through Somerled to Colla Uais, the mythical fourth century ancestor to whose descendants properly belong 'the headship of Ireland and Scotland'.[34] The counter-claim is couched in similar terms: to the Campbells belongs the headship of the Gaels. 'A good charter is the headship of the Gael'. 'The headship of the Gael of the island of Alba.' 'Lord of the Gaels is Gilleasbuig.'[35] In the 1550s Maclean's poet reflects Campbell claims when he says in elegant diplomatic verse that he comes 'with my finished poem to the King of the Gaels'.[36] Viewed against the background of events from the 1490s onwards the precise words of this Campbell poetry make an illuminating comment: 'A good charter is the headship of the Gael, whoever it be that has a grip of it; a people's might at this time it has exalted; it is the noblest title in Alba. Gilleasbuig, earl of the Gael has grasped the charter of the headship of the people; in his charter it has ever been of right to rule a willing people without self-seeking.' The use of 'charter' reminds us of a *locus classicus* in Clan Donald poetry: 'The broadsword's charter is the birthright of that bold people; often without seal's impression do they impose tax and tribute.'[37] It recalls also the bitter and often quoted words of Iain Lom in 1678: 'The sharp stroke of short pens protects Argyll . . . By falsehoods you deprived us of Islay green and lovely, and Kintyre with its verdant plains'.[38]

Hostility to Crown charters by those who suffered under the policies they endorsed was real enough and the Campbells were justifiably regarded as masters of such 'un-Gaelic activities'. The point to note, however, is that Campbell military and political ambitions are here backed by explicit claims at the diplomatic level of classical Gaelic bardic exchanges. Mr Ronald Black has shown that this particular Campbell poem was well known to the poets of Clan Donald. He adds: '. . . it exists in two manuscripts . . . To find a Scottish bardic poem in more than one manuscript is unusual; to find a poem in praise of Mac Cailein Mór written by two different MacMhuirichs seems on the face of it little short of amazing.'[39] Whatever the MacMhuirichs' reasons for preserving the poem so carefully, the implications of this Campbell *démarche* would certainly not elude them nor could its language fail to distinguish Campbell policy from that of others whose acceptance of the leadership of Clan Donald might well be less than total. Consequently, even the MacKenzies, who frequently played a part in the north comparable to that of the Campbells elsewhere (and who may have begun to pursue a distinctive course as far back as Harlaw)[40] never achieved a commensurate notoriety in the general tradition of the Gaels. It is frequently observed that no feud is as bitter as that between kinsmen. Yet tradition has preserved no memory of the consistently treacherous behaviour, from the Clan Donald point of view, of MacIan of Ardnamurchan who from 1494 until his death c.1518 'never failed to oppose the restoration of the Lordship by MacDonald claimants and throughout . . . was in close association with the Campbell earls of Argyll.'[41] Except at a private and local level the custodians of MacDonald tradition could not deal with this without making a fundamental shift in historical perspective. A larger ideological framework was required. It is a curious irony in view of the Campbell reputation for double-dealing that their notoriety should have been built up not so much perhaps by Campbell involvement in Scottish state affairs as, at the cultural level, by the plain speaking of the Campbells' poets with regard to the Headship of the Gael.

This interpretation may seem to put too much weight on the evidence of a few poems. My own view is that in Gaelic society one single composition of the kind I have quoted would be sufficient. We hear in tradition, often enough, how one taunt or one satire was registered, and recalled at the proper moment. It is quite likely that among the manuscripts that have perished through destructiveness and neglect there were other poems to rouse Clan Donald to an awareness of the Campbells' ultimate aim. At the same time we can only make an informed guess at what values might have been expressed in the lost poetry of Gaelic Scotland.

There is a well-known poem of incitement to battle addressed to Archibald, 2nd Earl of Argyll and Chancellor of Scotland, on the eve of the Battle of Flodden, where, along with other Campbells, he lost his life. It begins: 'The race of the Gael from the land of Greece', and draws upon Gaelic legendary history and mythology. Within the conventional form the author articulates his message: 'Meet it is to rise against Saxons . . . ere they have taken our country from us; let us not yield up our native country, let us make no gentle warfare; let us, after the pattern of the Gael of Banbha [i.e. Ireland] watch over our fatherland . . . [Saxons for a space raised] tribute from our country: [it was so done] through each man's fear; such is our mistrust . . . send thy summons east and west for the Gael from [Ireland]; drive the Saxons westwards over the high sea, that Alba may suffer no division.'[42]

The references to fear, mistrust and division may well reflect an underlying concern with the unity of the realm of Scotland, not just the Gaidhealtachd. Nevertheless the poem as a whole is very much a composition from the world of the 'sea-divided Gael'. Watson remarks on 'its fierce national spirit' and observes: 'there must no doubt have been many such poems, now lost to us, in connection with the Wars of Independence; one other, composed in 1310 . . . is found in the Dean's book.'[43] As a matter of fact this other poem, a panegyric to Eoin mac Suibhne of Knapdale, is by no means an unequivocal example of pan-Scottish propaganda: as it happens, it is from the Balliol or, as Watson puts it, 'from the English' side. The MacDonalds were of course deeply involved in the Wars of Independence but there is no evidence to suggest that the poets would have celebrated the Scottish rather than the Gaelic cause. In this connection it is of some interest that the tone of the *Clanranald History* (although perhaps affected by later events) in dealing with these stirring times is markedly detached. The writer merely notes that the MacDougalls took Balliol's side and the line of Raghnall son of Somhairle took that of Bruce.[44] By the sixteenth century Campbell participation in the affairs of state would naturally have brought something of the 'Scottish dimension' into their poetry, even if the poets still express themselves in figures of traditional rhetoric. But by the eighteenth century, under the pressures of Jacobitism, some MacDonald poetry, as we shall see later, is quite explicitly Scottish, not merely Gaelic.

It was established some years ago by Mr W.D.H. Sellar that the genealogy of Somerled's line is almost certainly authentic back to Gofraid son of Fergus, contemporary with Kenneth mac Alpin.[45] We have already noticed briefly how we can find even in oral, vernacular poetry occasional references to the Gathelus story and other learned lore, showing the sense of continuity of Gaelic history. In a pioneering study of classical Gaelic poetry W.J. Watson drew attention to the fact 'that while the MacDonalds vaunted descent from Conn Cétchathach . . . and Colla Uais . . . Mac Cailin's bards disclaimed Irish connection, and traced the line of Mac Cailin up to Arthur of the Round Table, emphasising the British origin . . .

'Thy pure descent, Giolla-easbuig, I could recount to Arthur every step . . . Ten generations from thee in the heroic warrior-host comes wondrous Cailin of lasting feats . . . eleven steps from wondrous Cailin to Arthur comely and pure of the Round Table, the best king throughout the world . . .'[46]

Elsewhere Mac Cailin is the 'heir of Arthur', 'of the blood of Arthur and Béine Briot'. Watson implies that this pedigree is to be taken as part of the rival claim that Campbell poets urge against MacDonald pretensions. In fact, as Professor Gillies has shown, the Campbells did not exactly disclaim Irish connection; rather they used different lines of descent as political or other needs dictated.[47] The MacDonald poets were aware of the Campbell pedigree: 'Brutus son of Silvius . . .. Descended from that Brutus are the British and Mac Cailein of Scotland and the whole race of Arthur son of Uther. It is that Brutus that used to be called Brutus the Repugnant, and the reason he was so called is that his mother died in bearing him and that he killed his own father with an arrowshot so that he could have the kingdom after him; his brother Silvius therefore banished him from Rome to the isle of Britain, hence the British are named after him . . .'.[48]

From the Campbell viewpoint the connection with Brutus the Trojan, grandson of Aeneas and eponymous hero of Britain has psychological as well as political advantages connecting them as it does with the Matter of Britain and the great cosmopolitan world of Arthurian romance and pseudo-history which enjoyed such a prodigious vogue in Western Christendom throughout the Middle Ages. In the eighteenth century, however, the MacDonalds would over-trump this Campbell ace.

Nearer home there were other advantageous connections to be made. The obvious one is with the British of Strathclyde whose capital of Dumbarton lay just beyond the limit of the modern Gaidhealtachd. The Campbells' claim to British ancestry however is not merely propaganda but does appear to have a basis in fact. Alexander MacBain suggested, somewhat tentatively, that their origins lay 'on the borderland of the Strathclyde Briton and the Gael'.[49] Mr Sellar's brilliant unravelling of Campbell genealogies strongly endorses a British origin and directs our attention to the Lennox and to one of the leading families of that part of Strathclyde.[50] The family is the Galbraiths: *Clann a' Bhreatunnaich*, 'The Children of the Briton'. Sellar quotes a Gaelic saying associated with them: 'The Briton from the Red Hall, the noblest race in Scotland.' In medieval Gaelic romantic tales the 'Fortress of the Red Hall' is King Arthur's capital. Smeirbi or Merevie or Mervin, 'a son of King Arthur . . . was born at Dumbarton Castle on the south side of the fort, in the place called the Red Hall . . .. He was called to by his by-name, The Fool of the Forest; he was a wild and undaunted person . . .'.[51]

Scholars of Gaelic and Welsh literature are well aware of the complex of relationships and correspondences that lie behind the Merlin of post-Geoffrey of Monmouth tradition. Among other elements, characters and places these involve the primitive theme of the Wild Man of the Woods, the madman who lives in the forest and possesses the gift of prophecy, and the court of Rhydderch Hael of Dumbarton around the end of the sixth century.[52] Mr Sellar surmises that the diverse forms of the name Smeirbi are all variants of Myrddin (Merlin). Now in the poem 'A good charter is the headship of the Gael' it is said: 'The headship of the

Gael . . . will be in the possession of one man of the nobility of Britain.' This recalls the prophecy of the one monarch who is to unite Scotland and England, attributed to Merlin in the form of the old rhyme *When Tweed and Pausayl join at Merlin's grave/Scotland and England shall one monarch have*,[53] and invoked in connection with the crowning of James VI as James I of England. However that may be, the sententious nature of the statement in the Gaelic poem does suggest the formulas of popular prophecy and the use of 'Britain' fits into the Campbell scheme of things.

In the poem, also, MacCailein is 'high judge over Scotland': in 1483 the first Earl of Argyll was appointed Lord High Chancellor of Scotland. Two years later Henry Tudor ascended the throne of England. As Kendrick puts it: 'The prophecy made to Cadwallader, last King of the Britons, that his people would once again possess the land of their fathers seemed to be fulfilled when, after a dramatic dynastic upheaval, a man whom Wales could call her son became King of England. The British History, in other words, had suddenly proved to be true, and we find that it was not considered inappropriate to include in fanciful designs for Tudor Royal Arms the quarterings Brutus, Belinus, and King Arthur.'[54] The new lease of life which Henry Tudor's accession to the throne gave the British History could not go unnoticed among men of learning everywhere; we know in fact that Campbell poets drew upon English sources from the form 'Cing Artur'.

The One Monarch prophecy is also attributed to Thomas the Rhymer:

The lands of the north sall a' be free
And ae king rule owre kingdoms three.

Thomas was as well known in Gaelic tradition as he was elsewhere. 'When Thomas comes with his horses, there will be a day of great havoc on the Clyde: nine thousand good men will be slain, and a young King will take the crown.'[55] The Clyde is the boundary between the Gaidheal and the Gall. In this prophecy, which is still current, Thomas has taken the place of 'the deliverer whose appearance precipitates terrible battles but who finally establishes a rule of peace . . .'.[56]

Thomas' name, as Dr Emily Lyle points out, has obviously become associated with the Legend of the Sleeping Warrior, the story which is probably most widely known in connection with the return of King Arthur.[57] Elsewhere in Gaelic tradition it is Fionn mac Cumhaill (Finn mac Coul) who is cast as the warrior who will one day return to save his people. Fionn is no doubt the earlier, though probably not the original, deliverer and has not been entirely displaced in popular lore by Thomas, originally only the prophet of the return. And in political poetry of the seventeenth and eighteenth centuries there is no mention of a specific saviour figure, only references to Thomas' prophecy of the ultimate triumph of the Gaels. In the tradition of the northern Gaidhealtachd Fionn and Thomas, in separate versions of the legend, both sleep with the ancestral dead in the fairy mound of Tom na h-Iubhraich, near Inverness. In a variant account, apparently centred on the southern Gaidhealtachd, Thomas is in Dunbuck Hill, which brings us back yet again to Dumbarton and Strathclyde. Here, presumably, Thomas has displaced Fionn or some other deliverer, perhaps King Arthur himself. Indeed, J.F. Campbell guessed as much when he comments on a saying current in Islay which makes Dumbarton the location: it 'joins true Thomas to a common British legend.'[58] In Lowland tradition Thomas and Arthur are both associated with the Eildon Hills. It is therefore not impossible that British beliefs in the prophesied saviour, coming through Strathclyde, provide the link between Thomas the Rhymer and Gaelic tradition. Whether this is so or not, the messianic theme is old in Gaelic: certainly older than the early fourteenth century, when Thomas was already known as a prophet, and older even than the thirteenth century, when the historical Thomas of Erceldoune lived.

In Ireland the birth of a child of destiny who would restore former glories is at least as old as the twelfth century[59] when it appears in the prophetic poem ascribed to St Berchan; and from the thirteenth century on references to him are common in professional verse. Among the numerous references to Scottish Kings in the Prophecy of Berchan there occurs: 'Welcome! welcome! if he it is, who has long been prophesied: a King of the Kings . . . Scotland will be full from his day. This will be a fair, long reign . . . for seven and two score years: with fruit upon slender branches, with ale, with music, with good cheer; with corn, with milk, with nimble cattle; with pride, with fortune . . . Battles will not stand against his face . . . God, the son of man, is faithful to him.'[60]

It seems reasonable to assume a connection between the still current Gaelic prophecy and that of St Berchan. Like prophetic utterances elsewhere it could be adapted or changed to fit changing circumstances, coming into prominence at various points of crisis in Gaelic history. The initial crisis was of course the anglicisation brought about by the marriage of Malcolm III and Margaret. The hostile reaction of the Gaels is well known. It would be remarkable if such a profound setback did not produce some formal expression of hope that the former state would be restored. However gradual the process, curtailment and ultimately withdrawal of court patronage of the *filidh* — the highest caste of poets and historians — would lead us to expect the first articulation to be made at that cultural level. Some time might elapse before a messianic hope became diffused throughout society. And there it would remain, merged with related popular beliefs, a prophecy on behalf of all the Gaelic nation, though doubtless given focus by the achievements and aspirations of Clan Donald.

In the seventeenth century the Civil War, which for the first time drew the Gaels into a major British military and political struggle, gave the prophecy a new dynamic. In a song of greeting to Montrose, Iain Lom refers to it: 'Were Montrose to come to Ireland to join forces with us . . . with King Charles' command, the fulfilment of that prophecy would bring us to life, as Thomas the Rhymer foretold.' He uses almost identical words in his lament for the Marquis of Huntly.[61] Quite clearly the prophecy is an established part of Gaelic tradition: the poet does not require to elaborate further. In the eighteenth century John MacCodrum alludes to the prophecy in his *Praise of Clan Donald*: 'Our friends and faithful kinsfolk would rise to fight with us . . . when the men of the Yew-wood awakened, who would come first but Thomas?'[62]

Just after Sheriffmuir Sileas MacDonald of Keppoch observes that 'Justice has gone and injustice has come . . . Thomas says in his prophecy that it is the Gaels who will win the victory; every brow shall sweat blood, fighting the battle at the river Clyde . . . .'[63]

Just before the 1715 Rising another Macdonald poet rallies the Gaels with the opening words 'This is the hour in which we will prove the Prophecy to be true'. Here, in *The Song of the Clans*, the messianic hope is identified with the Jacobite cause.[64] Another poem by the same author (*The Dream about the State of the Kingdom in the year 1715*) is a vision of foreboding.[65] None the less the poet is reassured that the final outcome will be in accord with the 'Prophecy of the Kingdom'. The words which are used for 'prophecy' in these poems contain the same root as in the normal generic term for the Otherworld in medieval Irish mythology and literature. The Otherworld is represented 'locally' in the *sìdhein*, the 'Fairy Hill' of which Tomnahurich and Dunbuck are both examples. To the present day certain shennachies will recall that the Fairy Hill is the source of prophecy as well as other, sometime ambivalent or even dangerous, gifts.

The association of saviour figure, prophet and fairy hill is given an added significance by the ideology of kingship in ancient Gaelic tradition.[66] The king is the centre of the cosmos: kingship has an Otherworld dimension and legitimate kingship has its source in the Otherworld; the true and righteous king (whose rule, in some of the narratives, is sanctioned by Otherworld personages) mediates between his people and the powers of the Otherworld, thereby conferring peace and fertility upon his realm as we have seen described in the Prophecy of St Berchan concerning the King who has long been foretold. There is a reflection of the Otherworld dimension of Gaelic nobility in a panegyric to Alasdair mac Colla: 'Not alike are trees of lineage from fairy hills and (?) domesticated Saxon knights.'[67]

Although my quotations have been from poets of Clan Donald it should be noted that the authors do not use the prophecy to press specifically MacDonald claims. Sileas of Keppoch in fact continues, after the reference to 'the battle at the River Clyde': 'England shall submit, however great her cunning, seeking peace from the king who is away from us'; and elsewhere: 'But arise Scotland, as one, before the English cut your throats . . .' *The Song of the Clans* is not only a muster-roll of the Gaels; the nobility of the Lowlands[68] are also numbered (though not by individual kindreds) among the Men of Scotland. Even before 1715 Scottish nationalism finds expression in the *Song against the Union* of 1707.[69] The author is Iain Lom, than whom no poet was ever more conscious of the status and dignity of Clan Donald. In a song to Sir Donald of Sleat[70] he emphasises the old obligations of vassals of the Lordship, which are all the greater, he implies, seeing that those clans owe their position now (in the last quarter of the seventeenth century) to the reckless generosity of the Lords of the Isles. This he puts as a sequel to his announcement of their unique right.

The specific claim of Clan Donald is expressed in the curious formula that they have a right to a 'House and half of Scotland'. This phrase, which occurs in a number of poems, is in certain respects difficult to interpret. Iain Lom and John MacCodrum introduce it in the same stanza with Harlaw, which may suggest that they associated the claim with that campaign. Another song links it with Domhnall Ballach, son of John Mor of Dunivaig, who along with Alasdair Carrach defeated the Earl of Mar at Inverlochy in 1431. 'Domhnall Ballach of the Rough Bounds who made a boundary of the House of the Harp-strings, at the half-way point of Scotland.'[71] This particular house — *Taigh nan Teud* — near Pitlochry, is well known in local tradition as marking the exact centre of Scotland. If this is in fact the place which symbolises the territorial claim, the formula may be very significant indeed. The concept of the sacral centre is known the world over; it is known in Gaelic tradition also and is associated with the sacred site of kingship. Thus, even if MacDonald and the centre of Scotland were only linked by popular tradition in relatively recent times, a good deal of interest would still attach to the interpretation. For one thing the site does not lie within the confines of the Lordship of the Isles at all but in the heartland of the ancient Scoto-Pictish kingdom. For another, since possession of the sacral centre confers a title to the whole territory, we should still have to assume there was at least a popular belief that assigned that right to the leader of Clan Donald. There is, however, one poem which appears to make an even larger claim. Writing soon after 1645, in classical Gaelic, the poet observes: 'Tax and tribute over Alba's greater half once again those folk shall have as right, or else the old division.'[72] The implication would seem to be that the Gaels, represented and headed by Clan Donald, will share Scotland with the Gall, provided their *de jure* right to the whole is acknowledged. Otherwise, they lay claim *de facto* to 'Alba'. There is no reason to suppose that 'Alba' here does not correspond to 'Scotland', at least 'from Orkney to Tweed'. It may be worth noting, especially if poets associated these claims with Harlaw, that the attitudes expressed may have a bearing upon the intentions of Donald Lord of the Isles towards the crown of Scotland.

In the same poem occurs the stanza: 'The Gael of Alba and Eire long ago were the same in origin and in blood, as our schools relate.' No shennachie, to the present day, would deny that commonplace. Yet in the eighteenth century we can detect in certain quarters a shift of emphasis. The Gaels of Ireland and Scotland are still related but what now begins to receive attention is the Caledonian antecedents.

In 1751 Alexander MacDonald published his collection of poetry *The Resurrection of the Ancient Scottish Language*.[73] The title of the book indicates the author's view of his own role as a refurbisher of the tradition in the aftermath of the Jacobite defeat. The Preface is in English, addressed to the English-speaking world in general, but directed in the first place 'to the inhabitants of the Lowlands of Scotland, who have always shared with [the Gaels] the honour of every gallant action, and are now first invited to a participation of their reputation for arts . . .'. MacDonald sees his people as 'a small but precious remain' of 'the Celtic nation . . . [which] once diffused itself over a great part of the globe. From its bosom have issued the conquerors of Rome, the invaders of Gaul, Britain, Ireland . . . once great and flourishing in Asia; and peculiarly distinguished, in having one of the holy epistles of the great Apostle of the Gentiles addressed to them . . .'. In 1776 Alexander's son Ranald, also writing in English, puts the matter succinctly in perspective for all Scots: 'The Gaelic language . . . was once the mother tongue of the principal states of Europe. It was in particular, and for a considerable length of time, the only language spoken by our ancestors, the ancient Caledonians.'[74]

Into such a scheme could be fitted the British History, the Arthurian descent, and the whole panoply of Campbell pretensions. Although this Caledonian or sometimes Pictish view of Gaelic origins came late and had little effect on traditional poetry it persisted among antiquarians and was subscribed to by one or two scholars into the twentieth century. In the late eighteenth century it helped to obscure important issues of the Ossianic Controversy.[75]

There are two poems of MacDonald's which I shall look at briefly. *The author's paean to the ancient Gaelic language* contains the first reference to Gaelic as the language of the Garden of Eden. MacDonald, however, does not intend this facetiously: he is in a line of European linguistic speculation which connected Celtic with Hebrew and ultimately produced the fantastic flowering of Celtomania.[76] (Even the Highland Society Dictionary of 1828 cites 'striking affinities from the Eastern languages'.)

MacDonald observes that Gaelic existed before the Flood and still flourishes in spite of the 'great ill-will of the Gall'. It was the language of Scotland: of Lowlander and Gael, peasant and prince, cleric and layman. Malcolm Canmore spoke it: Gaelic was the language of the Court. There follows a list of the virtues of Gaelic, including its power in satire and flyting, of which MacDonald himself was no mean exponent as his anti-Campbell verse for one thing shows.

The other composition is his *Song of the Clans*, a species already noted in connection with 1715. Both these poems of Jacobite propaganda take a convention of panegyric, that of listing the Allies, real or ideal, of the kindred that is being celebrated, and develop it to its highest degree so that it becomes a pan-Gaelic roll-call.

Both MacDonald poets include the Campbells; Alexander placing them immediately after Clan Donald and addressing the Duke of Argyll in terms of elaborate praise, in full awareness of what the political and military strategy of the House of Argyll had been and was likely to be, at least in the near future. There were, of course, Campbells on the Jacobite side in both '15 and '45 and Sileas of Keppoch acknowledges the part played by the Glenorquhy branch of the great clan in the first Rising. But she is equally conspicuous in her hostility to the House of Argyll and in her awareness of where 'The Campbells', as if generically speaking, are to be placed.

There are, naturally, different degrees of directness of attitude to be found throughout the poetry. There is the fine denunciatory metaphor of a (seventeenth century?) song: 'The sickle's stroke on the stubble upon all who live of the Campbells!' Or there is the overt suspicion that the Campbells, although part of the Gaidhealtachd, will not support the '45: 'The whole of the Gaidhealtachd will be brave and bloody in battle; and should the Campbells not come, we don't think much of that pack!'[77] By contrast, the *Songs of the Clans* are diplomatic overtures.

The diplomatic function, particularly of classicial Gaelic poetry, is well-known. Mr Black suggests that the Campbell composition *A good charter is the headship of the Gael* survives in two MacMhuirich manuscripts for the very reason that it 'reflects the poem's usefulness to MacDonald envoys.'[78] Although this can scarcely have been the author's first intention he may well have been aware of the possibility. He is in fact using a sophisticated diplomatic code capable of conveying ambiguities as well as clear information. Here, in a document which asserts the supremacy of the Campbells over all other Gaels, he observes the proprieties and in a list of the allies and supporters of the Campbells places Clan Donald at the top. This of course is far removed from *Real-politik*. The formal approach is much on a level with Alexander MacDonald's address to the Duke of Argyll in 1745, or indeed with his eirenic overtures to the Lowlanders in the introduction, in English, to his collection of 1751, for in the obscure interior of the book, his untranslated poems contain messages of a different kind. If it is true that the book was ordered to be burnt by the common hangman MacDonald obviously succeeded in getting these across!

The rhetoric of classical Gaelic poetry, in which panegyric with its convention of enumerating friends and allies occupied the most elevated heights, was reproduced to an astonishing degree in the vernacular poetry of Scots Gaelic. But this 'traditional' poetry is by no means composed of a single strand: it draws upon many sources, among them the craft of the simple praise-singer — the original bard. In its registers we can see an ancient and conservative inheritance constantly renewing itself and constantly reflecting the changing circumstances of history. Moreover, the poets whom we regard as its leading practitioners were in some instances scions of aristocratic houses or in others were warrior bards; in one way or another their involvement in social affairs was intimate and personal. And although they had no more to lose than members of professional orders of *literati*, the conventions of their art makes their propaganda on behalf of society seem less formal and less detached than that of their professional brethren. We have noted that they borrow occasionally from mythical history and the like. But on the whole what we are aware of is the pressure of contemporary events. Yet the expression of this is organised in an inherited panegyric framework.

The earliest dateable Gaelic song (still sung) is *Pìobaireachd Dhomhnaill Duibh*, a panegyric associated with the Battle of Inverlochy of 23rd June 1429.[79] A paean it may be: 'The Macintoshes fled, the MacMhuirichs fled but Clan Donald stayed.' But it also contains the verse: 'Today, today, today has gone against us; today and yesterday and every day has gone against us.' Even if this verse were a later accretion and if it were conceded that the verse expresses only the view of Clan Donald the statement could still be taken as an epitome of the theme that runs through so much of Gaelic tradition.

I leave it to those who know that tradition intimately and in all its manifold variety to judge. It seems to me that there is a strong undercurrent, surfacing occasionally, that expresses the feeling that we are the dispossessed of Scotland. When our poets act as our spokesmen they give evidence of a siege mentality.

I have tried to show elsewhere that panegyric is not only a genre in Gaelic but also a pervasive style. Its mandatory gestures obviously derive from praise of the warrior aristocrat. Now there is a persistent myth that what is popularly called 'clan society' was some sort of primitive democracy without distinctions of social class. In reality there was a high degree of economic stratification: the popular conception would at most apply only to the upper stratum. Gaelic poetry, however, does not reflect this as sharply as we might expect, especially when we remember how strictly the main classes were divided in the Isles at least as late as the last quarter of the sixteenth century. Of those who tilled the soil 'nane are chairgit or permittit to gang to ony oisting or weiris in all the haill Isles, but are commandit to remane at hame to labour the ground . . . And in raising or furthbringing of thair men (to war) . . . na labouris of the ground are permittit . . . except only gentlemen quhilk labouris not . . .'[80] In some areas this class structure may have survived the legislative enactments of the post-'45 period; in others it was perhaps modified much earlier. The growing demand for fighting men, for instance during the Civil War, would tend to have this effect. The parallel process began in Ireland in the second half of the sixteenth century when Seán Ó Néill in Ulster armed the peasantry. The extension of the privileges of a weapon-bearing élite would involve some participation in the aristocratic values of the older warrior class. There may in addition always have been an openness of communication between classes. Moreover a poet might be of low economic status but through family connections of relatively high caste. (Mary MacLeod is one instance.) At all events, the record of vernacular verse from the seventeenth century onwards shows that the values of the aristocracy had diffused themselves throughout Gaelic poetry. On internal evidence alone it is often impossible to tell apart the poems of peasants and aristocrats. But occasionally the predilections of the 'gentlemen that labouris not' find overt, clear-cut expression. In the early seventeenth century in Lewis the mother of one of the MacAulays of Uig, a renowned hunter, says in her elegy to her son: 'Born to roam the cold mountains, you chose the noble life: your fields were unploughed, your cattle-folds untended'.[81] Later in the same century Gilleasbuig, brother of Sir James of Sleat, describes 'the churles whose occupation is the cas-chrom'.[82] But in assessing the value of poetry as evidence of social attitudes we also have to take into account the selectivity of collectors. The gentlemen who compiled the great manuscript collections of the eighteenth century would probably agree with 'Ossian' MacPherson's criticism of Gray's Elegy, as reported by James Boswell: 'Hoots! To write panegyrics upon a parcel of damned rascals that did nothing but plough the land and saw corn!'[83]

The primary function of panegyric, then, is to celebrate the aristocrat and this remains its focal point. Its diction is codified in sets of conventional images most densely concentrated in the heroic elegy composed at the point of crisis brought about by the death of a leader — precisely when it was most necessary to reaffirm the traditional values of society. But the heroic eulogy contains the same topics. These are introduced and re-introduced until a densely woven texture of imagery is produced in which every phrase, every word almost, is charged with significance. The code uses various forms of address to the subject of the praise poem with patronymic and territorial styles. There are stock descriptions of personal beauty; of the warrior as defender of his kin, as lover, hunter, horseman and seaman. His social roles, his generosity, the magnificence and hospitality of his household are all celebrated in a variety of recurrent impressionistic images. As a hunter of noble game he is accompanied by his hounds, attended by his retinue, and he carries the weapons that are also formally listed in descriptions of war. There are numerous references to the warrior's justice, his mildness to his own people, his piety and loyalty. In descriptions of the household, with its drinking, its blaze of wax candles, dice and chessmen, music of harps and viols, gold and silver vessels, we have vivid scenes of conviviality that remain undimmed after the passage of centuries. There are shipboard scenes also which combine roles of seaman and warrior in vignettes which, like the description of the household, involve conviviality and project indeed a microcosm of society. When this protector dies, his people are likened to motherless lambs, a forest swept bare by storms, a ship at the mercy of the elements, or a hive of bees robbed of its honey.

Territorial styles — of Moidart, Keppoch, and so forth — lead naturally to other names, among them famous fields of battle, of which one of the most important is Harlaw. Such names have an evocative power in other cultures; in Gaelic this has been drawn into the central stream of poetry. Sometimes non-Gaelic warriors are given epithets from the common stock — *Iain Dubh nan Cath*, 'Black John of the Battles', for instance is Graham of Claverhouse. The process mediates between an alien or hostile world and an intelligible order, endowing those heroes' names with potency in native terms. Partly through genealogies, partly through lists of allies, and through place-names, there is generated in this poetic tradition a complex sense of territory, not just the territory to which the poet belongs but also a sense of a more extended territory which is at the least potentially friendly; or if it is potentially hostile, according to the circumstances of a given time, its hostility is capable of being subdued by a rehearsal of great deeds enacted in alliance. The poetic 'map' which the bards draw with place-names is comparable with the 'map' of political unity; less dominating perhaps, less vividly and precisely drawn, but the function is effectively the same. The native Gael who is instructed in this poetry carries in his imagination not so much a landscape, not a sense of geography alone, nor of history alone, but a formal order of experience in which all these are merged. What is to a stranger an expanse of empty countryside — magnificent or drab according to prevailing notions — to the native sensibility can be a dynamic, perhaps even heroic, territory peopled with figures from history and legend.

Throughout the whole range of the poetry conventional images pass before us like waves on the sea, endlessly recurring, formed in the same creative matrix, each a reflection of others, each one individual. They remind us of those that have passed; they prepare us for those that are to come. The rhetorical systems which contain these elements, interlocking and lighting up, as it were, in their entirety no matter where we make contact, could not fail to keep alive the unity of the Gaelic nation.

The traditional circuit made by poets from one patron to another reinforced the sense of cultural solidarity. The famous tale of Iain Lom's trip to Inveraray after the Battle of Inverlochy illustrates, even if it is fiction, how poets were held to enjoy diplomatic immunity.[84] At that level there must always have been a good deal of social and artistic communication no matter what hostility might exist at other levels. Alexander MacDonald mentions his friendship with Colin Campbell of Glenure (The Glen of Yew). 'I like Colin of Glenure', he declares and then cannot resist adding, 'I wish he *were* yew and not alder'.[85] These are respectively 'noble' and 'base' woods in Gaelic tradition; the significance of Tom na h-Iubhraich (Knoll of the Yew-wood) has already been noted. In such exchanges the Campbells are disadvantaged in more ways than one. A considerable amount of poetry from Campbell territory has survived but there is a noticeable dearth of vernacular propagandist verse, especially in the ancient declamatory measures which W.J. Watson called 'strophic metre'. (This is the favourite non-classical bardic form for concentrated propaganda.) It is as if the original professional bard (who occupied a relatively lowly position) had not been encouraged to develop his art to the level at which we find it in the work of Mary MacLeod, Eachunn Bacach Maclean or Iain Lom himself.

The growth of that kind of poetry is to be seen as a reaction to the threat of dissolution of a conservative Gaelic society. As we have noted there was still rigid stratification in the Isles in the late sixteenth century — just before the emergence of the 'new' vernacular poetry.[86] By that date Campbell policies had produced a less conservative social order which was more resilient in the face of threats to Gaelic identity. Hence this sort of psychological prop was not so highly valued. But even if the humble praise singers had risen to higher status, their attitudes might occasionally hark back to a time before the *literati* had begun to claim the 'headship of the Gael' for the Campbells. It is interesting to see how Duncan Ban Macintyre reacted to the Jacobite victory at Falkirk in 1746. Duncan, who was a Campbell panegyrist on numerous occasions, fought with his Campbell masters on the Hanoverian side and his two songs on the event are full of praise of the 'enemy', above all, praise of Clan Donald. The second, composed in the aftermath of Culloden, is whole-heartedly Jacobite, looking forward to the next Rising in terms not unlike that of the *Song of the Clans*. One verse begins, 'All the Gaels who were in Scotland would drive King George from his place'; the song ends, 'We shall all be of one mind . . . in your cause, Charles Stuart, for it is your crowning that will bring us peace'.[87] Rob Donn, among the Whig MacKays, echoes much of what Macintyre says; finally, on the death of the Prince in 1788, William Ross wrote the last genuine Jacobite poem composed in Scotland. The bardic tradition remained Royalist no matter which side the bards' patrons or masters might take.

It is interesting that in current oral tradition Robert the Bruce is the only monarch who is represented as a Gaelic speaker. I suspect that he once played a conspicuous part in Gaelic historical legends. In the traditions of Rathlin (the Gaelic of which is Scottish rather than Irish) he is the Sleeping Warrior, the Saviour King; and the whole background of the story is Scottish.[88] In another context, Bannockburn features in Thomas the Rhymer's non-Gaelic prophecies. According to Barbour's *Brus*, when the Bishop of St. Andrews heard that Robert the Bruce had killed the Red Comyn, he expressed the hope that Bruce was the great King prophesied by Thomas.[89] An adage that is still remembered in Gaelic, from the Outer Hebrides to Strathspey, seems like a fragment from that time: 'So long as a sapling grows in the wood there will be treachery in the Comyns'.[90] It was a Douglas who 'saw a dead man win a fight'.[91] The Goodman of Inbhirchadain in Rannoch says: 'I have heard men read from many a prophet in addition to the Rhymer that James has warriors who can perform brave deeds after death'.[92] The lost traditions of Scotland could perhaps have revealed unsuspected connections at that level between Gaidheal and Gall. As it is, what we have in Gaelic tradition is a vision of Alba in which the Galldachd is the country of a people of alien dress — black coats and hats; or they are mere tillers of the soil; or they are gloomy whisky-drinkers instead of high-born topers of red wine.

But Gaelic tradition also is fragmentary and our record of vernacular poetry, in which popular beliefs are most likely to be reflected, almost entirely unknown before the sixteenth century. To take just one of the points raised in this discussion, the dream lore that uses animal symbolism makes the pig the symbol of the Campbells. This suggests immediately the Boar's Head crest but it does not follow that the crest reflects primeval tradition. For in the same system of animal symbolism the deer represents the MacKenzies. Now if the goat[93] and not the deer were the original MacKenzie totem, it is plain that the interpreters of dreams were quite capable of keeping abreast of new developments. On the other hand it is highly significant that the two great figures of Diarmad and Arthur are both associated with the boar. Diarmad is the boar-slayer; Arthur the hunter of Twrch Trwyth, another magic and venomous boar.[94] Moreover there may be a lost common background to the Fionn/Arthur figure in his aspect of Saviour of his land, asleep in the fairy mound or with the ancestral dead, and Diarmad's apparent identity with Donn, the god who rules the Otherworld of the dead.[95] The Otherworld dimension of kingship would be of relevance here. The shennachies who drew King Arthur and Diarmad of the Feinn into Campbell genealogies would certainly have access to far richer popular traditions than are available to us. My speculation, admittedly very flimsy, is that a complex of popular beliefs, which probably cannot be unravelled now, underlay the constructions of Campbell shennachies. Political and similar motives would inspire the genealogists but popular belief could point the way and validate the constructs. It is also to be noted, however, that popular beliefs could be regarded by some genealogists as primitive and odious. According to tradition, the MacLeods, for instance, took any allusion to the Horse as a grave insult. In the case of the Campbells, I suggest tentatively that the beliefs they drew upon involved, on the one hand, a Boar or Swine totem and, on the other, an Otherworld personage who confers legitimacy on the ruler. In the latter connection even the name *Marbhan* (which to the present day would be immediately understood to mean 'The Dead One') may be significant.[96] *Marbhan*, incidentally, keeps as pet a white boar. Swine in general have Otherworld associations, not only in Gaelic mythology. We can at any rate draw attention to the fact that popular genealogical tradition constantly forges links, more or less in that manner, between names.[97] Thus MacCorquodales are held to come from Lewis on the basis of the resemblance between *Torcadal* and *Torcal*. The Macleods of Lewis are the Seed of Torquil.

Whatever the truth may be in the present instance, it is pleasant to think that long ago some shennachie may have drawn conclusions that in certain respects parallel those of modern scholarship! This sees Arthur as the British counterpart of Fionn and sees Fionn's wife Grainne, who elopes with Diarmad, as originally one of the manifestations of the loathly hag who turns into a beautiful young woman in the narratives that deal with the Sovereignty of Ireland. Professor MacCana writes: 'It is indeed possible that Arthur was a British leader . . . but if he was, it is nonetheless clear that the traditions which subsequently gathered about his name belonged to the same fund of insular mythology which gave rise to the legend of Fionn Mac Cumhaill'.[98]

What we have looked at briefly here indicates that tradition has many tiers of information. The survivals of belief are one. At quite another level is the synthesis into which poets resolve the antithetical processes of Gaelic history.

This remained ideal but nonetheless gave a continuity, and what can only be called a national perspective to literature, of such importance that it is impossible to imagine the twentieth century renaissance — in prose as well as in poetry — coming into being without it. It is also worth pointing out that in the Gaelic view the past is not seen in a golden glow. The view has indeed been conditioned by the Clearances, the Evangelical Movement, the Land Agitation, and by the perspectives created by the British Empire. But there is an inherent strain of realism in Gaelic historical tradition as there is in Gaelic poetry. There are historical sagas that show the vices and shortcomings of great men as well as their generosity and valour. A period of the past is known as *Linn nan Creach* — the Age of forays and plundering. In common usage it refers to a fairly distant past. Its limits, however, are indeterminate. Perhaps a plausible *terminus ante quem* could be set in the mid-eighteenth century. It is very likely that the *terminus a quo* is to be found in the time when the control exercised by the Lordship of the Isles was removed by the actions of the government of Scotland.

ABBREVIATIONS

BCG	Bardachd Chloinn Ghill-eathain. Eachann Bacach and Other Maclean poets. Edited by Colm Ó Baoill.
BG	Bardachd Ghaidhlig. Edited by W.J. Watson.
BSC	Bardachd Shìlis na Ceapaich. Poems and Songs by Sìleas MacDonald. Edited by Colm Ó Baoill.
GSMM	Gaelic Songs of Mary MacLeod. Edited by J. Carmichael Watson.
HP	Highland Papers.
OIL	Orain Iain Luim. Songs of John MacDonald, Bard of Keppoch. Edited by Annie M. MacKenzie.
PTWH	Popular Tales of the West Highlands. J.F. Campbell.
RC	Reliquiae Celticae.
SB	K.A. Steer and J.W.M. Bannerman Late Medieval Monumental Sculpture in the West Highlands. Appendix II.
SGS	Scottish Gaelic Studies.
SHR	Scottish Historical Review.
SJM	The Songs of John MacCodrum. Edited by William Matheson.
SS	Scottish Studies.
SVBD	Scottish Verse from the Book of the Dean of Lismore. Edited by W.J. Watson.
TC	Turner's Collection of Gaelic Poetry.
TGSI	Transactions of the Gaelic Society of Inverness.

REFERENCES

1. A. Sinclair, *An t-Oranaiche*, p.126.
2. *Edmund Spenser: A View of the Present State of Ireland*, ed. W.L. Renwick, p.62. cf. Angela Partridge *Wild Men and Wailing Women* in *Éigse*, Vol 18, pp. 25-37.
3. A. & A. MacDonald, *The MacDonald Collection of Gaelic Poetry*, p.31; cf. p X.
4. A. Sinclair *op. cit.*, pp. 131-5.
5. Discussion in SS, Vol. 12, pp. 37-8.
6. OIL, p. 193. cf. Clanranald History, RC, Vol. 2, pp. 154-5: 'All the islands from Man to the Orkneys were in the possession of the Norsemen.' Shetland is not mentioned.
7. A.O. Anderson, *Scottish Annals from English Chroniclers*, p. 202; cf. p VIII.
8. G.W.S. Barrow, *The Kingdom of the Scots*, p. 362 ff.
9. SVBD, p. 214.
10. K.H. Jackson, *The Duan Albanach* in SHR, Vol. 36, p. 125 ff.
11. Duncan Campbell, *Reminiscences and Reflections of an Octogenarian Highlander*, pp. 136-7.
12. *Burt's Letters from the North of Scotland* (1876 ed. Jamieson), Vol. 2, pp. 106-7.
13. v. TGSI, Vol. 50, p. 440.
14. GSMM, pp. 57-9.
15. BG, p. 247.
16. GSMM, p. 95.
17. SJM, pp. 129-31.
18. BCG, p. 15.
19. HP, Vol. 3, p. 268.

20. SB, p. 201.
21. RC, Vol. 2, pp. 214-5.
22. RC, Vol. 2, pp. 156-7.
23. v. D.S. Thomson in TGSI, Vol. 43, p. 276 ff.
24. Ed. Brian Ó Cuív in *Éigse*, Vol. 8, pp. 283-301. Apparently Raghnall's ship was named *An Eala*, 'The Swan', which according to Skye tradition was also the name of Domhnall mac Iain mhic Sheumais' ship. He is the subject of the panegyrics mentioned above; notes 3 and 4.
25. SB, p. 206.
26. *ibid.* f.n 7.
27. SVBD, p. XVIII. But cf. TGSI, Vol. 29, p. 205.
28. E.g. waulking songs.
29. SB, p. 205.
30. SVBD, p. 3.
31. SVBD, p. XVII.
32. *Collectanea de Rebus Albanicis*, pp. 23-32.
33. SVBD, p. 90 ff.
34. A. & A. MacDonald *op. cit.*, p. 6.
35. TGSI, Vol. 29, pp. 214-8.
36. BG, p. 259.
37. SGS, Vol. 2, p. 77.
38. OIL, p. 143.
39. TGSI, Vol. 50, pp. 329-330.
40. Wm. Matheson *Traditions of the Mathesons*, TGSI, Vol. 42, p. 153 ff. v. p. 160.
41. SB, p. 210.
42. SVBD, p. 161. 'Drive the Saxons back' is perhaps the sense.
43. SVBD, p. 290.
44. RC, Vol. 2, p. 157.
45. SHR, Vol. 45, pp. 123-42.
46. TGSI, Vol. 29, pp. 215-6.
47. TGSI, Vol. 50, pp. 256-295.
48. TGSI, Vol. 50, p. 330.
49. Skene *Highlanders of Scotland*, p. 421.
50. SS, Vol. 17, pp. 109-25. In addition to the Galbraiths, the MacArthurs, one of the 'three septs' of the Campbells according to Black's *Surnames of Scotland*, are worth investigating if only because Gaelic tradition everywhere claims that they are the oldest *fine* in Scotland.
51. PTWH, Vol. 3, p. 96. cf. Note 59.
52. v. J. Carney, *Studies in Irish Literature and History*, p. 129 ff.; p. 385 ff.; and references. A.O.H. Jarman, *The Legend of Merlin*. The name *Merrin/Meirbi/Smerbi*, etc may be connected with *Marbán*, discussed by Carney, *op. cit.*
53. A.O.H. Jarman *op. cit.*, p. 28.
54. T.D. Kendrick, *British Antiquity*, p. 35.
55. J.G. Campbell, *Superstitions of the Highlands and Islands of Scotland*, p. 271.
56. E.B. Lyle *Thomas of Erceldoune: the Prophet and the Prophesied* in *Folklore*, Vol. 79, pp. 111-21.
57. 'The Legend of Barbarossa': v. Stith Thompson, *Motif-Index of Folk-Literature*.
58. PTWH, Vol. 4, p. 35.
59. J. Carney *Cath Maige Muccrime* in Myles Dillon (ed.), *Irish Sagas* pp. 152-66: v. esp. p. 160. The deliverer is 'The Red-handed One', etc. Carney remarks on 'the reference most likely being to the bloodshed that will precede the glory of the messianic era.' The colour Red, which symbolises blood and death, recurs remarkably often in Gaelic legends of the Sleeping Warrior: v. Dáithí Ó hÓgáin *'An e an t-Am fós é?'* in *Béaloideas*, Vol. 42-44, pp. 213-308. The 'Red Hall' of King Arthur may involve the same symbolism. Red Knight and Round Table both appear in a story of *Ceann Aistear* (probably a corruption of *Cing Arthur*) recorded in Nova Scotia by Professor Kenneth Jackson, SGS, Vol. 6, pp. 178-83; pp. 186-7.
60. A.O. Anderson, *Early Sources of Scottish History*, Vol. 1, pp. 447-8; v. ed. *Zeitschrift für Celtische Philologie*, Vol. 18, pp. 1-56: Verses 148-151. The phrase *go mbuair mbra(i)s* translated 'with nimble cattle' may mean 'rutting cattle'.
61. OIL, p. 29; p. 53.
62. SJM, p. 131.
63. BSC, p. 43.
64. BG, p. 149 ff.
65. TC, p. 138 ff. The song may represent a surfacing of a sub-literary current connected with the Irish *Aisling* (Vision) poetry, on which v. Gerard Murphy, *Notes on Irish Aisling Poetry* in *Éigse*, Vol. 1, pp. 40-50.
66. v. Tomás Ó Cathasaigh, *The Semantics of 'Síd'* in *Éigse*, Vol. 17, pp. 137-155.
67. SGS, Vol. 2, p. 85.
68. As in BG, 3rd ed.
69. OIL, p. 222 ff.
70. OIL, p. 146 ff.
71. BG, p. 282.
72. SGS, p. 77.
73. The 1802 ed. is a reprint of the very rare 1751 ed.
74. Ranald MacDonald *Eigg Collection*, Preface, p. V.
75. v. SS, forthcoming.

76. Paul-Yves Pezron's *L'Antiquité de la Nation et la langue des Celtes* (1703), translated into English in 1706, is one of the important sources. Macdonald may well have known it.
77. TC, p. 185.
78. TGSI, Vol.
79. v. Ranald Nicholson, *Scotland: The Later Middle Ages*, pp. 315-6.
80. Skene, *Celtic Scotland*, Vol. 3, p. 428 ff.
81. *Celtic Magazine*, Vol. 2, pp. 478-85.
82. Traditional text.
83. Quoted by Barrow, *Kingdom of the Scots*, p. 368.
84. OIL, pp. XXIX-XXX.
85. Traditional text; v. further on the yew, etc. SGS, Vol. 7, pp. 184-192; esp. p. 189 ff.
86. For discussion of some of the questions involved, v. SGS, Vol. 11, pp. 3-23.
87. A. MacLeod (ed.) *The Songs of Duncan Ban Macintyre*, p. 2 ff; p. 408 ff.
88. Dáithí Ó hÓgáin *art. cit.*, p. 217; p. 224.
89. E.B. Lyle *art. cit.*
90. *Nicolson's Gaelic Proverbs* ed. Malcolm MacInnes, p. 139. 11. There are also traditional variants.
91. I owe to Mr Matthew P. MacDiarmid the suggestion that the line 'I saw a dead man win a fight' is to be understood in connection with the belief in the Sleeping Warrior and related traditions.
92. BG, p. 283.
93. TGSI, Vol. 39-40, p. 193 ff.
94. v. N.K. Chadwick, *The Lost Literature of Celtic Scotland* in SGS, Vol. 7, pp. 115-83 for general background.
95. Gerard Murphy, *Duanaire Finn*, Part 3, p. 360, *s.v.* 'Donn'; R.A. Breatnach, *Tóraigheacht Dhiarmada agus Ghráinne* in Myles Dillon (ed.) *Irish Sagas*, pp. 138-51; esp. p. 149 ff.
96. cf. Note 52.
97. In this connection, v. Gerard Murphy *op. cit.* p. 197: 'Appendix F. On the use of non-essential resemblance to establish real influence of one story on another.'
98. Proinsias MacCana, *Celtic Mythology*, pp. 110-15; esp. p. 115.

Old High Church, Inverness
•West Tower
X78

Index

Kisimul Castle, Barra
X'81